THE ACOUSTIC GUITAR GUIDE

THE ACOUSTIC GUITAR GUIDE

EVERYTHING

YOU NEED

TO KNOW

TO BUY AND

MAINTAIN A

NEW OR USED

GUITAR

Revised and Updated

Larry Sandberg

FOREWORD BY ARTIE TRAUM

Library of Congress Cataloging-in-Publication Data

Sandberg, Larry

    The acoustic guitar guide : everything you need to know to buy and maintain a new or used guitar / by Larry Sandberg—2nd ed., rev. and updated.

      p. cm.

    Includes bibliographical references (p.)

    ISBN 1-55652-418-8

    1. Guitar. 2. Guitar–Maintenance and repair. I. Title.

ML1015.G9 S3 2000

787.87'19—dc21   00-031788

Cover photo: Guitar and bass guitar by Harry Fleishman
Photo by John Youngblut, courtesy Harry Fleishman
Cover and interior design: Lindgren/Fuller Design
Line art by Fred Hickler, based on computer drawings by Larry Sandberg

©2000 by Larry Sandberg
Foreword ©2000 by Artie Traum
All rights reserved
Second edition
Published by A Cappella Books
An imprint of Chicago Review Press, Incorporated
814 North Franklin Street
Chicago, Illinois 60610
ISBN 1-55652-418-8
Printed in the United States of America
5 4 3 2 1

CONTENTS

❺ How Your Guitar Works I: Where the Action Is

❻ How Your Guitar Works II: Body Language

❾ Pickups and Amplification

❿ Used, Vintage, and Modern Guitars

⑪ At the Point of Purchase

⑫ Taking Care of Your Guitar

PART II: Market Survey

⑬ Guitar Manufacturers

🅮 Custom Luthiers

🅯 Selected Importers, Distributors, and Manufacturers of Student, Mid-Line, and Laminate-Body Instruments

FOREWORD

This is the Age of Acoustic Guitars: a time of fine luthiers, pick-players, fingerpickers, strummers, alternate tuning freaks, and a generation of what can only be called the great unplugged. Our current romance with guitars started to take shape in the 1960s when thousands of young people with proto-Luddite tendencies sought to discover America's gentler past through Appalachian folk music, country blues, and Woody Guthrie ballads. The pickaxes that unearthed this deep mine of folk music were acoustic instruments: banjos, mandolins, and, of course, guitars. In those days, hipsters sought out funky pre-war Martins, scratched-up Gibsons from the 1920s, turn-of-the-century Washburns, and any old guitar with deep scars and character. Character was what acoustic guitars were about: the more beat up, the better they seemed to sound. And, of course, everyone knew that aged wood meant more resonance, more warmth, and more passion.

Acoustic guitars have always had a place in the American parlor; however, since the 1960s, their influence on American music, and music around the globe, has become profound. From the resurrected recordings of Robert Johnson, Son House, and Skip James to the influential brilliance of James Taylor, Doc Watson, Joni Mitchell, Richie Havens, and CSNY, the place of the acoustic guitar in pop music has been sealed forever. Now, with the turn of the century, guitarists have incorporated the styles of Earl Klugh, Pat Metheny, Tony Rice, Alex de Grassi, Preston Reed, and many other innovative players into the world's musical consciousness.

That Larry Sandberg should come to write *The Acoustic Guitar Guide* was no surprise to me. Larry and I were best friends in high school and his passion for the acoustic guitar was undeniably inspiring to me. Not only was he an exceptional player with that mysterious gift of "touch," he was also one of the first players I knew who actually composed for six strings and arranged traditional pieces like "Buck Dancer's Choice." Larry's interest in music started with folk music but he easily gravitated to classical and flamenco players like Julian Bream, Segovia, and Sabicas, and jazz maestros Charlie Byrd, Kenny Burrell, the MJQ, and even Ornette Coleman. This wide range of interests makes Larry the perfect person to describe the potential of the guitar and how to choose, fix, analyze, and play them.

When the first edition was published in 1991 I thought it was a snappy looking book, but one I'd only browse through. I didn't expect to be pulled into the text but nevertheless I found myself reading it and learning a lot of things I thought I already knew. When you've been playing and reading about guitars as long as I have, there's a tendency to think you know it all. The first edition of *The Acoustic Guitar Guide* was smarter, faster, and more interesting than I'd thought possible. I shouldn't have been surprised; my old buddy Larry Sandberg knows his stuff and he knows how to write.

There was some information in the book that immediately caught my notice. Sandberg's descriptions of the various woods used in guitar making and the way they are sawed, finished, and glued together was eye-opening. I found his discussion of strings, pickups, and guitar maintenance equally interesting. My favorite chapters were about the history of guitar companies and luthiers, including Martin, Taylor, and Santa Cruz. I'm always curious about how people got started in doing what they do.

These days, because we're in a renaissance of guitar building, playing and interest, there are more great, affordable guitars around than ever. You don't have to seek out pre-war instruments to have an exceptional, or even a decent, guitar. Unlike in the 1960s, good instruments are now available at prices to fit every budget. The stores are so full of well-made, easy-to-play, inexpensive guitars that Larry Sandberg's guide is more essential now than it was just ten years ago. It will help you maneuver through the hype and avoid costly mistakes in either buying or repairing your instrument.

The second edition of *The Acoustic Guitar Guide* is welcome indeed. Whether you're an experienced musician or an absolute beginner trying to navigate your way through the complicated world of guitars, this book is a must. It will lead you to answers. It will separate commercial hype from the truth. It will help you make decisions about purchasing, repairing, and maintaining your instrument. Not every book can do this, but you are in good hands—literally—with Larry Sandberg as your guide.

—Artie Traum, Bearsville, New York
February 2000

Artie Traum at the Philadelphia Folk Festival, 1984. *Photo by Larry Sandberg*

Artie Traum has been a performer, songwriter, recording artist, writer, instructional video teacher, clinician, and record producer for almost forty years. Beginning in the Greenwich Village and Woodstock folk scenes of the early 1960s, he has performed as a soloist, accompanist, or with his brother Happy Traum with many of the best-known acoustic artists of our times, including Bob Dylan and The Band. After a string of Rounder albums featuring his work as a singer-songwriter, he turned to instrumental music. Among the several albums featuring his guitar work, the 1993 Shanachie release Letters from Joubée *spent months on the "adult alternative" airplay charts, cresting at number one for six weeks.*

ACKNOWLEDGMENTS

Thanks to all my friends and colleagues who have shared their knowledge and insights about the guitar with me over the years, especially Edward Dick, Janet Feder, Harry Fleishman, Max Krimmel, Jon Lundberg, El McMeen, Eileen Niehouse, Larry Pogreba, David Rubio, John Rumley, Charles Sawtelle, Marc Silber, Larry Shirkey, Kit Simon, Denny Stevens, Artie Traum, Harry Tuft, Donny Wade, and Steve Wiencrot. Thanks to my teachers: Bill Bell, Dale Bruning, Happy Traum, and Dick Weissman. Thanks to editor Richard Carlin, who first suggested this book; to Yuval Taylor, who proposed and edited the present edition; to Lisa Rosenthal, who managed its production; and to Gerilee Hundt for her art direction. Thanks to Abbie Lawrence for being the wife of an author and musician.

And thanks, finally, to those who have allowed me to use their photos. These include, in addition to many of the names above, Byers, Schwalbe & Assoc., Flying Fish Records, J. W. Gallagher & Son, George Gruhn, LaSiDo, Linda Manzer, C. F. Martin & Co., Saga Musical Instruments, and Santa Cruz Guitar Company.

This edition is dedicated to the memory of Charles Sawtelle.

—Larry Sandberg
Denver, Colorado, February 2000

INTRODUCTION

How to Use This Book

This book will help you to buy a steel-string acoustic guitar and to understand how it works once you have it. Even if you already own a guitar and have no intention of looking for a new one, you'll find lots of information here that will help you get the best out of it—and out of yourself as well.

The main focus is on flattop acoustic guitars with six strings—the kind of instrument that most people think of when they think of the guitar. Other kinds of guitars are also briefly described, but this book is really about steel-string flattops, which are the epitome of the American acoustic guitar.

Redundancy

You're welcome to read through this book cover-to-cover if you care to, but you probably won't. This seems to be the kind of book you'll want to treat more like a business consultant than like a steady date. On the theory that you'll be visiting it from time to time to look up specific details, it mentions things more than once if you'll probably need the information in more than one context. Or, to paraphrase the old saw, anything worth saying is worth saying twice.

Money

Except through luck or trickery, a really good guitar is going to cost you a fair bunch of money—money that's hard to earn, or that you are reluctant to spend, or that you just may not have right now. Since the ideal is one thing and reality is often another, this book offers sensible, balanced advice and recommendations for entry-level and midrange buyers.

Words

There are lots of reasons why one guitar is different from another. Size, shape, wood, and design all play a part; in fine guitars, so does the magic of the individual craftsperson's touch. The way you learn about guitars is not by reading books but by playing and handling lots of instruments until you can hear the difference between rosewood and mahogany, between a boomy guitar and a balanced one, and so on. A book can never teach you to hear the difference between a played-in, old guitar, a brand-new guitar with a sound that hasn't opened up yet, and a new guitar that will *never* open up. What a book can do is explain that these differences do exist, and that you need to learn why they exist and how to recognize them.

So don't try to memorize a lot of words out of this book. Instead, use it to teach yourself what to look for when you visit music stores to try out various guitars. Make it your business to do so. Memorize the feel and sound of the guitars instead of the words about them.

You'll also come to understand it is not just the bracing, the choice of wood, the strings, or the instrument's size that make a guitar play and feel the way it does; rather, it is the way all these factors combine and relate to each other in each individual instrument.

Because so many factors are interdependent it's not always easy to explain something without referring to something else that doesn't get explained until a later section. For that reason this book includes a hefty and detailed glossary at the end of the book where you can look up any terms you may not know. Use it! In fact, you can probably learn a lot about the guitar, or review what you've learned from this book, just by reading through the glossary.

Generalizations

The more you know about a field the more difficult it becomes to make any statement about it because all the exceptions and anomalies that you've encountered flood your mind. It can lead to paralysis. It can also lead to bad writing with an abundance of hedging, ambiguity, and a proliferation of the words *usually, as a rule,* and *generally speaking.* I've indulged quite heartily in *generally speaking,* but even so, this book contains plenty of blanket statements to which there are numerous exceptions. This is especially true of the many specifications concerning the dimensions of parts and adjustments. Always remember that general information is for your guidance but that the instrument you hold in your hand may be unique.

While a general reader may find this book to be quite technical at times, luthiers and other industry professionals will be quick to notice that it stops short of being as technical as it could be. It's a matter of common interest that guitar tops seem to work best when they're made of fairly stiff wood. I think everyone should know this. But I don't think an elaborate discussion of, for instance, how to measure stiffness-to-weight ratios and of their curious but debatable significance, is necessary in this book.

Second Edition Notes

In preparing the second edition I've gone over the first edition line-by-line, updating facts and accommodating changes in public taste and the guitar market wherever necessary. In the case of occasional major shifts in my own taste or opinions, I've generally pointed out the change and explained why it occurred. I've corrected several errors of fact that readers were kind enough to point out to me and I've tried to clarify any writing that seemed obscure.

Most importantly, I've enlarged Part I in several respects. In many small places I've added more information, expanded on my opinions, or enlarged the treatment of a subject, all told making the book somewhat larger. In addition the chapter on acoustic guitar amplification has itself been considerably amplified in order to keep up with the times. Many new photos have also been added.

Part II, the Market Survey, has on the other hand been streamlined considerably. I've kept, and in many cases updated and enriched, information on the major guitar companies and their histories and philosophies. But where once there was detailed, but quickly outdated, information on the various models available from each manufacturer, you'll now find listings of the makers' Web sites so you can make sure with a click of your mouse that the information is always up-to-date. The listings for companies that are merely importers of instruments made by anonymous factories along the Pacific Rim have also been condensed, since these companies lack rich histories and manufacturing philosophies. Again, Web sites have been listed, along with the proviso that, though I may have given these companies short space, you should not necessarily give them short consideration in making a purchasing decision.

The first edition also contained a list of acoustic guitar stores; this too has been eliminated. There were too many omissions, since I couldn't possibly find out about each one, and including each one would have made for too long a list to print. There were too many listings that went out-of-date as stores folded or changed address. It was unworkable. Again, the Web comes to the rescue. If your local phone book isn't helpful enough, you can look there for help. Here's a big hint: check out the guitar manufacturer's Web sites, which you can find the addresses for in this book. Many of them have dealer locations listed on their sites. By looking at high-end manufacturers, you can more quickly track down the location of "boutique" guitar shops in your area. But don't forget the surviving funky, small guitar shops as well. They're harder to track down but they can hold some real surprises.

PART

1

All About the Guitar

The Guitar Through History

ANCIENT ORIGINS

Sound is produced by motion, and the stringed instruments almost certainly owe their origin to the twang heard in the motion of the ancient hunter's bowstring. One day an early artistic genius, too impractical to invent the wheel, must have discovered that the sound of the bowstring could be enhanced by attaching a resonating chamber—perhaps a tortoise shell—to the bow. From the bow come the three main types of stringed instruments that are recognized by musical instrument scholars: the harp family, where the sound of plucked strings is indirectly transmitted to an attached sound chamber like our old friend the tortoise; the lyre family, where fixed-pitch strings are attached directly to the sound chamber; and the lute family, where the pitch of the strings is altered by pressing them against a neck that is attached to the sound chamber. Being the analytical sorts that they are, scholars divide the lute family into lutes proper (with round backs), and guitar-type instruments (with flat backs)—not to mention banjos, mandolins, the Japanese *samisen*, the Chinese *pyiba*, the Greek bouzouki, the West African *kora*, and all the other manifold shapes of plucked string instrument that human ingenuity has created.

The earliest known stringed instrument seems to be the one that ultimately gave the guitar its name, even though it was a member of the lyre family: the Assyrian *chetarah* of circa 2000 B.C., with five strings fixed to a tortoise-shell resonator. The first documentation we have of an instrument in the lute family comes from about seven hundred years later. By then Egyptian tomb carvings and pottery paintings showed men and women playing the *nefer*, which looks something like a loaf of bread with a broomstick for a neck. Presumably it sounded better than it looked, or at least tasted better. Perhaps it was this instrument that inspired Jimi Hendrix to eat his guitar.

From about the same time we have Hittite carvings from Turkey showing an instrument even more guitarlike in appearance. Later, the

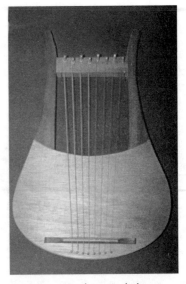

Contemporary lyre made by Edward V. Dick. *Photo by Larry Sandberg*

3

ancient Greeks came up with their own version of the lute. Called the *pandoura*, it was never as popular with them, or with their successors the Romans, as were the *kithara* (harp) and *lyra* (lyre).

THE DARK AND LIGHT AGES

We don't know much about what went on during the Dark Ages after the fall of Rome—after all, there's a reason we call them the Dark Ages. But by the Middle Ages we have ample evidence of many exciting changes: a proliferation of bowed instruments and the musical and technological development of the lute in the high Arabic culture of Spain and North Africa. (The Arabic word *al-'ud*, meaning "the wood," is where our word *lute* comes from.) The Arabic term for a flat-backed lute, *qitara*, probably originating with the Assyrian *chetarah*, seems to have been the immediate source for the Spanish word *guitarra*.

While the round-back lutes became courtly professional instruments, fiddles and the flat-backed guitars became the instruments for ordinary folks. Illustrated manuscripts, church frescoes, and stone carvings from the fourteenth through the sixteenth centuries show men, women, biblical figures, and angels performing on instruments of the guitar and violin families with names like *gittern, cittern, cithara, fidels, rebec, viol, vielle,* and *vihuela.* Some of the actual players of the day, however, were less than angelic. In a blast from the fourteenth century the English preacher John Wycliffe complained of musicians who used "veyn songis and knackynge and harpynge, gyternynge and dauncynge, and othere veyn triflis to geten the stynkynge love of damyselis." Some things never change.

The Renaissance and Baroque periods were a time of continuing variety in stringed instruments with all sizes and shapes of lutes, guitars, and fiddles moving in and out of fashion. The *Syntagma Musicum* of Michael Praetorious and the *Musurgia Universalis* of Athanasius Kircher, which for all practical purposes you may think of as the *Buyer's Guide to the Musical Instrument Industry* for the years 1620 and 1650, showed page after page of drawings of lute- and guitar-like instruments. In these catalogs, the various round-back lutes still outnumbered the flat-backed, guitarlike instruments, which had names like *quinterna, cythara,* and *mandora.* This is not surprising considering the lute's courtly preeminence and the fact that some of the greatest music of the time—the lute compositions of John Dowland, for example—had been written for it.

Like the lute, most of the guitar-family instruments of this time were "double-strung": that is, they were fitted with pairs of closely placed strings as on today's twelve-string guitar, tuned at the unison or, in the case of some bass strings, at the octave. One finger pressed down both strings at the same time. Such groups of strings are called "courses," a handy term that can apply to any grouping of strings from one up to three or even more, though I've never heard of an instrument with more than three strings to a course.

The lutanist Anthony Rooley.
Photo courtesy Byers, Schwalbe & Assoc.

Often for greatest melodic clarity, the highest course was a single string. (This is the normal way lutes are strung.) There was little standardization of instrument configurations, or even of their names, at this time. At the beginning of the 1500s in Spain two instruments emerged: the *vihuela*, with six courses of strings, and the simpler *guitarra*, with only four courses (which corresponded to the four inside courses of the *vihuela*). The *vihuela*, with its two extra courses, was more suited to the expression of composed counterpoint and therefore was generally associated with professional court musicians and their noble patrons. The music of Narvaéz, Mudarra, Milán, and other such sixteenth-century *vihuelistas* is still regularly performed in transcription by concert guitarists. The easier-to-play *guitarra*, on the other hand, was a more popular instrument associated with minstrels and the lower classes. It was common to see a *guitarra* hanging in a barbershop for the use of waiting customers, and the instrument appears in the hands of tavern musicians and peasant folk in the work of painters like Velázquez and the Brueghels.

Instruments at this time had strings made of sheepgut. Sheepgut was also used for frets, which were tied around the neck and fingerboard. The *vihuela* was typically tuned (low to high) G-C-F-A-D-G, while the *guitarra* was tuned C-F-A-D. But by around 1600, guitars were being made with five courses of strings tuned A-D-G-B-E, which has remained the standard tuning for the guitar's five highest strings ever since. Guitars at this time (and into the nineteenth century) were smaller in size and less full-figured in shape than they are today.

During this period after 1600 the lute acquired many more strings—even extra bass strings attached to an extra neck—and became increasingly complex, unwieldy, and temperamental. The archlute and theorbo, instruments with many extra low strings, ruled the high-tech roost, but were difficult to play and even to hold. It was a well-worn witticism that lutanists only tuned, never actually played. Meanwhile, the five-course guitar, known in Spain as the *guitarra castellana* (Castilian guitar) and throughout the rest of Europe by its Italian name of *chitarra spagnuola* (Spanish guitar), was played so much by all classes of society that eventually it drove the lute and *vihuela* players out of business. Even the common people could play it. The guitar's currency extended throughout Europe by the end of the fifteenth century and even such exalted personages as King Louis XIV of France and King Charles II of England were devotees. (What an all-star band *they* would have made! Unfortunately, their managers didn't get along.)

THE DEVELOPMENT OF THE MODERN CLASSICAL GUITAR

The guitar remained popular in Spain during the 1700s but declined in other parts of Europe as the harpsichord became more fashionable. (At one point, the guitar experienced a brief resurgence among English

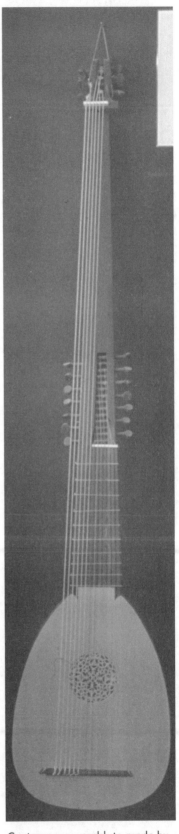

Contemporary archlute made by Edward V. Dick. *Photo by Larry Sandberg*

gentlewomen, who almost brought the harpsichord industry to bankruptcy when they sold off their instruments in droves. The shrewd harpsichord manufacturers put short shrift to the fad by distributing cheap guitars among shop girls, ballad singers, and other such vulgar lowlifes, soon driving the embarrassed gentry back to their keyboards.)

Although guitars with six courses of strings had occasionally begun to appear in France and Spain, it wasn't until almost 1800 that the sixth (low E) course really caught on. At about the same time guitarists began to abandon double-stringing, resulting in the six-string E-A-D-G-B-E configuration that remains standard to this day. (Other historical offshoots include the twelve-string guitar and the amazing variety of guitarlike instruments of all sizes and shapes with single-, double-, and even triple-strung courses that are used in Spain and Latin America.)

The nineteenth century saw a new trans-European revival of the guitar, even in Germany, the last stronghold of the lute. Almost everyone took it up: the composers von Weber, Schubert, Rossini, and Berlioz; the songwriter Thomas Moore; the writer and politician Giuseppe Mazzini; the violinist Niccolò Paganini; all manner of lords and ladies; budding romantic poets; young lovers; and even just plain folks. The Duke of Wellington's officers brought home guitars from Spain and France after the Napoleonic Wars, so once more they became fashionable in England. Paris, Vienna, and Berlin were seized during the second and third decades of the century by what the French called *la guitaromanie,* and there was plenty of work for a new crop of international teachers and performer-virtuosos like Matteo Carcassi, Dionysio Aguado, Ferdinando Carulli, Mauro Giuliani, and Fernando Sor. Their concert and didactic pieces are still performed and taught today.

Although guitars at that time had the twelve-fret neck that is still standard on classical guitars today, they were small in body size and in voice as well. They were typically constructed with tops reinforced by several braces (wooden struts) running laterally under the top, parallel to the bridge. This transverse bracing pattern fulfills the basic function of keeping the guitar from warping or pulling apart under pressure from the strings, but it doesn't contribute much to sound. Even Sor, who encouraged luthiers to experiment with lighter woods in order to achieve greater resonance, only had transverse-braced guitars to play.

But fashions come and go. By 1850 the guitar had once more retreated to its traditional refuge, Spain. It was vanquished in the rest of Europe by a new and domineering fad: the powerful modern piano, and its popular new stars Chopin and Liszt. It was fitting that in Spain, the guitar's spiritual home, the instrument should be reborn in modern form.

The basic form of the classical guitar as we know it today was achieved by a carpenter-turned-luthier named Antonio Torres (or, more formally, Antonio de Torres Jurado; 1817–1892). By 1850 Torres had developed a revolutionary, seven-strut, fan-shaped bracing pattern for the guitar's top and enlarged its body size and fingerboard length. The result was an astounding improvement in projection, dynamic range, and tone quality. Visually, he established a set of proportions for the instrument's shape that has never been surpassed for grace of line, and he cut down on the excessive inlay and ornamentation that had burdened many earlier instruments. He was also the first important maker to routinely use geared tuning pegs rather than violin-style wooden pegs held in place by friction.

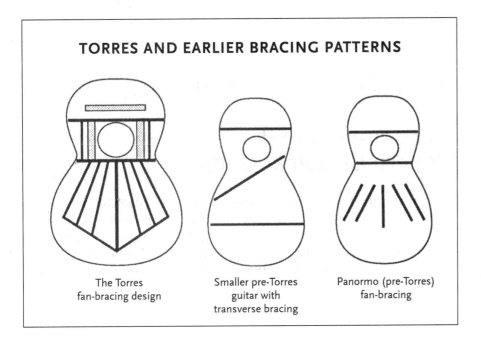

TORRES AND EARLIER BRACING PATTERNS

The Torres
fan-bracing design

Smaller pre-Torres
guitar with
transverse bracing

Panormo (pre-Torres)
fan-bracing

We owe the present state of classical guitar music to Francisco Tárrega (1852–1909), the guitarist, composer, and transcriber who laid the foundation of contemporary technique, and to the late Andrés Segovia (1894–1987), who established contemporary standards of repertoire and performance. It's likely that neither of them would have been able to make their contributions had it not been for the design achievements of Torres. Although modern luthiers continue to develop and diverge from the Torres design, it's still accepted as the root from which all other shapes have sprung.

C. F. MARTIN AND THE AMERICAN GUITAR

The guitar has been present in America since colonial times. Benjamin Franklin and the first secretary of the navy, Francis Hopkinson, both played. In Latin America, of course, the Portuguese and Spanish settlers brought over all manner of guitars and *vihuelas* from Iberia. They were readily adopted by the native peoples, who developed them into many new forms.

Modern classical guitar with oval sound hole made by Edward V. Dick. *Photo courtesy Edward V. Dick*

The classical guitar had a small following in America during the nineteenth century and the names of the leading teachers of the era are still known to us. They lived mainly in cities like New York, Philadelphia, and Cincinnati, where the traditions of upper middle-class European culture were actively preserved. Probably most of the guitar music played and taught in nineteenth-century America was in the now nearly forgotten "parlor guitar" genre, which featured light classical arrangements of European and popular American melodies.

The nineteenth century also saw the emergence of C. F. Martin & Company (now called the Martin Guitar Company) as the leading manufacturer of American guitars, a position it retains to the present day. (See Chapter 13, page 226, for a more complete history of the Martin Company.)

Guitar maker Christian Frederick Martin emigrated from Saxony to the United States in 1833, bringing with him a mastery of pre-Torres guitar design in the Viennese style. By the 1850s he had developed a new bracing pattern based on two large struts that crossed like an *X* slightly below the bridge. Like the Torres fan-brace, it was an improvement over the transverse-braced sound of the German and French guitars, and by the end of the nineteenth century many other American makers were copying it.

As it turned out, Martin's X-brace wasn't as effective for the classical guitar sound as the Torres design. Meanwhile, though, something else was happening in American music that made the Torres guitar irrelevant. Beginning around 1900, steel strings, with their brighter

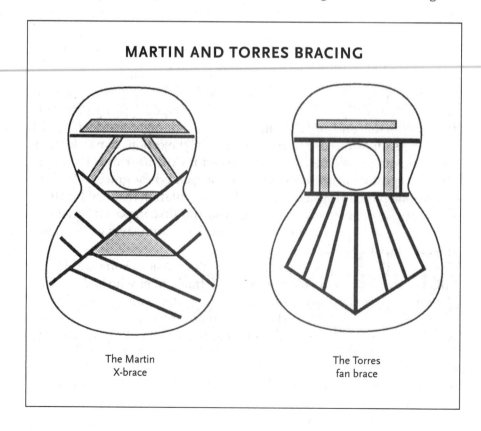

MARTIN AND TORRES BRACING

The Martin
X-brace

The Torres
fan brace

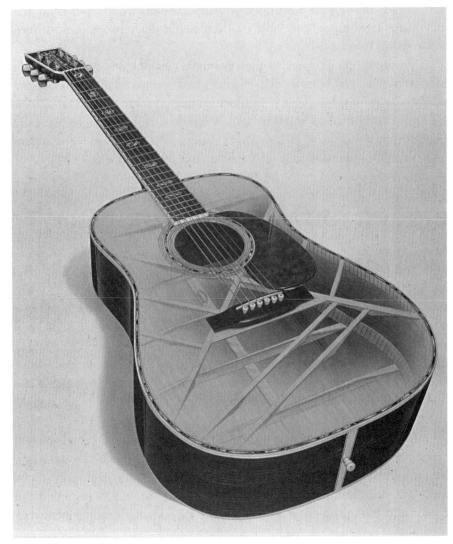

C. F. Martin's mid-nineteenth-century X-brace concept survives in this modern Martin D-45 guitar. *Photo courtesy C. F. Martin & Co.*

sound and a response more suitable for strumming, began to replace gut strings in popular use. The Martin X-brace could withstand the higher tension of steel strings and enhanced their brighter sound. By the end of the 1920s steel strings had almost completely replaced gut except among classical guitarists and the X-brace had been adopted as the industry standard for steel-strung guitars.

THE EARLY YEARS OF THE STEEL-STRING GUITAR

The guitar was a relative newcomer to American popular and folk music, following the banjo by several decades and the fiddle by several centuries; however, once steel strings came in, its place was assured. By the time 78-RPM recording became popular in the 1920s, blues singers had already developed a number of brilliant regional and personal guitar styles. The guitar had also by then achieved a place in southern white string band music.

The first few decades of the twentieth century saw guitars getting increasingly larger. Nineteenth-century guitars were tiny by today's standards, and even the largest ("auditorium-size") guitars of the late 1920s are now thought of as small by most guitarists. But thanks to pioneers like the early country music singer Jimmie Rodgers, the guitar was increasingly being used as a solo accompaniment for the voice.

BIGGER GUITARS FOR THE 1930s

As the guitar began to find a place in the new musical styles of the twentieth century, players wanted instruments with powerful, booming bass notes to provide a strong bottom for vocal accompaniments and to provide bass runs and fills in string band music. Martin and Gibson, as well as long-gone makers like the now-classic Bacon & Day, Prairie State, and Euphonon companies, turned increasingly to the production of larger instruments during the decades from 1900 to 1930. As a rule, the sound balance of bigger guitars becomes bottom-heavy and the fullness of the high notes often thins out somewhat, but that's what most people wanted (and still do).

In 1931 Martin first introduced a deep, wide-bodied, broad-waisted model that they named the "dreadnought" after HMS *Dreadnought*, which became famous after it was launched in 1906 as the largest and most advanced battleship of its time. Few guitars since have equaled the power and bass projection of the best of the classic dreadnoughts that

The progression of Martin guitar sizes in a variety of styles and vintages. Left to right: model 0-21, c. 1920; model 00-42, early 1930s; model 000-18, late 1930s; model D-28, mid-1950s; and model D-45S, 1937. *Photo by George Gruhn, courtesy Gruhn Guitars, Inc.*

came out of the Martin factory during the first decade of their production. The dreadnought shape (like Martin's other innovation, the X-brace) is so widely copied that it's now an industry standard. Martin made dreadnought-style guitars for other marketers before 1931 but it was not until that year that they aggressively marketed the style under their own name. (See Chapter 13, page 230, for more on the dreadnought.)

The other major guitar manufacturer, Gibson, developed a large-bodied but narrow-waisted design called the "jumbo," which eventually evolved into the classic J-200 model. Eventually Gibson also developed its own versions of the dreadnought, which were also somewhat confusingly catalogued as "jumbo" guitars. But Gibsons have always had a completely different sound from Martins: sweeter, less boomy, usually not as loud, and often with a fuller, though less brilliant, sound on the high strings.

But while the tastes of early country music singers and guitarists were turning toward the bottom-heavy sound balance, blues guitarists continued to favor instruments with sound balanced toward a thick, full high end. The 1920s and 1930s saw the flowering of the great country blues stylists whose influence pervades today's music. Their music was based mostly on melodies and licks played on the high strings while the bass strings supplied a thumping rhythmic undercurrent; therefore it was important that the sound of the bass strings not dominate the high strings. A combination of taste and racial economics joined together in leading blues guitarists to prefer the thicker high notes and thuddy basses of Gibsons and of lower-priced instruments like the Regals and Stellas of that time rather than the clearer, brighter, and more expensive Martin sound. Many blues players even used "resophonic" guitars, in which metal resonators produce strong highs ranging in character from throaty and twangy to thick and syrupy (see Chapter 2, page 29, for more on resonator guitars).

Around 1930 it became fashionable to make guitars whose bodies began at the fourteenth rather than the twelfth fret. In other words, there were two extra frets that could be reached by the player's fingers because the body was shortened. Classical guitars and a very few steel-string models are still made with twelve-fret necks. The designers did this by flattening out the shoulders to shorten the body a little, rather than by adding frets or making the neck longer. This takes a small amount of cubic volume out of the upper bout.

The extraordinarily powerful Martin dreadnoughts of the 1930s are the most sought-after guitars on the vintage acoustic instrument market today; however, superb instruments of other shapes and sizes also came out of the Martin factory during this time. The Gibson product line was more varied in quality level (their low end was lower than Martin's and their high end not generally as high), but many great instruments also came out of their factory in Kalamazoo, Michigan. Those who prefer the old Gibson sound to the old Martin sound, among whom are many country blues players, can also find satisfying instruments from this era.

THE 1940s AND 1950s

The late 1940s and the 1950s were the low point in the recent history of the acoustic guitar. Even the classical guitar world could support only one performer, Segovia, as a full-time concert artist of international stature—and even so, he was viewed as something of an oddity rather than as part of the musical mainstream. Mainstream pop had some use for archtop guitars (mostly to enhance the punch of a dance band rhythm section), but almost none for the acoustic flattop guitar. In Nashville the acoustic guitar was used for the most part for rhythmic texture or informal accompaniment; in the studios and on the road the electric guitar and pedal steel ruled the lead and solo roost. In blues, in jazz, in rockabilly, and in early rock, the electric guitar was experiencing a healthy and vital period of development.

Electric guitar was in; acoustic guitar was out. It survived only in isolated rural pockets, among the few professional practitioners of blue-grass and acoustic country music who could make a living in those days, and in the small urban folk music scene, mostly affiliated with left/ labor politics and songmaking, which was lying underground, ready to burst forth in the 1960s.

Martin deserves a lot of credit for holding the acoustic guitar fort during the late 1940s and early 1950s. The Martin Company was really the only game in town for new, high-quality, acoustic guitars in those days. The people at Gibson had their minds on electric guitars. The Guild company started up in the early 1950s and eventually made good flattops, but their business at first was concentrated on archtops and electrics. Decent-sounding but more poorly made guitars were also available at this time from lesser makers like Favilla and the Swedish Goya firm. Cheapies came from makers and distributors who used names like Harmony, Kay, and Regal—names that had been around for decades, and which are still used from time to time by today's marketers for Asian import lines. And don't forget the Silver-tone guitars from Sears Roebuck and the Airline guitars from Mont-gomery Ward, which were usually made by Kay, Harmony, or other factories. There are thousands of guitarists out there whose first instrument was a Silvertone.

THE FOLK BOOM AND BEYOND

At the end of the 1950s the Kingston Trio achieved mainstream, com-mercial success singing more-or-less folk songs while strumming a guitar, banjo, and tenor guitar. (The tenor guitar is a four-string instrument tuned like a tenor banjo and was used mostly by jazz banjoists of the 1920s who couldn't manage the changeover to six-string guitar.) The Kingston Trio convinced entertainment industry moguls that there was a buck to be made with acoustic guitars. Guitar sales began to pick up. Changing demographics and a shift in the tastes and social standards of the college generation created a strong base of support for the new trend, which tapped into the latent left/labor folk music underground for ideas and inspiration. Young talents emerged, old talents were dragged out of the woodwork, and singers with guitars in their hands began to appear regularly on the college circuit. Folk festivals became popular on campus as well as in high-end venues like Newport. Suddenly guitars were making a lot of bucks and a lot of friends, too. Guitars meant freedom and sex. Everybody wanted to play. Even the classical guitar market began to expand, reaching proportions that would have been thought impossible in 1960. The folk boom and subsequent development of rock put guitars into millions of hands and moved the mainstream sound of American pop music from the piano-, band-, and orchestra-oriented thirty-two-bar song form (conceived mostly in the flat keys) to guitar-driven, blues- and folk-song forms conceived mainly in sharp keys. It has been a major revolution.

Musicians used a motley assortment of guitars in those days. If you were just starting out you could pick up a used Harmony or Kay for next to nothing; or, if you had a little more change in your jeans, a Goya or Favilla. You could get older Martins and Gibsons at prices that would make you laugh (or maybe cry) today. You could always count on finding a dependable guitar to play when you went visiting. Whether new or used, Martins and Gibsons were the guitars most professionals and aspirants wanted in those days, though some were attracted to instruments from the relatively new Guild company.

The music of the Beatles divided the folk music community. Traditionalists, with their numbers swelled, returned underground but not so far underground as in the 1940s. Protest music remained in the forefront because it was so important to the civil rights and antiwar movements. But when Bob Dylan went electric a lot of folkies went with him. (He'd always been interested in rockabilly and country music, but to admit this too soon in the purist, folkie circles that gave him his start would have been bad politics.)

Many of the brightest developing talents of the folk music boom turned to electric music, giving birth to hybrid groups like Buffalo Springfield that profoundly influenced the sound of music today. At the same time many rockers also became influenced by acoustic music: many early Beatles tunes were clearly conceived on acoustic guitars, and witness John Lennon's acoustic sound on later songs like "Norwegian Wood." Many of the brightest developing talents coming from non-"folk" markets also began to play a hybrid music influenced by the folk movement. For example, look what happened to the group who backed up barroom, rockabilly singer Ronnie Hawkins, later a minor cult figure. They went to work for Bob Dylan and, for want of a better name, eventually started calling themselves The Band.

Ironically, it was probably the electronic impact of the Beatles that permitted the acoustic guitar to maintain its position as a separate but equal partner to the electric guitar. The new sound-mixing technologies used in multitrack recording and stadium-level amplification permitted the acoustic guitar (miked or with a pickup) to still be part of an electric band. Without that technology the acoustic guitar might have been relegated to amateur and subculture use. Instead it has remained an important part of the musical mainstream even as synthesizers and samplers become more common in newer musical forms like hip hop.

The 1960s brought about a renewed interest in making guitars as well as in playing them. Many youngsters, able to establish careers in guitar repair because of the huge number of instruments that had been sold, began to explore the art of luthiery, with the result that they were able to produce instruments of fine quality by the 1970s, and to establish their reputations by the 1980s. Today's proliferation of guitarists with money to spend, helped out by repair work on the hundreds of thousands of instruments that have found their way into people's hands over the past twenty-five years, gives the luthiers a strong-enough market to survive. (See Chapter 14, page 248, for more about what contemporary luthiers have to offer.)

The increasing number of skilled craftspeople made it possible for newer American companies (like Collings, Larrivée, Santa Cruz, Taylor, and the redefined Gibson company) to successfully take on Martin by staffing factories capable of turning out production-line instruments of high quality. Even newer companies, like Bourgeois, Goodall, and Breedlove, emerged as powerful market contenders in the years before the millennium.

THE NOSTALGIC BABY BOOMER MARKET

With guitars as with other goods, the baby boomers who created new markets in the 1960s have come of affluent age, once more creating new markets since the 1990s. (As Yogi Berra is reported to have said, it's déjà vu all over again.) Hundreds of thousands of people learned how to play guitar in the 1960s. Tens of thousands kept on playing and became good at it. Now they've reached—as marketers are so fond of saying—their prime earning years, and have no problem coming up with the $2,000 or so it takes to buy a pretty good guitar.

The 1990s saw new technologies to match this bulge in the market. In that decade, CNC (computer numerically controlled) machines have largely replaced hand labor in many of the operations that go into making guitars—even high-end, so-called "handmade" guitars. Robots, programmed to perform many cutting, carving, routing, and shaping operations, are now as prevalent in the guitar industry as in any other. Some makers rely on them more than others, and, in the case of high-end, "handmade" guitars, critical shaping and assembly is still in fact done by hand even though certain operations may have been performed by robots.

CNCs have their pros and cons. On one hand, they make it possible for some very good guitars to reach the market at affordable prices. Coupled with standardized wood grading, they make it possible for manufacturers to achieve a high (though not absolute) level of consistency within each model range. They certainly solve the problem of neck inconsistency. In pre-CNC days, one guitar might feel radically different to play than another, because hand-shaping varied greatly from neck to neck. Now all the necks on one model feel very much the same, and, if you happen to like that neck, it's a good thing.

The con, of course, is that as the designer achieves prominence over the craftsperson there is an overall sameness, a leveling off of the individual character of instruments pretty much in proportion to the amount of CNC work done on a given model by a given manufacturer. Even so, this may not be such a bad thing after all. Say what you will about old world craftsmanship—and everything you say will be correct—watching robotic tooling at work is an amazing thing. Combined with thoughtful design it helps conserve wood and achieve consistent tolerances that permit innovations to be put into practice.

The demand for more guitars coupled with changing economics has also led to a growing import market. The Japanese jumped in with inexpensive, plywood student guitars as demand grew during the 1960s. A familiar pattern of development followed: the quality of Japanese products improved and cheaper products of lower quality started coming out of Taiwan and Korea. Now the quality of these products has begun to improve as well and places like Singapore, Indonesia, and China have become players in the guitar market, supplying instruments marketed and, in some cases, designed by North American, Japanese, or Korean firms. Cheap and in some cases exploitative labor combined with CNC technology have made the Third World a major player in the inexpensive guitar market.

Offshore production has also led to an interesting phenomenon: the reincarnation of American brand names from the past now used to market foreign-made instruments. The names of American manufacturers Epiphone, Regal, Gretsch, Washburn, and DeArmond have all been resurrected for import models.

But, to recapitulate, one of the most interesting results of robotized CNC technology has been the ability of manufacturers to present guitars of relatively consistent quality at each price point—that is, consistent both within each manufacturer's line and among manufacturers. Certainly there are going to be some exceptions, better and worse. The last time I made a round of stores to play guitars in preparation for this edition I came across a good instrument from one of the major manufacturers for $900. Not a sum to part with without thinking twice, but not a lot for a good guitar—a guitar that sounded, to me, more satisfying than other instruments twice the price. It played nicely, too. A distinctive, truly great guitar? No. A serviceable instrument I would not be ashamed to perform with or use on a recording session? Definitely so. A good, replaceable guitar to travel with? Definitely.

So bless you if you can hear the difference and spot the bargains and save yourself from the occasional dog. But if you can't, you can probably be more certain now than at any earlier point in guitar-buying history that you'll be getting an instrument of a quality that matches your dollar.

NEW SOUNDS FOR A NEW GENERATION

New styles of music have also brought about changing tastes in instruments. A generation of players used to the fast, smooth feel of electric guitar necks and fingerboards have pressured many manufacturers to offer similar-feeling acoustic guitars, while the technical and stylistic demands of ragtime, contemporary Celtic, new-age, and other "new acoustic" fingerpicking styles have called for a new breed of fast, resonant instruments with longer sustain and a more singing tone. The preconceptions and prejudices that almost entirely killed off the small-bodied guitar in the marketplace have been somewhat rectified and manufacturers are now making it at least a little easier for players to rediscover the sweetness of small-bodied guitars.

The increased demand for electric sound has also increased the popularity of acoustic guitars with aftermarket pickups and of the electro-acoustic guitar with built-in electronics designed entirely for an amplified environment.

The baby boomers' respect for the past creates a tension in the instrument market between the new and the old. Some guitarists must have Martin (or Martin-like) or Gibson guitars because that's what they always wanted. Some must even have instruments that directly copy vintage models. Others are more willing to accept innovations in luthiery concepts.

While baby boomers, now with money to spend, propel today's market to a significant degree, succeeding generations have affected it as well. Generation X and the following generations have made a difference. They will affect it even more as they become more affluent. But already they've made a difference. Once tastes in acoustic guitar sound—and appearance—were influenced by the 1960s folk generation and by that generation's idols among the traditional musicians of the pre–World War II era. Now a whole new set of influences is at play, including not just new generations of performers but also innovations in musical styles, in recording techniques and concert-hall amplification, and in the newly found role of the amplified acoustic guitar in ensembles including electric instruments and drums, where acoustic guitars once could not coexist.

GUITARS IN A WORLD OF SCARCE RESOURCES

As the guitar market moves into the twenty-first century it must—along with the rest of the world—deal with the question of diminishing natural resources. Already we are many decades past the point where fine grades of the favored traditional guitar woods—rosewood from Brazil and spruce from the subalpine regions of Europe—have become too rare to be used on any but limited-production guitar models. The same may soon happen to today's standards: Sitka (Pacific Northwest) spruce and Indian rosewood. Woods unheard of a few years ago are now in common use; for example, nato instead of mahogany for guitar necks. Veneers and laminates (in other words, plywoods) have replaced solid woods on all but high-end guitars, and in fact are so typically used by the guitar industry that it's hard to tell from catalogs, merchandise labels, and dealers' sales raps exactly what it is you're buying. The Ovation company has for many years been in the unique marketing position of offering guitars made of synthetic materials, and it's hard to imagine that all the traditional manufacturers, even those with the most conservative image, aren't also casting an experimental eye in the direction of synthetics. If they're not doing so now they will be in the future. They'll have to.

The guitar first began to achieve the form in which we now know it during the 1700s and since then has been bouncing in and out of fashion every few generations. Its enduring appeal seems to lie in its intimacy, relative simplicity, and musical fullness. You can get more music out of a piano but at a greater cost in money, space, learning time, and portability. Only a few people ever learn to play the guitar really well but most people can learn to coax satisfying music out of it with only a short learning curve. It may be the friendliest of musical instruments.

② It Takes All Kinds

FOLK GUITAR: THE STEEL-STRUNG SOLIDBODY FLATTOP

This book is about the steel-strung acoustic flattop guitar. Some people also call it the folk guitar. It's versatile, it's accessible, and it sounds good whether you strum chords or play individual notes, whether you use a flatpick, fingerpicks, or bare fingers. You can use it to play country songs, traditional folk songs, blues, and new-age music. You can use it to express many styles of pop, jazz, and rock. You can learn to accompany your singing, you can strum rhythms, or you can play solos. It comes in different sizes and shapes, each with a slightly different character. The steel-strung flattop guitar is probably the kind of guitar you want. It's the kind of guitar most people want. But let's take a quick look at some other kinds of acoustic guitars just to make sure you won't be happier with one of these instead.

THE TWELVE-STRING GUITAR

If six strings aren't enough for you, you can always try more. The twelve-string guitar is played just like a six-string except for the small adjustments in touch, style, and musical concept that you may have to make. Its twelve strings are mounted in six pairs, called courses. In each of the two highest courses the strings are tuned to the unison (the same as each other), but in the lowest four courses the strings are tuned in octaves. Even though twelve-string guitars are built to be extra sturdy, they're usually tuned a whole tone (two frets) lower than six-strings in order to help reduce the amount of tension on the instrument's neck and body. Some players even like to tune yet another tone lower, which can make for a deep, bassy, growly sound.

This Santa Cruz dreadnought-shaped guitar typifies the kind of high-quality, steel-string guitar available in today's market. *Photo courtesy Santa Cruz Guitar Co.*

The sound of the twelve-string guitar is full, resonant, and apt to be a bit messy in the wrong hands. It can be a very rich-sounding accompaniment for singing with simple strumming (as with John Denver and John McCutcheon, for example). Tuned low, it adds an important texture to many styles of Mexican music. It can be a uniquely expressive instrument in the hands of a skilled stylist (such as Leadbelly, Willie McTell, Marc Silber, Pete Seeger, Michael Cooney, and Leo Kottke).

Many of the old bluesmen adapted the twelve-string guitar to their own sound by using only nine, ten, or eleven of the possible strings, in one combination or another. By leaving one, two, or three of the upper courses strung singly, it's possible to achieve a clearly expressed melody on top and a rich, highly-textured bass accompaniment. The twelve-string was the signature guitar sound of the great American traditional songster Huddie Leadbetter, otherwise known as Leadbelly. He strung his instrument with unisons in the highest three courses, octaves in the fourth and fifth courses, and a double octave in the sixth course.

A Martin twelve-string guitar.
Photo courtesy C. F. Martin & Co.

If you admire the music of the twelve-string guitar then there may be one in your future, but I'd advise you to get a six-string first. The six-string is much easier to learn on and is more versatile. Almost everyone who enjoys the twelve-string enjoys it as a second instrument. And remember that although the twelve-string has only twice as many strings as the six-string, it seems to take four times as long to tune.

Twelve-string guitars are now available from several of the major manufacturers but it wasn't always so. Although a fair number of twelve-strings were made by low- and midrange American manufacturers in the late nineteenth century, and Martin made a handful of experimental prototypes in the 1930s, Gibson, Martin, and Guild didn't turn out production-model acoustic twelve-strings until the folk boom of the early 1960s.

The great classic country blues guitarists who used twelve-strings, like Leadbelly and Willie McTell, played instruments made in the 1930s and 1940s by lesser manufacturers like Stella and Regal. In the 1950s and early 1960s twelve-string players had to make do with cheap, undependable Mexican models or have custom conversions made on sturdy six-strings. Today the 1960s folk boom has faded, but good twelve-strings are easier to come by now than ever before because their sound has become an accepted texture in contemporary music. The instrument itself has changed as well. Some models are like the twelve-strings of old: heavy, brash, hard-to-play monsters that boom and jangle and handle like a jeep. But others are more like sports cars: airy-sounding, meant to be responsive to light strings, with slender, more comfortable necks.

THE CLASSICAL GUITAR

If you're serious about learning to play the music of Bach, Sor, Tárrega, and Brouwer, this is the instrument to have. It's built and braced to work with nylon strings. Steel strings aren't right for playing traditional classical guitar music. (See Chapter 1, page 5, for the history and nature of the classical guitar.)

On the other hand, the classical guitar's nylon strings don't provide the tonal resources that blues, country, traditional, and new acoustic styles demand. They just aren't designed to have a bright ring when strummed. A few stylists with a highly individual touch—Chet Atkins, Guy van Duser, Willie Nelson, and (sometimes) Jerry Reed among them—have found ways of using nylon strings to play these styles of music, but they're really not for most people. I wouldn't recommend you get a classical guitar unless you have a very good reason to think you'll be happy with one. Or unless, of course, you want to play classical guitar music.

There are, however, two exceptions. If you're looking for a cheap, kid-size instrument for your youngster to start on, it's easier to find and cheaper to buy one of the off-brand, Asian-made, classical instruments than to get a steel-strung model. For most kids, nylon strings will do just fine for starters. Even some grownups seem to take better to a classical than to a steel-strung guitar.

Classical guitars are smaller than most steel-strung guitars and have broader fingerboards. The purpose of the broader fingerboard is to increase the space between the string so that the picking hand can exercise greater finesse in its choice of strokes, affecting nuances of tone.

Good classical guitars are built much more lightly than steel-strung guitars. Their necks aren't reinforced the way steel-strung necks need to be. Nylon strings don't put as much energy into the top, so the top and bracing have to be much lighter in order for the strings to set them vibrating. Don't *ever* put steel strings on a classical guitar. The guitar just can't take it. You'll destroy the instrument, and quickly, too.

Fine steel-strung guitars are in their prime by the time they reach fifty years of age, but fine classical guitars, because of their lightness, tend to burn out their voices by then and have to be retired.

THE FLAMENCO GUITAR

Flamenco guitars are essentially a subset of the classical guitar adapted especially for the Spanish Gypsy music called "flamenco." They're often built a bit more shallow than classical guitars, with some other minor structural differences, and are traditionally equipped with wooden, violin-style friction pegs to make the headstock lighter. This makes it easier to balance the instrument on the player's lap in the traditional fla-

Classical guitar by Harry Fleishman with non-traditional cutaway to facilitate playing on the highest frets. *Photo by John Youngblut, courtesy Harry Fleishman*

Flamenco guitar by Vicente Sanchíz. Note the light color of the maple sides. *Photo by Larry Sandberg*

menco playing position, where the guitar is held more erect than it is for classical or folk playing.

The traditional body wood for flamenco guitars is Spanish cypress, a softwood, rather than the rosewood or other hardwoods used for classical instruments, though sometimes sycamore or maple is used. These woods give flamenco guitars a sharp, brittle sound that cuts right through hands clapping, castanets tapping, bottles clinking, shouts of "olé!," and dancers' feet pounding on the floorboards. The essence of flamenco rhythm is in the forceful strumming patterns called *rasgueados*. Flamenco guitars are made to sound tight and punchy when you strum them hard—just the opposite of classical guitars, which sound airy, messy, and generally untogether when you ask them to do the same job. (In fact, the better a classical guitar is at producing plucked sounds, the worse it generally sounds when strummed.)

Flamenco guitars are special-purpose instruments. They're superb at what they do best but not many people like them for other kinds of music. For some players their cutting quality makes them more adaptable to country, contemporary, and bluesy sounds than a true classical guitar is. But, like classical guitars, they burn out in the course of their careers—even faster. It must be the flamenco spirit.

BARITONE GUITARS

The baritone guitar has a longer neck than usual and generally has a larger body as well. With its longer string length, it's designed to be strung in open tunings (which generally use strings tuned lower than usual) or to be tuned down to the regular tuning intervals, but four or five pitches lower than standard tuning. This gives the instrument tonal and playing characteristics all its own; it's not just a low guitar.

Depending on how you tune it and how long the string length is on your particular model, you might choose heavier-than-usual strings. Some string companies offer special baritone and open-tuning sets.

BASS GUITARS

Perhaps you've seen a *guitarrón* in a Mexican mariachi band. It's the instrument that looks like a jumbo guitar on steroids. In recent years several American and offshore manufacturers, including Alvarez, Epiphone, Guild, Martin, Taylor, and Washburn, have been turning out somewhat more manageably proportioned versions of these acoustic bass guitars. Like regular string basses they have four strings tuned in a relationship corresponding to the lowest four strings of the guitar. As a rule they come with pickups and work best plugged in, since they're fairly weak sounding. (You really need an instrument with the cubic volume of a string bass to get a big bass sound.)

If you're interested in playing bass and have a commitment to acoustic sound you might enjoy trying one of these instruments, although a real string bass or a regular electric bass would probably be more satisfying for most people in terms of sound.

Electric basses are also tuned like the lowest four strings of the guitar and since they're held the same way, most guitarists find them fairly easy to adjust to mechanically. (Adjusting to them conceptually is another story; the bass requires its own way of thinking and of relating to other instruments.) Occasionally you see an acoustic bass used professionally but their main market is for home music makers who are mostly guitar-oriented but like to have a low end in their ensembles. Adding a bass, especially one as convenient as this sort, can really improve the sound of homemade music.

Acoustic bass guitar by Harry Fleishman. *Photo by John Youngblut, courtesy Harry Fleishman*

ARCHTOP GUITARS

How Archtops Work

The archtop guitar owes its design to the violin. Instruments of the violin family have tops and backs that are carved from a thicker board into an arched shape rather than being cut flat. A master builder will tune the top and back while carving them, tapping them from time to time to judge the sound and determine where and how much the

Archtop guitars by John Rumley. *Photo by Larry Sandberg*

wood should be graduated (thinned). On cheaper mass-produced guitars, the sides and back are made of steamed plywood that is pressed into shape.

Most archtop guitars now use violin-like, *f*-shaped sound holes, which were popularized in the 1920s on Gibson's classic L-5 guitars and F-5 mandolins created by the legendary designer Lloyd Loar. Before that, archtop guitars and mandolins followed Orville Gibson's original design with a round or elliptical sound hole.

Flattops and archtops both look like guitars and walk like guitars, but they quack like two entirely different animals. Underneath the top of the flattop is a complicated system of bracing struts, while archtops use only two long struts called *tone bars*. The strings of flattop guitars are held in place by pins in the bridge whereas the strings on archtops merely rest on the bridge and then run into a holding bracket called the *tailpiece* that screws into the end of the guitar.

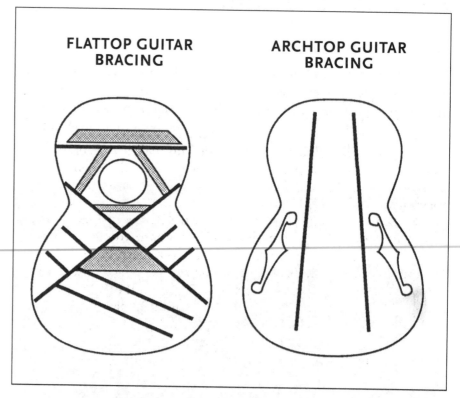

FLATTOP GUITAR BRACING **ARCHTOP GUITAR BRACING**

Modern archtop guitar by Linda Manzer. The appearance of this instrument shows great appreciation for tradition but, because Manzer is no slave to tradition, it also incorporates original elements, most notably an original design for the f-holes. Manzer often builds archtops far more modern in appearance than this one. *Photo by Mark Brickell, courtesy Linda Manzer*

As a result of these structural differences the soundboards move according to different physical principles. An archtop soundboard moves up and down whereas a flattop soundboard moves in complicated, twisting patterns that vary depending on the pitches being produced. As a result the sounds produced by either instrument have different characters and occupy completely different musical spaces in ensembles. In addition, the pressure of the strings on archtop guitars (and violin-family instruments, for that matter) is *im*plosive, forcing the body joints in on themselves. But on flattops the string tension is *ex*plosive, pulling the instrument apart rather than compressing it.

The original function of the archtop guitar was to provide a punchy, supportive beat in the rhythm section of big bands—a beat that was felt by the other players more than it was heard by the audience. It accomplishes this not by overwhelming the other instruments but by projecting cannonballs of compressed sound that find their way into spaces between the other instruments.

The Great Archtop Guitars

The archtop guitar replaced the four-string banjo in jazz rhythm sections. As American music moved out of the 1920s, the sound of the banjos used in early jazz bands was too clanky and unpliable to keep up with the new textures and rhythms that were emerging. Yet the original round-hole, archtop guitars were too slow to speak, too wooly-sounding, and too lacking in clarity and projection to be an effective substitute. When Gibson designers Lewis Williams and Lloyd Loar perfected the f-hole, archtop guitar in the 1920s, it was the right instrument in the right place at the right time.

In their heyday the great archtop guitars came from the Gibson and Epiphone factories and from the workshops of John D'Angelico and Charles and Elmer Stromberg. Most Gibsons and some D'Angelicos are good for jazz single-line and chord-style solo playing. Epiphones (a product line of mixed quality and characteristics), Strombergs, the Gibson Super-400 models and some other Gibsons, and many D'Angelicos are generally more suited for punchy, rhythm section work.

F-hole guitars of one sort and another were also made by other companies, including not only the cheapie producers like Harmony and Kay, but also high-quality manufacturers like Martin, Prairie State, and Vega. Some of these instruments had arched tops but flat backs. Most of these instruments did not achieve great favor in their day or ours. They are sought more as collectibles and curiosities than as player's instruments.

Electric Archtops

As electrified instruments became more popular from the 1940s on, the factories let the quality of their acoustic guitars become inconsistent, though of course many very fine instruments continued to be made. Gibson and Epiphone began to mount pickups in the top of the guitar. This cut down on the tops' projection, which didn't matter if the instrument was going to be played amplified all the time. But once you start doing this you have to ask: why bother to do a fine job of top-carving in the first place? (If you want to electrify a finely made, acoustic archtop guitar without messing up the top, the way to do it is with a "floating pickup." This is a pickup that mounts on the end of the fingerboard or on the pickguard without interfering with the top.)

While the electric archtop depends more on its pickups and amplifier to determine its sound, it still has a character and clarity that

Another bow toward tradition on this modern archtop by D. W. Stevens. Strings on an archtop guitar are held by a "tailpiece"—in this case one of staggered design in order to increase tension, and therefore punchiness of sound, on the low strings. A similar tailpiece, known as the "Frequensator," was used on some guitars of the 1940s. *Photo by D. W. Stevens*

Archtop guitar by D. W. Stevens. Note the small pickup mounted at the end of fingerboard. *Photo by Larry Sandberg*

Contemporary f-hole design on an X-braced archtop by D. W. Stevens. Shape and placement of the f-holes is designed to maximize the vibrating surface area of the top. *Photo by Larry Sandberg*

makes it sound quite different from the contemporary-style, solidbody electric guitars generally used in rock and blues. Oddly, many electric-oriented archtops sound quite dead when you play them acoustically but just great when you plug them in.

The mainstream jazz and 1950s rockabilly sounds (especially the rockabilly sounds of Gretsch guitars) are both creatures of the electric, f-hole guitar, and you can't really duplicate them on solidbodies or on electrified flattops except (to a reasonable degree of accuracy) by digital modeling—the use of digital tone shaping available in some amplifiers and sound processing devices.

The Contemporary Archtop

In the present day the baby boom generation's seemingly infinite capacity for nostalgia has created new interest in archtop guitars as well. From offshore producers we now have a number of CNC-made, electrified models, many of journeyman quality, to choose from. From limited-production shops and custom luthiers come instruments that rival or exceed the great archtops of the past in quality. Some are built along traditional lines in terms of bracing and sound quality as well as visual quality, mimicking the gorgeous art deco appearance of archtops of the past. Others are modern in appearance, or sound quality as well, even to the point of using flattop-style X-bracing to produce a more singing, less chunky tone. At this point in the evolution of the archtop any maker must choose some point on the spectrum between the chunky, explosive quality of the dance-band rhythm guitar and the lyric, singing quality of the guitar used for jazz soloing. Somewhere within this dual heritage lies the perfect guitar for every player.

Is an Archtop the Guitar for You?

If you have to ask, the answer is almost certainly no. The archtop guitar simply doesn't sound right with most forms of contemporary acoustic music. To today's ears it doesn't find a sonic space within most contemporary ensembles. It doesn't seem to surround or support the voice properly when accompanying modern song styles. It doesn't ring enough and it speaks too thickly and, on heavier instruments, too slowly. But it's still unsurpassed for re-creating the authentic sounds of swing and for clarity and elegance in executing mainstream jazz styles. Many professional flattop guitarists own an archtop model that they play when it's called for or for a change of pace. Today players adapt modern styles to the archtop and makers adapt their guitars to modern styles.

Among the well-reputed North American luthiers and shops making fine acoustic archtop guitars today are Steven Andersen, Bob Benedetto, Linda Manzer, John Monteleone, the Santa Cruz Guitar Company, Dennis W. Stevens, and John Zeidler. The Gibson, Guild, and

Heritage companies are sources of well-made, factory, acoustic and electric archtops. Among offshore companies, Epiphone and Gretsch offer satisfactory instruments in lower price ranges. The fine work of the late James D'Aquisto, once John D'Angelico's apprentice, bridges traditional and contemporary builders.

SOLIDBODY AND SEMI-HOLLOWBODY ELECTRICS

In the late 1940s the Fender company pioneered solidbody electric guitars by producing the guitar model now known as the Telecaster. Fender later came out with another model, the Stratocaster, featuring three pickups and a contoured body, which has become the most popular—and most copied—solidbody guitar style. In a solidbody guitar the sound is totally electric. The body, being solid wood, offers no acoustic resonance, but its mass causes the vibrations of the string to sustain for a longer period of time. Since it isn't dissipated into the top or an air chamber, vibrational energy tends to stay in the string. In addition, the relationship between the attack and decay parts of the sound tends to be smoother in solidbody guitars. (See Chapter 3, page 42, for more information about the attack and decay parts of sound.)

Albert Collins playing a solidbody Fender Telecaster. *Photo by Larry Sandberg*

Gibson soon followed Fender with its own solidbody lines, including the classic Les Paul design with its characteristically fat tone. Gibson also pioneered a series of semi-hollowbody guitars that, like B. B. King's Lucille, combine a solid wood strut down the middle of the body with small air chambers on either side. Although the tone of electric guitars also has a lot to do with electronics and how you set them, semi-hollowbody guitars characteristically have a darker, fatter tone, less sustain, and more abrupt attack than solidbodies do.

In many ways, electric archtops respond to the touch like acoustic guitars. Solidbody guitars don't. They're really very different instruments—as different as a clarinet is from a saxophone—even though they're played similarly. Solidbody electric guitars are great for playing electric music but not for sitting around the kitchen quietly enjoying friends. It only makes sense to start out on an electric guitar if you're sure you want to play in an electric band. Otherwise the acoustic guitar is a much better starting point for most people. If you're committed to electric music, you may be happier going directly to an electric guitar, even though an acoustic instrument is in some ways a better way to start. Fortunately, most people have a pretty good sense of where they want to start, and it makes sense to follow your heart and your inclinations.

Remember also that, as with any amplified instrument, your amplifier and other electronics play as great a role in your final sound as the guitar itself does. (See Chapter 9 for more information on pickups and amplification.)

HAWAIIAN AND OTHER LAP-STYLE GUITARS

Playing the guitar with a slide, lap-style or Hawaiian-style. The player is Bob Brozman and the playee is a National Tricone. *Photo by Larry Sandberg*

The instrument called the Hawaiian guitar can be any guitar, as long as it's played face up, flat across your lap, with raised strings and a slide. Koa and mahogany, sweet-sounding woods that are also favored for ukuleles, are the body woods of choice for the true Hawaiian sound. Resophonic guitars like the bluegrass Dobro are often held and fretted in the Hawaiian *manner*, but most Hawaiian *people* who play Hawaiian *music* seem to find that an all-wood guitar is better suited to their style. (See page 29 for more information on resophonic guitars.)

It's common to use medium-gauge strings on these instruments, so as a rule they're sturdily built and may have square necks for maximum strength. Since they're intended to be played exclusively with a heavy steel slide, they usually have an extra-high nut and saddle to keep the strings well away from the fingerboard even when weighed down by the slide.

Beautiful California-made Weissenborns fetch top dollar on the vintage market and contemporary copies from limited-production luthiers aren't cheap either—nor should they be. But if you'd like to try out a lap-style guitar, you can satisfy your curiosity cheaply. An old ten-dollar junker from the flea market or music store basement will do for experiment just as long as it's sturdy enough not to explode when you put the strings on. Because you'll be playing with a steel slide, it doesn't matter how bad the action is. In fact, the worse it is, the better. If it's still not bad enough, a couple of bucks will buy you a removable gadget called a "nut extender" or "extender nut," a grooved metal collar that sits over your nut and raises the action to a height suitable for slide playing. You'll also need a slide. A heavy glass bottle or length of metal tubing will get you started but ultimately you'll find a store-bought one more satisfying. For decades most players' favorite slide was the Stevens brand steel with its comfortable, grooved finger-holds, but recently the Shubb company has marketed a similar version with a rounded end that makes it easier to move from string to string. Most acoustic guitar players prefer to keep away from the large, heavy, "bullet" steels that work better on electric pedal steel guitars. (See page 29 for more information on pedal steel guitars.)

An extender nut like this one can convert any guitar for Hawaiian-style playing with a slide for a pittance. *Photo by Larry Sandberg*

Sometimes it's worth the effort to convert a good-quality Hawaiian guitar back to a regular one. Just get the high nut replaced with one of regular height. If you're lucky, the neck will be straight and you'll be ready to play. However many of these instruments may also need fairly extensive surgery to be playable. Often, after enduring years of heavy string tension, they'll need to have the neck taken off and reset at the proper angle. And, if they've got square necks, a luthier will have to recarve them to a standard contour.

Why go to all this trouble and expense? Because period Hawaiian guitars were built to optimize the thick, syrupy tone on the high strings that country blues players love. Some of the better instruments from before World War II turn into superb country blues guitars when they're rebuilt.

THE PEDAL STEEL GUITAR

Sometime in the 1930s somebody got the bright idea of building a solidbody, amplified, Hawaiian-style guitar and, on some models, adding one or two extra strings. These instruments are called *lap steels*. Then someone else got the bright idea of mounting lap steels on legs so they could be played standing up. (Steel virtuoso Waldo Otto calls his instrument the "electric table.") Then others got the idea of shortening the legs so the table could again be played sitting down, this time with a bunch of knee levers and foot pedals to change the pitch of different strings as the instrument was being played. And of course there was now enough room on the tabletop to include two completely different necks, each with eight or more strings and each in completely different tunings with different knee-lever and pedal configurations.

The result is the modern "pedal steel guitar," which has evolved so far away from the guitar that it's a completely different animal. It's a specialized, challenging, and highly virtuosic instrument requiring the soul of a musician mated with the mind of a chess master.

RESOPHONIC GUITARS

The twangy resophonic guitar gets its sound from a metal resonator built into the body. In a regular flattop guitar, the vibration of the strings sets the entire top in motion. In a resophonic guitar the vibrations pass instead into what is basically a glorified pie-plate mounted under the bridge. It's called the "cone," and, like the cone of a loudspeaker it amplifies the vibrations it receives. Since it's metal, it adds a metallic twang and a somewhat echoey quality to the sound. Resophonic guitars are usually quite loud. The concept of the cone resonator was intended by its designers primarily as an amplifying device, and its distinctive tone was strictly secondary. These days it's the tone that's highly valued. If it's merely loud you want, you can get it by turning a knob. A resonator guitar is a poor choice for a first guitar unless you're absolutely sure it's what you want. But later on in your development it could be a stimulating second instrument—especially for playing country blues.

In order for the cone to amplify most effectively, a good deal of string energy has to be transmitted to it. Therefore resophonic guitars are usually strung with medium to heavy strings and are solidly built to withstand this tension. In fact they're usually so thick and solid that the tops have a negligible acoustic function—it's the cone that does all the work. Because there's not much you can do to the body that would affect the instrument's sound, resophonic guitars are the perfect candidates for inlay designs, engravings, paint jobs, and other kinds of ornamentation, some of which have extended the boundaries of taste.

You can play resophonic guitars with a slide or just like a regular guitar, but a slide brings out the best in them. In fact the combined

Ron Mesing with a wooden-bodied, Dobro-style, resonator guitar. *Photo courtesy Flying Fish Records*

sound of slide and resonator cone is, like shrimp and garlic, a marriage made in heaven.

The best known resophonic guitar is the Dobro brand model, played lap-style with a slide in bluegrass and sometimes in country music. The Dobro name, a trademark of Original Musical Instruments (OMI), comes from the company's founders, the DOpyera BROthers. To the Dobro company's chagrin, "Dobro" has in common usage become the generic term for a lap-style, resophonic guitar, which other companies now also make. The Dobro company also makes resophonic guitars designed to be held the usual way.

The other resophonic archetype is the all-metal-bodied instrument originally sold under the National brand name. While bluegrass and country players mostly prefer the Dobro sound, blues players mostly prefer Nationals.

The original Dobros and Nationals were made from 1927 through 1941. (Electric guitars and the shortages of the war years combined to bring sales to a halt.) In the ensuing years a few odd resophonic-style models were marketed by the companies, which purchased OMI's parts and stock.

As usual, the story gets a little more complicated. Thanks to tangles in the corporate history of the two brands there are some older metal-bodied instruments labeled "Dobro" and wooden-bodied instruments labeled "National." And when OMI cranked up operations again in 1959 it started producing both wooden and metal instruments under the Dobro name. So when you hear the words "Dobro" or "National" they could be referring specifically to the manufacturer or generically to the type of instrument.

The history of OMI in its post-1959 incarnation has been speckled, with several changes of brand name ownership and manufacturing procedures, but during the 1970s the company stabilized and again established itself as the major manufacturer of resophonic guitars. More recently the Dobro brand name was purchased by the Gibson company.

Dobros and Nationals differ not only in having wood versus metal bodies but also in details of cone design, which has a profound effect on tone. Not only are the cones themselves differently shaped, but in Dobros the cone is connected to the bridge indirectly by a strutwork apparatus called a "spider," which looks like a skinny, six-legged cousin of a gas burner grid. Dobros also have an ornamental covering called a "cover plate"—another pie-plate, but this time with perforations—that fits over the resonator cone and spider. When you look at a Dobro, the metal plate you see is the cover plate. You have to take it off or look through its holes to see the actual cone. Nationals may have either one large or three small cones.

Because resophonic guitars are heavily strung, they're usually plucked with fingerpicks rather than bare fingers and are often built with stout necks. On instruments intended to be played lap-style the tuning pegs may be mounted with the pegs facing up for convenience and the necks may be square for maximum strength. It's safest not to go heavier than medium-gauge strings on any but the square-necked models.

New resophonic instruments are available from a number of companies, including Gibson's Original Acoustic Instruments Division in Nashville and the National Reso-Phonic company in California, as well as from limited-production and custom shops. Offshore models, of lower price and quality, are also available.

With a little luck and some elbow grease you can find a used resophonic guitar made by OMI in its post-1959 incarnation at a reasonable price. Sixties models made by Gretsch under the Gretsch and Sho-Bro names and using genuine Dobro parts can also be good. Seventies models from R. Q. Jones are fine instruments but they usually have asking prices to match. Unless you happen across an uninformed seller, instruments from the original 1927–1941 period are pricey collectors' items subject to the forces of an expert market that values cosmetic condition and ornamentation as well as minor historical and design features too specialized to go into here.

Other excellent instruments from the 1930s include those made by the Regal company, otherwise a maker of mostly nondescript guitars, under license from OMI. Minor companies also made lower-quality, resophonic-style instruments during the 1930s. Others have continued to make instruments of varying degrees of quality through the present day.

Resophonic instruments are sturdy on the outside but the cones and spiders are fairly fragile and can easily be damaged by shocks or heavy-handed adjustment. What with all the nuts, bolts, pie-plates, spiders, and other unusual creatures that inhabit them, they're also subject—much more so than regular guitars—to all sorts of irrational buzzes and rattles. These problems are best sorted out by dealers or

Fanciful modern resonator guitar by Larry Pogreba. The cover plate is the hubcap from a 1954 Packard Clipper; hubcap guitars are a Pogreba specialty. Also note the built-in magnetic pickup. *Photo by Larry Pogreba*

Cyndi Cashdollar plays a wooden-bodied resonator guitar Hawaiian-style standing with a strap while Bob Brozman sits with a metal-bodied resonator guitar held Spanish-style. *Photos by Larry Sandberg*

A Saga DG-250 Django-style guitar. *Photo courtesy Saga Musical Instruments*

repair people who are experienced in resophonic instruments. You can learn in time to do your own servicing. In fact, you'll have to. But get some advice along the way.

THE MACCAFERRI ("DJANGO") GUITAR

This distinctive instrument was the brainchild of an eccentric Italian luthier and guitarist named Mario Maccaferri. It was marketed during the 1930s by the Henri Selmer company of Paris (better known as a manufacturer of fine wind instruments), and is best recognized as the instrument that contributed to the unique sound of the great Gypsy jazz guitarist Django Reinhardt. Django was the quintessential Maccaferri player.

The original Maccaferri guitar of 1930 had a wooden inner sound chamber within its lower bout—a body within the body, as it were—and a sound hole shaped like a *D* in order to accommodate the sound chamber. The interior sound chamber was open at the end next to the sound hole but a saucerlike sound deflector bounced the sound around inside the body for a while before it actually got to the hole. Four longitudinal straight braces (similar to the two straight braces of archtop guitars) supported the top and the strings were supported archtop-style by a tailpiece rather than a pin bridge. The result was a brilliant, throaty, highly sustained single-line sound, and a compressed, punchy chord sound with little separation.

In 1937 Maccaferri bowed to consumer pressure and went from a twelve- to a fourteen-fret neck. This resulted in a reproportioned body shape that compelled him to omit the inside sound chamber. The fourteen-fret guitars, produced until Maccaferri came to the United States in 1940, are still Maccaferri-sounding, but not as Maccaferri-sounding as the original models with the sound chamber. In all about 750 twelve-fret and 350 fourteen-fret Maccaferris were made, which makes them prime collectors' items.

In the original Quintet of the Hot Club of France, Django first played lead guitar on a large, D-hole, twelve-fret model but later moved to a small, oval-hole, fourteen-fret model. The quintet's pair of rhythm guitarists played D-hole models. As a result the D-hole became stereotyped as a rhythm model. To my taste, however, it has a greater and more satisfying variety of tonal resources than does the oval-hole model. The later models were marketed by Selmer. As a result the D-hole models are often called Maccaferri guitars and the oval-hole models Selmer guitars, though not everyone observes this careful distinction.

Although Maccaferri began his career as a concert artist, his mind had primarily a technological bent. He was among the first makers to use laminate backs and sides. In his later years he became infatuated with plastics and turned to the invention and production of plastic woodwind reeds in addition to pretty much sewing up the market on plastic guitars and ukuleles. If you remember the rows of plastic novelty ukes, guitars, and miniature instruments hanging in dime stores during the 1950s and 1960s, then you've seen Maccaferri's work. At one time he even made some full-size plastic guitars.

The Maccaferri guitar has been of interest mainly to players working in the Django Reinhardt style although there's really no reason why it shouldn't be extended imaginatively into more modern styles. Its great sustain combined with an uncanny combination of warmth and brilliance makes it an extremely interesting instrument. It remains, however, a specialized sound and instrument and is not one to choose unless you know exactly what you're doing.

Today, high-quality Selmer- and Maccaferri-style guitars are available from several manufacturers including Michael Dunn in Canada, John Kinnard's Dell'Arte company in California, Maurice Dupont in France, and John LeVoi in England. Saga imports a less expensive model made to its own specifications. Some independent luthiers also make Maccaferri-style guitars for custom orders.

SYNTH GUITAR

The guitar can also be used to drive a synthesizer using the MIDI (Musical Instrument Digital Interface) protocol. Currently the guitar synthesizer that rules the marketplace and appears likely to maintain its position is the Roland system. However, its dedicated pickup is designed to be used with electric guitar strings and to be mounted on an electric guitar body. You can fudge one onto an acoustic guitar strung with electric guitar strings but it's not a good fudge.

The Godin company in Québec makes several models of acoustic guitar—in both steel- and nylon-string models—that are designed to drive the Roland synth unit using Godin's own built-in pickup system. These are worthy but little-known instruments. More information can be found at www.lasido.com. (See Chapter 13, page 224, for more information about LaSiDo.)

HARP GUITARS AND OTHER ODDITIES

Seven Strings, Ten Strings, and More

On a commission from jazz guitarist Pat Metheny, Toronto luthier Linda Manzer once constructed a guitar with forty-two strings strung on four necks (one six-string and three twelve-strings) running every which way out from the body. She called it the "Pikasso" guitar because it looks like one of those multiperspective guitar renderings the Cubists were so fond of.

The Godin Multiac guitar is especially designed to drive the Roland guitar synthesizer. *Photo courtesy LaSiDo*

Linda Manzer's "Pikasso" guitar. *Photo by Mark Brickell, courtesy Linda Manzer*

Guitar with more strings than you can count (much less play), by Edward V. Dick. *Photo courtesy E. V. Dick*

If your tastes are less extravagant, maybe you'll settle for only seven strings. Usually the seventh is an extra bass string tuned to B or A, which gives you the opportunity to add a lot more bottom to your playing. A few guitarists—such as swing player Bucky Pizzarrelli, Nashville jazz player Lenny Breau, the incomparable cocktail-jazz virtuoso George van Eps, and his protégé Howard Alden—have mastered the seventh string, and in their footsteps have followed a handful of acoustic flattop guitarists working with custom-made instruments or instruments adapted from wide-necked or twelve-string guitars. But most players find that six strings are quite enough trouble to master and, once mastered, they do the job just fine, thank you.

The seven-string guitar actually goes back over 150 years. At the peak of European *guitaromanie* around 1830, all kinds of experiments with novelty guitar shapes were going on; but there was also a lot of interest, especially in Russia, in ordinary guitars with anywhere from one to nine extra bass strings. (Such instruments were known in their time as "bass guitars.")

Today the ten-string guitar is experiencing a small revival. Classical guitarist Narciso Yepes and Latin/jazz guitarist Egberto Gismonti, for example, are known for their ten-string instruments, which look like a regular nylon-string guitar but with a neck almost twice as broad.

To play this kind of instrument you conduct business as usual on the highest six strings; the remaining four strings are all tuned to such extra bass notes as might come in handy in the piece you're playing so that, whenever you want some extra bottom, you just reach up with your thumb and pick one of the extra bass strings. Sometimes it may be convenient to fret one of them to get the note you want, but for the most part they simply provide extra open notes. In addition, they're great showbiz.

Ibanez makes seven-string, electric archtop models, but if you want an acoustic guitar with seven or more strings, start saving your money for a custom instrument.

The Harp Guitar

The late new-acoustic stylist Michael Hedges briefly revived the nineteenth-century oddity known as the harp guitar, in which extra bass strings (and sometimes sympathetic strings) are added onto an extra neck or a lyre-like extension of the body. The idea actually goes back to lute-family instruments of the sixteenth century called the archlute and theorbo, but it wasn't until the 1790s that the idea was applied to the guitar. The 1790 model was called a "harp guitar" by its maker because the extension for the extra strings looked like a small harp grafted onto the guitar body. The name stuck.

An old Gibson harp guitar. *Photo by George Gruhn, courtesy Gruhn Guitars, Inc.*

Harp guitars had enough of a following to survive through the nineteenth century and into the twentieth. Gibson turned out over four hundred of them between 1900 and 1920 and the Larson brothers, important manufacturers of the early twentieth century, turned out a number of them under the Dyer and Stahl brand names. Even Martin made a few special-order models. But when the 1920s roared in they pushed harp guitars out of the way and there they remained until recently as mere curiosities.

On harp guitars the extra bass strings are unfretted. The player just plucks the appropriate open strings. On some contemporary custom models there are also extra, open high strings added below the high end of the fingerboard. (This, in essence, is a reinvention of the zither.)

If you're motivated to learn to play such an instrument, you'll either have to locate an old, collectors'-item harp guitar or have a luthier make a custom instrument for you. In either case you'd better start saving your pennies right now. You're unlikely, at least as of the time this book goes to press, to find an inexpensive, Korean import model at your local music store.

All this could change, though, if a harp guitar gets used in the next Garth Brooks video. You never know.

Multineck Guitars

Guitars with more than one neck, each one tuned its own way, also began to appear during the 1830s. They persist in one form or another to the present day. Nowadays you're more likely to find them made as electrics, but you can find acoustics too—though only as custom models. Most multineck guitars are ordered by professionals for very specific purposes. One player may need to go rapidly back and forth between six- and twelve-strings, another between a regular neck and a high-action, slide neck, others between guitar and mandolin, or regular

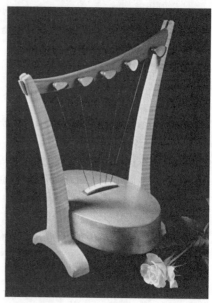

To be or not to be a guitar? Luthier Edward V. Dick makes these "sound sculptures" that combine luthiery skills and concepts with a sculptor's sensibility. *Photos by Larry Shirkey, courtesy E. V. Dick*

and open guitar tunings, and so on. Most multineck guitars are electric; the tension caused by two necks' worth of strings on a single body is stupendous. They look real sharp on stage, which is probably the main reason to have one.

AIR GUITARS

Since air guitars are invariably electric, they are outside the scope of this book and are not included here. However, because of its low cost, ease of playing, and quick learning curve, you should seriously consider whether the air guitar is the instrument for you.

3 Guitar Sound

Guitar makers design guitars in order to get a certain sound out of them. Or, sometimes, they decide what sound qualities they're willing to compromise in order to build a cheaper guitar. Before we look at how guitars are built we'd better learn how to describe the sounds the makers are aiming for when they build them.

We need to acknowledge at the outset that learning about sound from words is an impossible task. A book can't teach you what "balance" or "full-sounding" means. This is something that can only be taught by example and practice.

But a book can help you teach yourself. The way to teach yourself is to play as many different guitars as you can. Seek out guitars. Play friends' guitars. Play through a couple of walls full of guitars at a big box guitar store. Frequent the nearest high-end guitar shop. Many stores will be hospitable as long as you don't abuse the instruments or the owner's ears—especially if you're sincere about buying a guitar someday.

Another way a book can help you learn to hear the qualities of different guitars is by giving you a vocabulary you can use to sort out what you hear. Knowledge, after all, is power. Some of these word overlap. Some are used differently by different people. Some seem to be inconsistent or contradictory. All are at least to some degree subjective. Eventually, when combined with listening, they will fall into place.

TONE

"Tone" refers to the precise color of a note; that is, the qualities that make your guitar sound different from someone else's and even more different from a bassoon or trumpet. Tone quality is what people try to describe when they use words like "dark," "bright," "throaty," "harsh," "transparent, " or "sweet." At best they're only grasping at metaphors, but that's what metaphors are for.

Each of these Santa Cruz guitars has a different size, shape, and in one case a radically different configuration, and is made of different materials. To an experienced player, each will sound very different. Each is suited for a specific range of styles. *Photo courtesy Santa Cruz Guitar Co.*

Tone differences come about because musical instruments, just like the rest of us, obey the laws of physics whether we like them or not. When a string (or, in the case of other instruments, an air column or drum head, and so forth) is set into motion, it does more than vibrate along its entire length. It also splits up into smaller vibrating portions that give off their own sounds. The big, underlying vibration of the whole string is called the "fundamental," and the smaller vibrations are called "overtones." Each instrument has its own way of splitting up the smaller vibrations, of giving greater prominence to some of them than to others, and of leaving some out. The smaller vibrations affect each other as well and can recombine in complicated ways depending on which vibrations are present, which are not, and which are dominant over others. This is what gives each instrument its unique tone quality.

All guitars share some combinations of fundamental and overtones. That's what makes them all sound like guitars. But depending on how it's built and what it's built of, each individual guitar also has its own personal combination of fundamental and overtones. And that's why no two guitars sound alike, even though they both sound like guitars. Even though they may be the same model, the same size, and made of the same woods, each guitar is unique.

The main factor in a guitar's tone color is the material of its back and sides. To an experienced ear, rosewood is soulful compared to the other major body woods and it growls or shouts. Mahogany is sweeter and softer; it sighs or hums and, in the finest mahogany guitars, it sounds plump and round and beautifully balanced. Maple is as projective as rosewood but more brittle and astringent in tone and with less bass resonance.

TONE, TIMBRE, AND PITCH

Everyday language is used as much as possible in this book. But you should be aware that, in formal discourse, musicologists don't use the term *tone* quite the way we do in ordinary speech. They prefer the terms *tone color* or *timbre* for what we call *tone*. (*Timbre* comes from French and is pronounced "TAM-brah.") In correct scholarly language, "tone" actually means what the rest of us usually call a "note," meaning a sound you hear. Technically, *note* refers only to the dot on the printed page of music, not to what you hear. *Pitch* refers to the actual frequency of vibration of a given tone (or note, depending on whether you're speaking to me or to a musicologist).

VOLUME

"Volume" is how loud your guitar is. Sometimes it's called "amplitude." At its simplest, volume is an objective standard that audio engineers know as "sound pressure level" (or SPL), and measure with a decibel meter to tell them how loud a guitar is (the decibel is the standard unit of SPL). But in real life there's more than meets the meter, because subjective perception of other qualities such as balance and presence also play a part in how loud a guitar seems.

Volume is mainly a function of how freely the top of the guitar moves when driven by the strings, but a combination of other factors is also involved.

- The quality and thickness of the top wood and the way it's planed, braced, and finished determine the guitar's volume potential. The quality of the back and sides also plays a part because their rigidity determines how efficiently the air chamber of the body resonates.
- Heavier strings usually sound louder because they put more energy into the top than do lighter strings. However, some guitars—usually but not necessarily light, delicately built ones—seem to be able to absorb only so much string energy and will produce diminishing returns if you string them too heavily.

- Of course you have to play loud by applying your own energy to the strings to make them vibrate enough to move the top.
- All other things being equal, larger guitars sound louder. There's more top to vibrate and a larger sound chamber to reinforce the vibrations. But, because in the guitar world all other things are never equal, you can find dynamic small guitars that overwhelm big ones with stodgy tops.
- Finally, an instrument's capacity to absorb energy from the strings is affected by the mass of the neck and headstock. An odd but interesting phenomenon is that every so often you'll find an instrument that can be improved by putting heavier tuning machines on the headstock.

Volume may also differ from high strings to low ones. It's cheaper and easier to make a guitar with relatively loud bass strings and high strings that have only a weak, false jangle. Beginners are sometimes attracted to this sound because they hear the strong bass first, but they become dissatisfied as their ear, taste, and musicianship become more sophisticated. An instrument that's genuinely loud is loud all across its range, not just in the low notes. (See page 41 for more information on this subject.)

PRESENCE

"Presence" is another mysterious, subjective quality. It can make a guitar seem louder even though it may not actually read so on a meter. It makes the guitar sound full and all there.

The kind of volume that can be metered affects how far away you can move from a guitar and still hear it and is an index of whether or not one instrument can overwhelm another. But presence is more of a psychological factor that will make you and your friends feel surrounded by sound when you play in an intimate setting. Having to play too loud is a poor way to compensate for an instrument with insufficient presence.

A good measure of presence is how satisfying an instrument sounds when you play it softly. On a good guitar, softly played notes will have the same degree of authority as loud ones. Tone quality won't fall off along with the volume level. This sensation of fullness is closely related to balance and sustain and implies good tone quality as well.

Presence comes from the efficiency of the guitar's top. It seems that a guitar sounds fuller and more honest in proportion to the degree it depends on its top to produce its total volume, rather than on the resonance of its air chamber.

DYNAMIC RANGE

You'd think that in order to get the guitar to play more softly or more loudly, all you'd need to do is strum or pluck it softer or harder. But that's true only to a point. A great guitar goes from very, very soft to very, very loud, responding to every nuance of your touch. An ordinary guitar only goes from soft to loud, if that. Most cheap guitars go only from moderately loud to clangy.

The concept of dynamic range overlaps somewhat with those of volume and fullness and, as with those qualities, it's primarily a function of the guitar's top. An instrument without a full dynamic range will frustrate you when you want to add strong accents or emphasize the meaning of a song through loud and soft sections.

SEPARATION

"Separation" is the ability of an instrument to express simultaneously played notes so that they are perceived distinctly and individually rather than as a blended whole. In other words, when you strum an open E chord, is what you hear more like one glob of sound or six separate ingredients? An analogy might be to the flavors that make up a fine sauce.

It is hard to learn how to hear separation and harder still to express it in words, but it's an important factor in determining the "sound" of an individual stylist. How much separation you want is a matter of personal preference. However it's difficult to build a guitar with good separation and luthiers generally consider it an achievement.

Separation is also a function of the player's individual touch.

BALANCE

"Balance" is the relationship between the high and low notes in terms of fullness and volume. In a balanced guitar, the notes have equal authority throughout the entire range of the instrument.

Guitars that are overbalanced toward the bass are called "boomy." This may be a desirable quality depending on your style. If your main goal is to punch out bass notes in a bluegrass band, such an instrument might be perfect for you. Bass-heavy guitars also provide an extremely full sound when being played in a bass-note/strum style as the sole accompaniment to a singer. The total effect sounds much fuller when the bottom gets filled up with those big bass notes.

If you want to play by yourself in a quiet room or do a lot of melodic fingerpicking, you may find that you prefer a guitar that's balanced more toward the high strings. Instruments that sound this way are usually called just plain "balanced," notwithstanding the fact that, to today's predominant tastes, a slightly bass-heavy instrument is actually the norm.

The ideal, perfectly balanced guitar is one that gives you the opportunity to control the relative volume of the high and low strings through touch. To a beginner's ear a well-balanced guitar may sound flat and dry compared to a boomy one. Such guitars are harder to make and harder to find than imbalanced ones—especially bass-heavy ones. They're also harder to play, since they put more of the responsibility for how they sound squarely on you.

Balance is mostly a function of size. If all other factors are equal, as they never are, larger guitars tend to be bass-heavy (with dreadnoughts the boomiest of all), while smaller instruments tend to bring out the highs more strongly. The type of body wood also plays a part (mahogany is less boomy than rosewood) and a larger sound hole also tends to balance toward the highs. Balance is also a quality of the individual instrument, so that one rosewood dreadnought may be better balanced than another, seemingly identical, instrument.

SUSTAIN

"Sustain" is the sense of how long a note keeps sounding after you initiate it. Acoustic scientists divide a sound into two components: attack and decay. If the sound decays too fast, you have poor sustain. Instruments that have poor sustain lack a singing quality and cannot hold long notes or chords. Generally, sustain is a quality of fine guitars and is something you want but it may be more or less important to you than to the next person depending on your style. Some guitarists might even feel that a given guitar has too much sustain. The archtop guitars used in the dance bands of the 1930s and 1940s needed to have a percussive sound that gave a bouncy "chock-chock" lift to the rhythm section; too much sustain would muddy the beat. Guitars in traditional bluegrass ensembles need a similar quality to sound clean and so as not to compete for ensemble space with the mandolin. On the other hand, modern bluegrass guitar soloists often like a more singing sound when they solo on the high notes, so some compromise may be necessary. (No wonder bluegrassers are so notoriously fussy about their guitars!) Sustain is a desirable quality for many, perhaps most, but certainly not all, guitarists.

The vibration of the top is what gives you an honest, clean sustain that preserves all the components of the tone throughout its duration. Echoey sustain that depends more on the air chamber makes for a cheaper, less clean sound. You can learn to hear the difference. Sustain is also affected by many other factors including the lightness of the body, the mass of the neck and headstock, and the quality of the saddle and bridge.

If you're a beginner, it's hard to judge sustain on high notes because you need to build up enough strength to hold the string firmly against the fret in order to let the note sing for as long as the guitar will let it. Too-low action (strings set too low above the fingerboard) will adversely affect sustain. Experienced players also play with vibrato, which adds extra energy to the note and increases the sustain and singing quality. Factors outside the acoustics of the guitar itself, such as the condition of the frets and the age and gauge of the strings, may also affect the instrument's intrinsic sustain.

Sustain is one of the most important factors in creating the immediate impression—even to the unsophisticated ear—that a guitar does or does not sound good for the kind of music you want to play on it.

CUTTING POWER

"Cutting power" is the ability of an instrument to insert itself into spaces in an ensemble with other instruments, as opposed to overwhelming them through sheer volume. Therefore it also depends on the nature of the ensemble and the music being played. A swing band with horns, a bluegrass band, an old-time music band, and a band with a keyboard or an accordion or a cittern all leave completely different spaces to be filled and each may call for a very different-sounding kind of guitar.

Cutting power also depends to a large extent on the relationship between the qualities of attack and decay mentioned in the preceding section on sustain. In order to try to hear these qualities in your mind's ear, try to re-create in your mind the plunky sound of a banjo and to differentiate it from the more singing sound of an acoustic guitar. The banjo is an instrument with a very sharp attack and a short decay. The guitar has a smoother attack and a longer decay.

However it's still hard to make an acoustic guitar that really sings because there's an intrinsic banjolike quality in all plucked instruments. (The harpsichord, which is plucked, sounds banjolike. The piano, which is struck, sounds less so. Soundwise, the banjo is to the guitar very much as the harpsichord is to the piano. I believe it was Ralph Vaughan Williams who once described the sound of the harpsichord as that of skeletons dancing on a tin roof, but let's not get into that.) The result of this plucked heritage is that when you play the guitar louder you tend to increase the volume of the attack part of the sound; however, the decay part of the sound increases, far less proportionally. To a certain extent this relationship between attack and decay volume can be controlled by choice of woods, by bracing design, and even by string gauge.

Before today's new golden age of luthiery the standard of comparison in the acoustic guitar world was the 1930s Martin dreadnought. The extremely loud attack of this instrument gave it great cutting power in string band ensembles. Another standard was the Stromberg archtop guitar, with a sharp "chock-chock" attack that could be heard unamplified by every member of a twelve-piece band and that gave a lift to every dancer on the floor. Guitarists in those days needed to be felt more than heard. But it would be impossible for today's acoustic guitar soloists to sing their songs and dream their dreams on such a guitar. Contemporary guitarists need less attack and more sustain to play for ears that are used to the long, sustained notes of electric guitars.

Since cutting power depends on the sum of the qualities of the instrument and how they relate to the sum of the qualities of the ensemble you're playing in, it can only be judged from personal experience and as a matter of personal utility.

VOICE

"Voice" is the way the instrument projects its sound. It's possible to describe different instruments as slow or quick to speak and to say (for example, of a brand-new instrument that has not yet been played in) that its voice sounds contained.

Note that the term *voicing* is used in a somewhat different sense to refer to the way in which a luthier listens to the sounds of the top and bracing as they are being carved into final shape on a fine, handmade guitar. This, along with the body woods and the rigidity of the body, are the main factors in voice.

WRAPAROUND AND PROJECTION

"Wraparound" is the term guitar aficionados use to describe the ability of a guitar to wrap its sound back around you, as opposed to "projecting" it forward to the microphone or audience. Both are important qualities. Projection can be important not only for sounding full to your audience but also for making sure that your fellow band musicians can hear what you're playing. Wraparound is important for your ability to hear yourself in an ensemble and is one of the most important factors in your self-satisfaction. It's just more fun to hear a guitar that comes back around you, circling you with its warmth and fullness.

Try this sometime: get together with a guitar-playing friend and a roomful of guitars. Then study the way various instruments sound when you play them yourself and then when you hear them played at you. Some instruments might sound better (or louder, or fuller) played at you than when you play them yourself. These instruments might have a certain advantage in some performing situations but are less likely to satisfy you when you play or practice by yourself. You may also notice that, among equally well-made guitars, smaller guitars tend to wrap around more than larger guitars do.

YOU

Ultimately, the sound of the guitar will also be your sound. It's a function of your personal touch, the angle at which you pick, your decisions about string gauge, the kinds of picks you use (if any), the way you shape your fingernails, and so on. Instead of thinking of a guitar as having a certain sound in and of itself, it's best to think of it as having a sound that comes from an interaction between you and it. It's hard for a beginner to judge this. Experienced players can pick up a guitar and be able to say almost immediately, "This guitar is for me. It does what I want it to do. It says what I want it to say."

AMBIENCE

Where you play the guitar makes a lot of difference in how it sounds to you and to others. Your instrument will sound lighter, brighter, and in many ways more satisfying if you play in a room with bare walls and little upholstery or drapery; that's why many people like to play in the kitchen. A poor instrument might be quickly revealed as too harsh and abrasive-sounding under the same circumstances. Conversely, instruments sound mellower, warmer, and generally less powerful in a plush room.

FACTS AND IMPRESSIONS

Most of the qualities we've discussed can be reduced to quantitative measurements. If they can't, it's only because our technology isn't good enough yet. We can measure volume with an SPL meter. We can see the relationship between fundamental and overtones on an oscilloscope. We can analyze the vibration patterns of a moving top by sprinkling graphite dust over it or through holography.

Some of these measurements are useful to the quality-control engineers whose mass-produced guitars need to be as standardized as possible. Some luthiers also use this kind of quantitative data, although most prefer to work by touch and intuition. How they do it is their business. But your business is to go by sound alone. As a musician your first duty is to listen, for the simple reason that to listen is the *only* duty of your audience.

4 Wood, Finish, and Glues

PLYWOOD AND SOLID WOOD

Most Guitars Are Plywood

Most of the guitars made nowadays—and just about all new guitars with a list price under $1,000—have plywood backs and sides. The real cheapies even have plywood tops. If this comes as a surprise to you, it's because the guitar industry has not exactly been trumpeting the news around. In fact the guitar industry should be ashamed of the essentially deceptive way it skirts the issue in its advertising and sales literature. There's really no reason for it.

In the guitar world, plywood goes by the highfalutin name of "laminate," which implies (for the most part correctly) a higher class of goods than the stuff you get at the lumberyard. It boils down to the same thing, though: several layers ("plies") of wood are glued together. The guitar makers would prefer me to use the word *laminate* exclusively, but, since I'm not on anyone's payroll at the moment, in this book I use *laminate* and *plywood* interchangeably. Real, honest-to-god wood, the stuff that comes to you in unadulterated planks right off the log as God and Nature made it, is known in the industry as "solid" wood.

The Mystique and Value of Solid Wood

The spirituality of a laminate guitar is another story. Although it may offend you to discover that plywood is even used, much less that it's now standard, in the holy art of guitar making, you'd better remember that plywood is the standard construction material in most homes today, including possibly your own. You'd also better remember that almost all dark hardwood furniture these days is laminate (or "veneer," as they call it in the furniture trade). Just as with guitars, you've got to go either to a prestige maker or buy an antique if you want solid

wood—in fact, new solid-wood furniture is harder to come by than a new solid-wood guitar and is proportionately more expensive in relation to veneer furniture.

It also seems likely that fine solid-wood guitars will last longer, although solid woods of inferior quality will likely hold up over time no better than laminates.

If you need or want to feel that you own a "real" guitar, you'll need solid wood. A real wood guitar of fine quality is something that becomes an heirloom. It sounds better and it gets better with age. But there are a lot of guitarists out there playing away happily—and some of them very well and for good money—on their laminate guitars.

LAMINATES

Buyer Beware

Too many guitar manufacturers are careless about indicating that they use laminates, and dealers may not leap to point this out either unless they're trying to move you up into the all-solid-wood price range. Some businesspeople's business ethics allow omission but won't allow a lie in response to a direct question. So ask. Roughly the same standards seem to apply to the way veneer is treated by furniture dealers. (In the furniture industry, by the way, these terms are used a little differently. The word *veneer* generally implies a true wood surface ply while *laminate* refers to a synthetic surface ply, usually over a chipboard core.)

When you browse through manufacturers' catalogs or even read the labels on showroom guitars, you'll find that the way solids and laminates are labeled is often confusing. Some manufacturers are very clear, some inconsistent, and a few just plain shoddy. I suspect that this is due in part to sloppy copywriting and poor communication between the copywriting and marketing departments, in part to ignorance, in part to a desire to play down the term *laminate*, and in part to deliberate evasion. Standards need to be raised. Not the least of the problem is the way laminates are so often described in ads and catalogs as *fine woods*. Yes, veneer-grade rosewood and mahogany are fine woods, so it's probably legal to describe laminates this way. And laminates can differ considerably in quality, especially as to whether the inner ply is quality wood or some junk composite. But don't you get the feeling that someone is trying to play you for a fool? Much guitar advertising operates at the same level of moral validity as slapping a "low-sodium, low-cholesterol" label on a food product laden with artificial flavors and polysyllabic preservatives.

Perhaps you get the feeling by now that it's safest to assume that any wood not specifically labeled as *solid* is suspect as a possible laminate. You're right.

Even better would be to get the word *laminate* out of the closet. It's the standard industry material for backs and sides on low- and mid-price guitars, some of them pretty good, so why not admit it? As things stand now the manufacturers are silent about the quality of the wood they use in cores, glues, and other specs. If laminate comes out of the closet, they'll be able to compete with each other in the advertised quality of their materials and we'll all be better off. But for the time being a great silence hangs over all. Like political candidates who cannot admit that they will raise taxes, no manufacturer seems brave enough to take the first step toward acknowledging reality.

There's one more thing you need to know. Some manufacturers describe their tops as being of "select" spruce. This is a code word for laminate. (However, a top called just plain "spruce," if not specifically labeled as solid, might also be laminate.)

Laminate Construction

Guitar laminates are usually three-ply. The outer ply is a finished veneer of rosewood, mahogany, maple, or so on. Veneers are milled by a process called rotary cutting in which a thin, continuous layer is cut off the log in a way that resembles peeling the skin off an apple. Rotary cutting gives the wood merchant the greatest board-foot efficiency and therefore the greatest profit per log of any milling method. It also brings out the figure (ornamental grain pattern) of most woods more than other milling methods do. As a result laminate guitars may be more attractive, at least on the surface, than much finer instruments made of solid wood. (Veneers, of course, vary among themselves in quality and the best-looking ones wind up on the more expensive laminates.)

The center ply, or core, is glued cross-grained (with the grain going in a perpendicular direction) to the outer veneer layers. This imparts strength in the same way that gluing corrugated plies of cardboard perpendicular to each other imparts strength to cardboard cartons. Ideally the center ply should be of the same wood used in the inner and outer plies, although this may not be the case with inexpensive instruments. In cheap guitars it may even be junk wood or some kind of chip composite. We don't know. Only the makers know, and they're not telling. (Of course, you could break open the guitar and take a look.)

The inner ply, which is what you see when you look through the sound hole, should be the same wood as the outer ply. In some instruments, especially cheap ones, it obviously isn't. Generally a rather plain-figured cut of wood is used for economy, which is fair enough—beauty is only skin deep, so there's no reason to make the inside of the guitar look ravishing. Some makers do use an inner ply with some figure to it, which usually serves to make it harder to tell by looking whether the wood is plywood or solid.

Stability and Durability

When it comes to stability and durability, laminates come out well when compared with solid woods. They don't crack all the way through with dryness as solid wood can, but some (especially if of poor quality) may swell up and distort with humidity. In fairness, poorly seasoned solid wood would do this as well. As a general rule laminates hold up very well through climate changes and abusive treatment in the short run. The long-range behavior of modern guitar laminates is not well tested but certainly many ornamental laminates to solid wood bases on vintage furniture have held up over the years. So have the ornamental laminates on European guitars of the pre-Torres era.

On the negative side, plywood shatters rather than breaks cleanly when punctured, making it a repair shop nightmare. In the past most repair people advocated only quick-and-dirty work on laminate guitars; however, now that they've gone up in price and quality, it's become more worthwhile to do neat work. But what would be a small patch job on solid wood can mean cutting out and replacing an entire section of laminate. Some repair people—the ones who have managed to build up a busy trade exclusively in fine instruments—simply reject repair work on laminates.

The plies in laminate may also separate over a period of time, especially when subjected to abusive changes of temperature and humidity. Sometimes this can lead to a loose section, for example a knot, in the inside ply that creates a hard-to-locate rattle. Once located, though, it's easy enough to fix with a glue injection.

Detecting Plywood

How can you tell if any instrument is plywood? It's not always easy. For starters, ask the dealer or read the merchandise tags and sales literature. Then examine the guitar itself. Try looking for a knot, texture, or pattern in the wood on the back of the guitar and see if it corresponds to an identical pattern on the inside. Or try looking for plies in the wood on the inside edge of the sound hole. (A plastic binding around the inside of the sound hole may be a sign that the maker is trying to cover something up.) The appearance of plies around the edge of the sound hole is most difficult to disguise in the area under the end of the fingerboard, where you may be able to spot three (or, in very cheap guitars, two) plies. If you have an inspection mirror, take a good look at the underside of the top. Laminate tops generally have an obviously less-finished-looking, courser-grained inside surface. But it's not easy to learn from words. Comparing guitars is the best way to learn, but even so, a clever cover-up can be hard to recognize.

Laminate Tops

Only bottom-line guitars have plywood tops these days. You may also encounter plywood on the tops of older models from some companies that have more recently switched to all-solid tops. Plywood by its very nature is not effective for tops; it just can't vibrate the way a top must in order to sound good. Nonetheless, a properly designed all-plywood guitar can have an adequate sound for a beginner and would be acceptable if fairly priced. Some makers even believe that it's theoretically possible to build a plywood-bodied guitar that will sound every bit as good as ones made of the finest solid wood, even as it matures over time. But it hasn't been done. Plywood-top guitars also tend to be cheaply built in every way and do not sound good. Buy one if you must. Avoid them if you can. As a beginner you're more likely to succeed with a better instrument.

Solid tops sound better and also improve with age if they're made of decent wood to begin with, so most manufacturers, in response to competition, now offer solid tops but compromise on the back and sides to keep costs down. Buying a guitar with a solid top but a laminate back and sides is a perfectly reasonable way to go. The plywood back and sides usually keep such a guitar from sounding really good but such instruments can still sound better than a bad all-solid-wood guitar.

Laminate Backs and Sides

Plywood backs and sides are another story, because a guitar's back and sides have an entirely different acoustic function from that of the top: to maintain the rigidity of the sound chamber and help project the sound. A good laminate guitar, though offensive to purists, can sound better and be more durable than a poorly made solid wood guitar.

Among recent American high-quality manufacturers, Guild began to use laminates for the backs and sides of some high-range models as early as the mid-1970s, with considerable success. The top-range offshore instruments, including the best of the Alvarez-Yairi, Washburn, Takamine, Epiphone, and Yamaha lines, with their solid tops and laminate backs and sides, are also widely used by professional musicians. Martin met the Japanese competition of the 1970s by introducing its low-end Sigma line of laminate guitars and more recently has introduced laminates to the low end of its own brand. Although the use of laminates in good-quality flattop guitars is a fairly recent development, plywood has also been used on journeyman-level, electric archtop guitars for well over a quarter of a century, and the original Maccaferri (Django-style) guitars had laminate bodies.

Many professionals use laminate guitars to perform with and they work just fine, especially for band players whose sound is not exposed or for players who plug in their guitars and can therefore control their sound quality through electronic modification.

Laminate Fingerboards

On a cheaply made guitar even the fingerboard may be made of plywood. Sometimes you can spot the lamination by taking a good look at the end of the fingerboard just above the sound hole. Maybe you'll be able to spot the layers of lamination or a cap of wood glued on over the fingerboard end to hide the layers. But if it's a good dye or cap job and you don't have a good eye, you could be fooled. A laminated fingerboard isn't a good thing: it's weak, it's potentially unstable, and it's a sign of cost-cutting that reflects on the whole guitar. It's acceptable only on the most inexpensive instruments, where you're getting what you pay for.

Laminate Necks and Headstocks

Sometimes necks and headstocks are made of several pieces of glued-together wood. These are also called "laminates," because technically that's what they are; but really they're a whole different kettle of fish. Lamination here is a strong, perfectly respectable, time-honored way of constructing these parts of the instrument. Often it's done ornamentally or to impart strength by juxtaposing cross-grained sections; even when the underlying motivation is to be able to use smaller remnants of wood by combining them, it's OK. (See Chapter 5, page 78, for more information on this topic.)

Materials and Tone

As we'll learn in greater detail in the course of this chapter, each kind of body wood has its own sound: mahogany is sweet, rosewood punchy, maple bright, and so on. But plywood guitars reflect these differences less consistently and less strongly than solid woods do—sometimes not at all. Whether or not a laminate accurately reflects the tonal qualities of the wood it's "supposed" to be made of is probably due to the type and quality of woods used for the core and inner ply; you'll find that well-made laminate instruments do offer perceptible tone differences between body woods.

SEASONING AND MILLING SOLID WOOD

Seasoning

This section is not about salt and pepper. Well-seasoned wood is not something that will help your chops or let you play tasty licks. Seasoning, also called "drying" or "aging," is the process by which the wood's natural moisture content is reduced after it is cut. Seasoning stabilizes wood to help it resist warping, cracking, shrinking, and expanding. How well the wood is seasoned is an important factor in how well your guitar will hold up over the years and also plays a part in tone quality.

Proper seasoning of fine wood calls for expert skill and sensitivity. Wood is seasoned either by air drying, which may take years, or by slow kiln drying, which may take weeks or months. The faster the kilning, the less stable the wood. At the extreme low end, very quick kiln drying is used only for junk wood like the stuff that's used for tomato stakes and orange crates. The less your guitar wood is like tomato stakes and orange crates, the better off you are.

A lumber kiln is essentially a shed into which you blow warm, dry air through logs or boards stacked so they have some air space between them. Some commercial woods are seasoned by chemical, electrostatic, or dehumidifying (air-conditioning) methods, but these woods aren't suitable for instrument making or any fine woodworking.

Many collectors feel that the excellence of fine nineteenth- and early twentieth-century guitars is due in part to the use of wood that was slowly air-dried with a degree of care that would be economically prohibitive today. But this is pure supposition, however reasonable, because no documentation survives of exactly how guitar woods were treated by Martin and other fine makers during that era.

Whatever the case may have been, almost everyone agrees that air drying is a superior method. While some wood suppliers claim that their kiln-dried woods are indistinguishable by hygrometer readings from air-dried woods, purists counter that hygrometers don't take into account the more gradual evaporation of resins, of the natural glues that hold wood grains together, and of other volatile components—a process that occurs during the much lengthier air-drying process. Three years is a typical time for air drying, although some luthiers air dry for much longer than that. At a minimum it should take at least one year so the lumber can go through at least one complete cycle of the seasons.

Whatever the advantages of air drying, the fact is that most guitar woods today are kiln-dried. Proper kiln drying is a patient process that depends on the skill of the kiln operator. It must achieve a precise balance between the rate at which the moisture evaporates from the surface of the wood and the rate at which the moisture is drawn to the surface from deeper within the wood. When these two factors are out of balance, the wood cracks or warps from uneven stress patterns. Guitar body wood, while only around $\frac{3}{32}$ of an inch thick, must withstand the force of many pounds of string pressure, so it must be free of faults. Only a small part of commercial lumber is kilned finely enough for luthiery use. The better the kilning, the more time and care went into it, so the more expensive it is. High quality kiln-dried wood is preferred by many factory makers for its consistency and predictability.

Seasoning doesn't end when the making of the actual guitar begins. In the highest-quality instrument making, the wood may be allowed to stabilize for several weeks or even months further between assembly stages. In addition, properly climate-controlled shops and factories maintain a relative humidity level of about 40 percent in order to keep the wood at the level to which it has been seasoned.

Nor does seasoning end when the guitar comes out of the factory. Fine instruments continue to mature indefinitely as elements of the wood and finish continue to age, aided by the actual "playing in" of the instrument.

MILLING LUMBER

Prime Cuts

Logs are round. Boards, tabletops, and pieces of guitar wood are flat. "Aha," you say, "someone must have cut the log." The process of cutting timber is called milling, as in saw*mill*, and it's pursued in a considerably more organized and scientific fashion than in the *Texas Chainsaw Massacre* or while carving the average Thanksgiving turkey. The following sections cover the subject in a somewhat simplified way and only consider those points that relate to guitar making.

Grain and Figure

The most obvious visual feature of wood is the surface pattern, which is caused by the growth rings that grow outward in concentric circles from the center of the log. Evenness of ring size is a sign of consistent climatic conditions that permit the tree to grow about the same amount each year, while evenness of coloration is a sign that seasonal shifts of humidity within the year were not extreme. However, each species of wood has its own characteristic cell structure that imparts a unique appearance.

When botanists talk about wood grain, they are referring to specific technical aspects of the alignment of the cellular structure within the wood. But when people like you and me talk about grain we usually mean the visual pattern of the growth rings. *Grain* is used in this colloquial way in this book.

In this sense grain is similar to the woodworkers' term *figure*, which is the overall visual surface pattern of a board. Figure results from a number of factors including climate and other environmental conditions, the method of sawing and the character of the grain structure of the wood species.

In addition to the growth rings in their concentric circles, wood also contains tissues called "medullary rays," which radiate outward from the center in a spoke-like fashion and serve the purpose of storing nutrients over the winter. Rays, as we shall see, are visually present in the wood figure only when certain kinds of milling are used.

Slab Cutting

If you're a wood merchant and want to make the most money per log, you'll rotary cut it for veneer as described earlier in the section on laminates. If you're producing boards, the most economical way to get them out of the log is by the method variously called "slab cutting," "flat cut-

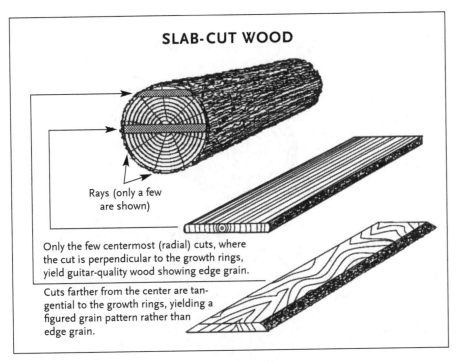

SLAB-CUT WOOD

Rays (only a few are shown)

Only the few centermost (radial) cuts, where the cut is perpendicular to the growth rings, yield guitar-quality wood showing edge grain.

Cuts farther from the center are tangential to the growth rings, yielding a figured grain pattern rather than edge grain.

ting," or "plank sawing." This uses up almost every available bit of the log so there's little waste.

In the board cut from the absolute center of the log the growth rings are perpendicular to the saw cut. This center board is called a "radial cut." It's the most desirable cut to use in a guitar because the perpendicular grain pattern makes the wood less likely to warp and distort with climate changes than in any other cut. It also promotes the best possible vibration patterns in the top.

As the cuts move farther from the center the pattern of the concentric rings becomes less and less perpendicular. These cuts are less desirable for guitars but suitable for less critical applications like furniture making. (Tabletops and bookcases are considerably thicker than the ³⁄₃₂ of an inch wood used in guitars so stability is less of an issue.) In addition, the cuts that are farther away from the center show the figure of the wood better. In general, wood that you would admire in cabinetry is not as good for guitar making as a plainer-looking piece of lumber—though some makers and buyers choose to go more for looks, anyway.

Quartersawed Wood

Slab cutting yields only one absolutely perfect, luthiery-quality board—the radially cut board from the center of the log. The next few cuts out from the center might also have grain close enough to perpendicular to be acceptable. But if luthiers and fine woodworkers had to depend on only a few boards per tree, their materials costs would be prohibitive. Fortunately there's another way of running the log through the mill called "quartersawing," which results in many more high-quality boards per log.

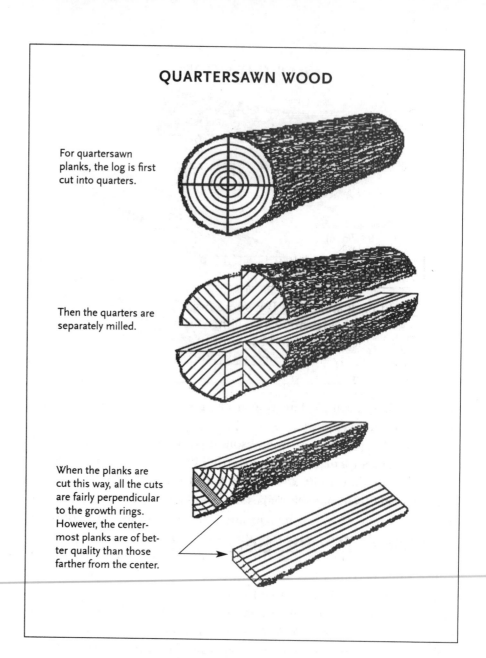

QUARTERSAWN WOOD

For quartersawn planks, the log is first cut into quarters.

Then the quarters are separately milled.

When the planks are cut this way, all the cuts are fairly perpendicular to the growth rings. However, the center-most planks are of better quality than those farther from the center.

Quartersawing is so called because the log is first cut into quarters, and then milled into boards in a close-to-radial fashion. As with slab cutting, only the very center cuts are radially sawed right on the money. But the rest of the cuts come out with the growth-ring pattern close enough to perpendicular to be acceptable for luthiery.

Remember, though, that quartersawing does not magically confer fine sound quality on a piece of wood. There are still lots of other things to consider: the tone quality and resiliency of the wood itself; how well it's aged; and how carefully the maker does the final shaping, thinning, and assembly.

Quartersawed wood, however, is always structurally superior to slab-cut wood because it's more stable as it ages. Therefore it's always the first choice for the tops, necks, backs, and sides of fine guitars. Ideally

WOOD WARPING PATTERNS
The degree of warping shown is exaggerated for visual emphasis.

The outer rectangle in the diagrams below represents the shape of the freshly cut plank before it shrinks over the years.

All wood shrinks over a period of years, but quarter-sawn wood shrinks evenly as it dries.

Slab-cut wood warps as it shrinks, creating additional problems for the guitar.

the bracing struts, bridge blanks, and even the inside blocks should also be quartersawed. But don't expect to find perfectly quartersawed woods in any but the most expensive guitars.

Tops should certainly be quartersawed if they are to qualify as fine. So should the back and sides. But some first-class makers use slab-cut wood for back and sides anyway—either for economy or because the maker gives higher priority to beauty of figure than to stability and acoustic value. A finely made guitar with a well-chosen piece of highly figured, slab-cut wood can look stunningly beautiful. But I cannot recommend paying serious money for a supposedly serious instrument in which all the woods are not quartersawed. These include the products of some quite accomplished luthiers who have opted for the figure of slab-cut wood over the stability of quartersawed wood, as well as some regular production models from high-end makers.

Bookmatched Tops and Backs

The tops and backs of fine guitars should ideally consist of two sections of wood that are "bookmatched." This means that they come from a single piece of wood about 3/16 of an inch thick that has been cut in half down the narrow dimension into two pieces each about 3/32 of an inch thick, and then opened out like a book. Bookmatched sections look nice because they mirror each other but their real importance is in the symmetry of grain structure. That means that both sides of the bookmatched joint will expand and shrink at equal and symmetrical rates over the years and that both sections will be acoustically equal.

Bookmatched veneer sections used on laminates look pretty but have no structural or acoustic value. They are merely a cosmetic feature.

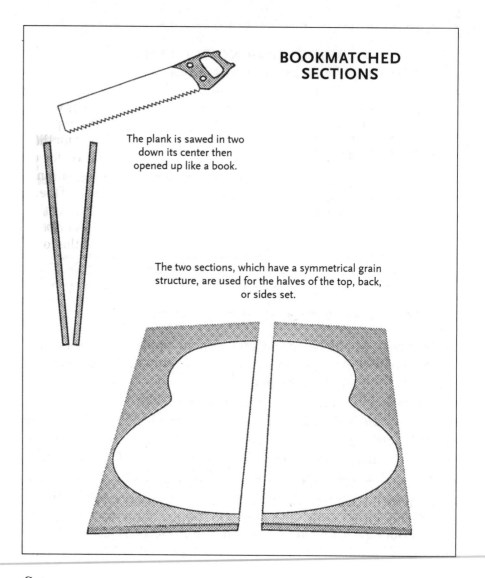

BOOKMATCHED SECTIONS

The plank is sawed in two down its center then opened up like a book.

The two sections, which have a symmetrical grain structure, are used for the halves of the top, back, or sides set.

Sets

Wood merchants furnish luthiers and factories with the material for the back and sides in what is called a "set": unfinished pieces cut to approximate size and ready for final trimming and shaping. In high-production factories the sets are usually procured and put together by the company's own wood-supply division; in fact, some makers both large and small even purchase raw logs and do their own milling or have it done specifically for them.

In instruments made with any degree of care the backs and sides of a set should be visually and acoustically compatible. But in the very finest guitar making the ideal set consists of back and sides from the same log. This gives the wood the same advantages that bookmatching does: all sections are acoustically identical and all are likely to shrink and expand at the same rate because they are matched in raw material and seasoning.

Matched sets from the same log are more expensive and harder to come by. Don't expect to find them on any but the most expensive instruments.

Blanks

A roughly shaped section of wood is called a "blank." Necks, bridges, heel blocks, and end blocks are all milled to blanks that approximate the piece's final shape. In mass-produced guitars they are machine-cut, but in finer guitars more handwork is used in carving them to final shape.

TONEWOODS

The word *tonewood* is used to describe instrument-building woods in general, although some violin makers use it only to describe the spruce for the top. In addition to the large, obvious piece of wood used for the top, back, sides, and neck of the guitar, smaller pieces are used for other structural components as well: the ornamental "binding strips" around the edges of the top; the "lining strips" that reinforce the edge joints of the sides with the back and top from inside the guitar; the "bracing struts" of the top and back; and the massive "heel block" (or "head block") and "end block" that support the joints where the two sides come together at the top and bottom of the body.

Wood Naming Conventions

Names of woods are confusing even to professionals. The lumber industry uses a hodgepodge of nomenclatures: native and vernacular names, trade names, names that reflect regional origins or ports of shipping, and different names for the same wood depending on whether it's been milled or is still on the tree. Guitar makers echo this imprecision and the names of woods used in instrument making are no less confusing. What violin makers usually call "Swiss pine," for example, is not pine but spruce, and these days it's most likely to come from Romania. "German" spruce might really be from Germany but it's also an acceptable term for describing European spruce in general. (What isn't acceptable, however, is to ship British Columbian Sitka spruce to Germany and then import it back as German spruce, and it's been done! Since German spruce sells for more than Sitka does, it's worth the trouble and shipping costs. An experienced eye can tell the difference, but can yours?)

The following table lists the major woods used in guitar making. It may help clarify things a little by correlating many of the trade and vernacular names with the Latin botanical names. Don't try to memorize it. Just remember that it's here so you can flip back to it for reference or amusement if you need to.

THE MAJOR GUITAR WOODS

FAMILY	COMMON NAME	BOTANICAL NAME	ORIGIN & COMMENTS
Cedar Cupressaceae	Western red cedar	*Thuja plicata*	Pacific Northwest. Also called British Columbia cedar, red cedar.
Ebony Ebenaceae	Gabon ebony	*Diospyros crassiflora*	West Africa. Also called African ebony.
	Macassar ebony	*Diospyros celebica*	Indonesia. Also called Indian ebony.
Mahogony Meliaceae	Honduras mahogany	*Swietenia macrophylla*	Central & South America. Also known as American, Amazon, or "genuine" mahogany, and differentiated commercially by country of origin.
Maple Aceraceae	European flame maple	*Acer campestre*	Parts of Europe.
	Rock maple	*Acer saccharum* & *Acer nigrum*	Eastern U.S. and Canada.
Rosewood Leguminosae	Brazilian rosewood	*Dalbergia nigra*	Brazil. Also known as palisander, *palo santo*, and *jacaranda de Bahía*. (Do not confuse with other jacarandas.)
	Honduras rosewood	*Dalbergia stevensonii*	Belize. May be used for bridges and fingerboards; not a body wood.
	(East) Indian rosewood	*Dalbergia latifolia*	India and Java. "Indian" and "East Indian" are loosely interchangeable.
Spruce Pinaceae	Sitka spruce	*Picea sitchensis*	Pacific Northwest. Also called silver spruce.
	European spruce	*Picea abies*	Most of Europe. Categories like "German" may be used generically.
	Engelmann spruce	*Picea engelmannii*	U. S. and Canadian Rockies. Sometimes spelled "Englemann."
	White spruce	*Picea glauca*	U.S. and Canada. Commercially differentiated as eastern or western white spruce, Québec spruce, Adirondack spruce, etc., depending on origin and port of shipment.
Rosewood Family Leguminosae	Cocobolo	*Dalbergia retusa*	Central America. Also called *granadillo*.
	Jacaranda	Machaerium villosum	Brazil. Also called *jacaranda pardo*.
	Koa	Acacia koa	Hawaii. The classic ukulele wood.
	Narra	Pterocarpus indicus	South Pacific. Also called *amboyna*.
	Ovangkol	Guibortia ehie	West Africa.
	Tulipwood	*Dalbergia frutescens*	Brazil. Also called *jacaranda rosa*.

Spruce

A resonant softwood of the pine family, spruce is the standard wood for guitar tops. It's also the favored top wood of violin makers, who sometimes refer to it as "Swiss pine."

European spruce is the top wood regarded most highly by guitar and violin makers alike. Mountain-grown logs from Switzerland, Bavaria, and the Carpathians have all been highly prized in the past, but recently much of the European spruce used for guitars, violins, and piano soundboards has come from Romania. The term "German spruce" may be used generically in the wood industry for any European spruce. What country the piece of wood actually comes from is not as important as its individual qualities.

Sitka spruce, usually somewhat ruddy in complexion, comes from the Pacific Northwest and is today the most commonly used wood for guitar tops. Sitka is a bit stronger and stiffer than other spruces and has a faster growth rate. Some luthiers feel that it lacks the tonal and projective qualities of other, more expensive spruces; others don't share this opinion at all.

Appalachian or Adirondack spruce is found from the Appalachian Mountains on into the western states and north into Québec. Some luthiers regard it as superior to Sitka. It has been suggested that Adirondack spruce (localized eastern white spruce) was the wood used on early Martin guitars; but, according to the Martin company, there are no records to verify or disprove that assertion. Gibson, on the other hand, is said variously to have relied on Michigan or Appalachian white spruce for its pre–World War II guitars.

Another highly regarded spruce is Engelmann spruce (*Picea engelmannii*) from the higher elevations of the Rockies and Pacific Cascades. It's much less common than Sitka and some feel it gives a more projective, resonant sound. Engelmann, incidentally, is also prized for large Christmas trees because of the perfection of its shape when grown tall.

Spruce is also customarily used for top bracing, though sometimes mahogany or another hardwood is used for the flat brace above the sound hole and beneath the fingerboard spatula. Sometimes other woods are used for bracing, either as an economy measure on cheap guitars or because a luthier just happens to like them. Spruce (or mahogany) may also be used for the end block and heel block.

SPRUCE MYSTIQUE

There are people who swear they can distinguish the sound of German, Adirondack, or Sitka spruce blindfolded. I can't claim to hear what they do. (Could it be because I've never tried the blindfold?)

Here's my problem. I have certainly heard a magic in some German spruce tops that I've heard nowhere else. It's a special clarity, a strength and transparency in the high overtones, and a sense that it's the wood, rather than the resonating air chamber, that's doing all the work. But I can't swear that I can always spot German spruce because I've also heard German spruce tops—on instruments from the finest makers, mind you—that have been absolute dogs.

On the other hand, there are hundreds, if not thousands, of Sitka-topped guitars made every year that sound good and better than good. Certainly better than a dog of a German-spruce instrument. Often enough you'll find a Sitka top that's a real knockout.

Recently I had to choose between two pieces of wood for the top of a custom guitar. One was a plank of Engelmann. It had as lovely, even, and close a grain as you'll ever see. The other was a plank of coarser-grained Sitka—much less a textbook example of great wood. But the Sitka came from a dismantled airplane built during World War II; in other words, over fifty years ago it was considered well-enough seasoned to be of aircraft quality and it's been curing ever since. Both planks were cut right on the quarter and the medullary rays glistened on both like moonlight on an icy lake. I had heard other guitars constructed by three different luthiers made from other sections of these same woods and it was perfectly clear that either would sound great. What was really remarkable was that when the luthier and I tapped out both planks, we could distinguish no real difference in tone quality! Which did I choose? Well, I picked one, and got just as wonderful-sounding a guitar as I'm sure I would have gotten had I picked the other. Why? Because the luthier's skill was the most important factor of all.

Just remember that the magic is in the wood, not the name. The finest German spruce may be the best of the lot but not all German spruce is the finest. Good Sitka is better than bad German. Good German is better than bad Engelmann. Good Engelmann is better than bad Adirondack. Good Adirondack is better than bad Sitka. Good Sitka is better than bad German . . . and the circle is complete. Listening to the instrument is what tells you whether it's got a good top or not. Reading the catalog specs does not.

Selecting Spruce for a Top

How well a guitar sings is determined by how well its top vibrates due to the quality and shaping of the surface and bracing as well as the quality of the wood itself. The sound of the top will improve with playing and with age. While it may take a decade or two for the top to really mature, you can hear the top of a brand new instrument begin discernibly to "open up" after only a few hours of playing.

You can learn to spot quartersawed tops by the appearance of the rays since rays only appear clearly in quartersawed or radially cut wood (see page 54 for more information about the grain and figure). They impart a certain lustrous sheen across the texture of the grain when you hold the wood against the light. It can be shown pretty easily by example but it's impossible to teach by words.

What a guitar maker looks for in spruce is a light color and a fine, straight growth-ring pattern. The lighter and darker parts of the grain lines, which represent the tree's spring and summer growth, should not be too highly differentiated in shade. (Extremes of shading indicate excessive differences in humidity between the wet and dry seasons of the growing year.) An edge grain structure of no fewer than twelve to fifteen lines per inch at the widest-grained portion of the board is considered the minimum standard for first-class timber. This ideal tends to occur in trees from near the treeline that have experienced healthy, consistent patterns of rainfall and temperature during their lifetime.

The edge grain widens somewhat across the width of the board, reflecting the fact that the outside growth rings of the tree get wider as the log increases in diameter. After the two halves of the top are split and bookmatched, it's conventional to join them with the narrower edge grain at the center seam. However, on some guitars—many vintage Martins in particular—the wider grain is at the center. Both methods seem to work equally well, although each undoubtedly has strong partisans.

A good guitar maker will judge the quality of timber not only by sight but even more importantly by how it rings when tapped and by its resilience and feel. A fine top requires a unique blend of stiffness and resilience that only the best woods provide. Therefore, in spite of everything said about appearances in the preceding paragraphs, you'll occasionally find a quite undistinguished-looking top on a great instrument and, even more often, a good-looking top on a mediocre one. So again: learn to use your ears! The luthier does.

Cedar and Redwood

Over the past few years makers have increasingly turned to western red cedar for tops on both steel-strung and classical guitars. Redwood, a similar wood, has also been used, more often on classical guitars than on steel-strings. A few makers have made tops half of redwood and half of spruce in order to take advantage of both characteristics. The two best-known practitioners of this style have opposite philosophies about which wood to use on the bass side and which on the treble.

Cedar and redwood may have a more brilliant tone than spruce on new guitars but some feel that the tone seems to stay where it is for the life of the guitar instead of growing richer with time as it does with spruce. The tone is more bell-like than that of spruce. Of course the sound of a good piece of cedar would certainly be preferable to that of a bad piece of spruce no matter what the characteristic qualities of each wood.

In the first edition of this book I wrote that "Cedar and redwood tops are not to my taste on steel-string guitars, but you should make up your own mind. Some excellent players use guitars with tops made of these woods." Since then I've made up my own mind too. Two years after I wrote that I had to pick the top wood for a guitar I was having made for me—a different one from that described earlier and by a different luthier. He left me alone with a half-dozen plates (sawed sections) of top wood to tap out. Bear in mind that I've had some, though not much, experience listening to tap tones in wood. One plate was cedar. In it I heard a lot more pleasing things going on than in the spruce plates, and they all sounded good together. So I picked it in spite of my bias against cedar. I wound up with a guitar that had exactly the sound I wanted. Was it the cedar I picked? Perhaps. I've since heard two other guitars with tops from the same billet and liked them too. But again, I think it had more to do with the luthier I picked, because he characteristically builds with an unusual sound I like very much and it was really *his* sound that I wanted and got. The cedar just helped.

Cedar from Europe and the Middle East and mahogany are used by many of Spain's foremost luthiers for the necks of classical guitars.

Harry Fleishman is a luthier who often makes guitars with tops that are half redwood and half spruce. Note also the fanciful rosette pattern on this instrument, which he originally made for himself; one of the elements of the rosette design is trying to escape, and one has in fact already escaped onto the top. It seems the elements, like the luthier himself, don't like to stay within the lines. *Photo by John Youngblut, courtesy Harry Fleishman*

Ceder is the wood of choice for flamenco guitar necks, where both its color and light weight go better with the cypress body. Nineteenth-century guitars, including Martins, had cedar necks, but mahogany and maple hold up better under the tension of today's steel strings. Cedar is also sometimes used for linings.

Rosewood

Rosewood is a dense, resinous, and extremely hard wood. It is usually considered the most desirable material for the back and sides of classical guitars and imparts a brilliant, cutting quality to steel-strung flattop guitars. Rosewood gets its name because the resins of the freshly cut tree give off a sweet, roselike fragrance. (Get your nose out of your instrument! The fragrance is long gone by the time the log has become a guitar.)

When struck, rosewood has greater resonance than any other hardwood, making it the wood of choice for xylophones and marimbas. It has a brilliant and highly projective sound with both a dark and bright side to it and a bit of a bark. It's most guitar players' wood of choice for many excellent reasons. But there are also good reasons to like the sounds of the other major body woods, maple and mahogany, so it's important that you form your own taste. For maximum projection the back and sides of the guitar need to reflect sound rather than absorb it. This is why very hard woods like rosewood and maple give a bright sound while the softer mahogany gives a sweeter sound.

From the builder's point of view rosewood has excellent structural as well as acoustic properties. It may be cut very thin without sacrificing rigidity (the most important factor in back and sides) and it lends itself well to the heat-bending process by which the sides are shaped. However, rosewood splits fairly easily along its grain if subject to climate changes. Re-gluing split sides and backs is a fairly common repair job and not much to worry about. Because it's a fairly open-grained (porous-looking) wood, rosewood is usually treated with a filler before staining and finishing.

Quartersawed, straight-grained, evenly colored, and simple-looking rosewood is best for guitars. Rosewood with a purplish cast, planksawed with a highly figured grain pattern, can be gorgeous in furniture but is structurally less suited for a guitar. But many value it for its cosmetic appeal anyway.

Brazilian rosewood is also known as palisander or by its Spanish name, *palo santo*. In Brazil it is also sometimes called *jacaranda de Bahía*, not to be confused with other jacarandas. Until the 1960s it was imported in the form of uncut logs. Martin and other manufacturers then milled it in their own U.S. factories. But in the late 1960s the Brazilian government, in an effort to develop its own milling industry, decreed that only milled lumber could be exported. Because sawmills find it much more profitable to mill lumber in forms more suitable for furniture than for guitars, guitar-quality Brazilian rosewood became rare and expensive. Now it has become even more expensive because, as a result of rainforest destruction, it is listed as an endangered species and international shipping is prohibited under CITES (the Convention on International Trade in Endangered Species). Some remaining stocks of Brazilian rosewood can still be found in custom and limited-production instruments, where it commands a premium price.

Martin switched to the lighter-colored East Indian rosewood for its standard production models in 1970. Now the Indian wood is getting hard to come by as well. The Indian government prohibited shipping of whole logs in the mid-1970s, also in order to stimulate the growth of its own domestic milling industry. In addition India's forest-growth rosewood has been significantly depleted and most Indian rosewood we see these days is a lighter, plantation-grown variety. Note that the terms "Indian" and "East Indian" rosewood are used interchangeably in the guitar industry.

Many guitar makers and players feel that Indian and Brazilian rosewood sound similar. Some feel Brazilian sounds a lot better, using the sound of vintage Martins to prove their point—a good point, but one that fails to take into account the issues of top woods and bracing patterns as well. One luthier I know says Brazilian sounds different from Indian, but not necessarily better.

Conservative purists certainly prefer the appearance of Brazilian wood and feel (whether or not out of mystical preconceptions) that it does somehow sound better. One of the traditional standards of comparison has been a fifty- or sixty-year-old Brazilian rosewood Martin. To someone like me who grew up with Brazilian rosewood, the Indian stuff just doesn't look right and that's all there is to it. I expect I'll go to the grave with this bias about appearance—but not about quality. As I think back on the three dozen or so most interesting and distinctive flattop guitars I've ever encountered, some have been Brazilian, some Indian, some mahogany, some other woods; some have been new, some old.

Rosewood is a hard-enough wood to be used for bridges and fingerboards, though the more expensive ebony, being harder still, is for some a better choice and is used on more expensive steel-strung guitars. Classical luthiers prefer rosewood bridges, which sound sweeter. Rosewood is also used for bridge plates, as is maple.

Honduras rosewood (also called *nogaed*), a slightly different species, is also used for bridges and fingerboards as well as for marimba bars, guitar laminates, and furniture making. But it's generally not used as a solid wood for guitar bodies because it doesn't bend well to shape the sides.

The various rosewoods are in great demand not only as furniture veneers but also for turned bowls and trinkets (rosewood lends itself well to lathe-work) and for fine knife handles. Brazilian rosewood is also highly sought after for these uses as well as because of its beauty.

Rosewood Substitutes

The following woods are similar to rosewood and in some cases are relatives. For the most part they are inferior to rosewood either acoustically or structurally; for example, some exude pockets of sap when the wood is steam-bent for sides. Therefore they are not generally used for solid-wood guitars but instead are used as veneers for laminates, where they are attractive and sometimes even look like Brazilian or Indian rosewood.

Amboyna (another name for narra).

Bubinga (African rosewood).

Cocobolo (also called *granadillo;* from Mexico). May be used as a solid wood as well as veneer; some luthiers think highly of it for back and sides.

Jacaranda (also called *jacaranda pardo*).

Louro Preto (another Brazilian wood).

Narra (also called amboyna; from the Philippines).

Ovangkol (a dark African wood about midway between rosewood and mahogany). Often appears in slightly different spellings.

Tulipwood (another type of jacaranda known as *jacaranda rosa.* Also used for marimbas.

Mahogany

The best guitar mahogany is "Honduras" mahogany. As with many other names, this is an industry term and the wood may come from Latin American regions other than Honduras proper—even from Brazil. It's sometimes also called American mahogany. Like rosewood, it's open-grained and hence usually treated with a filler before final staining and finishing.

Philippine mahogany, sometimes used on cheap instruments, is a lighter, more porous, tonally inferior wood. European mahogany, while beautiful for furniture, isn't suitable for guitars.

Mahogany is softer and lighter than rosewood and doesn't have nearly as good a reputation as rosewood does—except among those many guitarists who, like Doc Watson and Leo Kottke, prefer its warmth, balance, and sweetness to the brilliance of rosewood. In some ways, you could say that a mahogany guitar is to a rosewood as a chamber-music violin or recorder is to a solo instrument. Or as a Guarnerius violin is to a Strad. Big rosewood guitars are notoriously difficult to mike and to record because of their boominess; many studio guitarists and engineers prefer mahogany instruments for exactly this reason.

Generally, mahogany is less projective, which is to say less loud. That doesn't mean that a mahogany guitar may not be the guitar for you. It also doesn't mean that some mahogany instruments may not be very loud indeed.

There's a saying that "It's no shame to be poor, but it might as well be." The same could be said about being mahogany. Its bad rep probably started because (as just about everyone agrees) its relative lack of brilliance is most apparent in classical guitars. The Martin company may also have played a part. Martin's sonic values have always been very rosewood-oriented and as a rule Martin and the makers it has influenced reserve their best spruce and greatest degree of attention for their rosewood instruments. (In spite of this you'll find some mahogany Martins out there that will knock your socks off—especially among the older ones. And there are a number of makers, the Gibson company and Harry Fleishman among them, who have never stinted in giving mahogany first-class treatment.)

Mahogany is sometimes used for tops on mahogany-bodied guitars. In the old days before laminates it was used especially on economy models. It produces a warm, balanced tone with a smaller voice than spruce's, which can nonetheless be very satisfying. Sometimes there can be an admixture of brightness or even tinniness—it seems to vary from instrument to instrument. As a rule mahogany-topped guitars don't put out enough sound for professional use. However, you'll sometimes come across pre-war, mahogany-topped Martins and Gibsons that can overwhelm many modern guitars.

Mahogany is the most commonly used wood for guitar necks because of its superior strength and stability under the kind of stress the strings produce. Straight-grained, quartersawed Honduras is best. A neck that's not quartersawed is simply not going to hold up well over the long run. Grain structure running the length of the neck is the sign of a quartersawed neck blank.

Mahogany may also be used for back bracing, for the flat brace on the top above the sound hole, and for linings, end blocks, and heel blocks.

Maple

Maple is a strong, stiff, projective wood for back and sides, as loud as rosewood but with more cutting sound. The big band archtops were generally maple guitars. If you're familiar with electric guitars, you'll know what it means to say that maple is to rosewood as a Telecaster is to a Les Paul. Maple doesn't bring out the bottom of low tones as much as rosewood does, which makes it less successful in small-bodied guitars than in larger ones, where the body size helps reinforce the bottom.

Antonio Torres used maple on some of his instruments and it's also sometimes used for flamenco guitar bodies (though cypress is standard). The Gibson, Guild, and Santa Cruz companies in particular have made some very successful maple guitars, and in recent years Martin has turned to maple as well. (Although C. F. Martin himself did some work in maple, the Martin factory until recently hadn't touched the stuff for well over a century.)

Maple comes in several patterns, called "flame," "quilted," "curly," or "bird's-eye" according to the figure. They, as well as cosmetically less pleasing unfigured maple, work well on guitars and have been used for

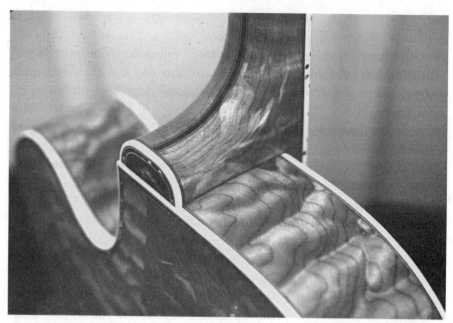

Exceptional figure shows up in this quilted maple on a D. W. Stevens archtop guitar.
Photo by D. W. Stevens

the backs and sides of the world's greatest violins, cellos, and basses for over three hundred years.

Maple is also the wood of choice for mandolin-family and archtop guitar bodies, which are inspired by the design of the bowed instruments. When these instruments are built to the highest standard, their backs must be tuned to the tops by careful carving and shaping. Because of its hardness and pliability, maple surpasses all other tonewoods for this sort of carving.

Maple's density makes it a good choice for bridge plates. It's also sometimes used for necks on guitars with maple and other light-colored bodies because it's more suited cosmetically for such instruments than mahogany is. Because maple is not quite as stable for necks as mahogany, it's often laminated with cross-grained ebony or rosewood strips, which add strength and look good as well.

Maple used on fine guitars may be either American rock maple or European flame maple. Japanese maple is similar to American maple. Red and silver maple are softer and are not generally used as solid woods but may be used as veneers.

Koa

Koa is a Hawaiian wood that came into fashion—especially for use in ukuleles and Hawaiian guitars—during the Hawaiian-music craze of the 1920s. It projects fewer lows than rosewood and fewer highs than mahogany, offering a compressed, woody midrange sound. In some ways it combines the qualities of rosewood and mahogany. Koa fell from favor after its Hawaiian novelty value faded at the end of the 1920s, but its visual beauty, combined with the increasing rarity of other woods, explains why it was revived by Martin and other makers during the 1980s. At its best koa's figure is extremely beautiful, like deep flame maple with a tropical complexion. However, koa export has been restricted by the Hawaiian government, so it may go the way of Brazilian rosewood.

Sometimes koa is also used as a top wood on koa-bodied guitars, in which case its midrange tendencies are even stronger. Koa-topped guitars have a voice all their own: soft, warm, sweet, sometimes with a slight abrasive edge, but not particularly crisp, clear, or well-separated—maybe something like a mahogany top as heard through a mist.

Walnut

Walnut is sometimes used for bridges and at various times in the past was used for bodies, though rarely. Taylor instituted a line of walnut-bodied instruments in the 1990s and now several other makers offer high-end walnut guitars as well. Its sound is similar to maple but not as projective. There are so few walnut instruments from the pre-war years that it's still an untried wood; nonetheless, ecological and supply situations are going to force us to get used to untried woods.

Ebony

Ebony is an extremely dense wood, better even than rosewood for fingerboards. Most experienced players easily discern the firmer feel of an ebony fingerboard. You'll also find that after years of playing, a rosewood fingerboard will show considerable signs of wear where ebony will not. (Making sure to keep your fretting-hand fingernails short is the best way to avoid fingerboard wear.) However, ebony is a brittle wood and over time it cracks more readily than rosewood. Filling cracks in ebony fingerboards with a mixture of epoxy and ebony dust is a common repair job.

Ebony's density also makes it a superior sound transmitter for steel-string guitar bridges. However, classical guitarists prefer rosewood for its sweetness with nylon strings.

The most desirable ebonies are the almost jet-black woods from Ceylon and Gabon in West Africa, colloquially called "Gaboon." Many guitar makers also use the more variegated Indian and Macassar woods dyed black for the sake of appearance. In any case, little ebony of any kind is totally black, so almost all is dyed. All ebonies are sufficiently hard, though the Ceylon and Gabon woods are somewhat harder and less porous. Ebony isn't very grainy in any case, but the less grain you can see, the better.

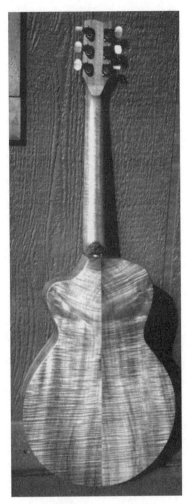

This guitar by Larry Pogreba shows off the deep tiger flame figure that can be found in koa.
Photo by Larry Pogreba

Other Woods

Ash is used for linings and occasionally for bodies, with tonal characteristics resembling maple's. The few ash-bodied guitars I've played (not enough to make a safe generalization) have been extremely quick and vivacious and quite enjoyable to play, though not profound. (Yes, guitarists sometimes sound like wine tasters when they get to talking about instruments. And just as ridiculous: I admit it.) Quilted ash is a very beautiful wood with a flame-like figure as deep as that of the finest maple. Ash is also used often in laminate cores.

Basswood may be used for linings.

Birch and sycamore are occasionally used as maple substitutes, especially as veneer facings.

Cherry, as both solid and laminate, is sometimes used for back and sides.

Cypress is used on the back and sides of nylon-strung flamenco guitars to give these instruments their distinctive, sharp cutting edge and piercing strummed sound. It is not used for steel-string guitars. I imagine it would sound tinny and jangly with steel strings.

Nato is a Pacific wood used as a substitute for mahogany on the necks of less expensive guitars. Sometimes it's also used for bodies. It's less stable than mahogany, but a nato neck with adequate truss-rod reinforcement should be dependable enough for a reasonable price.

Pear and walnut may be used for bindings and are hard enough that they are sometimes used for fingerboards, where they are usually "ebonized": dyed and treated with epoxy resin or some other hardening filler to impersonate ebony. They are also occasionally used for backs and sides; pear sounds similar to mahogany and walnut somewhat closer to rosewood.

Pine, willow, or poplar are sometimes used for the heel block, end block, and linings—especially on less expensive instruments.

White holly, boxwood, and other ornamental woods are used for bindings, as are various plastics and ivoroid cellulose nitrate or cellulose acetate.

Spruce and other softwoods, generally thought of as top woods, have also been used experimentally for guitar bodies.

FINISH

A beautiful piece of wood requires a beautiful finish to bring out its deep, gemlike inner glow. But finish is more than cosmetic: it also inhibits moisture absorption by the wood and protects the surface.

Stain and Filler Preparation

Guitar woods are customarily stained before finishing and, in the case of relatively porous woods like rosewood and mahogany, a filler may be rubbed in as well. These are standard cosmetic practices shared with furniture makers and other woodworkers. Once the stain is dry the instrument is ready to be finished. Of course if the instrument is going to have color lacquer applied then it won't be stained.

On cheap guitars the stain may be mixed in with the finish and sprayed on in one step. Cheapie guitars—usually minor-brand, offshore products—are typically sealed with a heavy layer of polyester finish, which is excellent on boat hulls but doesn't much help guitar acoustics. Often the bridge will be glued directly over this finish, which makes for a weak joint. (In fine guitar making, the bridge is glued to bare wood before the entire top is finished.) Polyester finish grows crystalline and brittle with time and eventually the bridge comes loose. Therefore, the cheap manufacturer may use bolts to hold the bridge down, which adversely affects tone and resonance.

Nitrocellulose and Acrylic Lacquers

Today's standard high-quality guitar finish is sprayed-on nitrocellulose lacquer. This may not be the case for much longer in mass-produced domestic guitars, however, since OSHA doesn't much like the stuff. A lacquer spray booth is a dangerously inflammable environment. Some makers now use, or at least are experimenting with, acrylic lacquer, which is also used on autos. Many feel it works as well on guitars as nitrocellulose does and that it's more suitable for color finishes.

A high-quality lacquer job may consist of six to twelve thin coats, each finely sanded and buffed before the next is applied. A cheap lacquer job might be one heavy-handed pass through the spray booth or maybe even past the spray robot. A good lacquer job leaves a thin, hard finish that allows the wood to vibrate freely and possibly even enhances its sound qualities. A cheap lacquer job acts like a blanket, deadening the guitar, and is more easily subject to finish checking (small cracks in the finish due to sudden temperature change).

Compare cheap guitars with fine ones and you'll learn to see the difference in finish quality. However even fine guitars from the best modern makers are too heavily finished these days. However popular taste demands a slick appearance and makers are afraid of losing sales.

For the few who do prefer a less glossy look some makers offer decent-looking low-gloss or matte "satin" finishes. Remember, though, that a low-gloss finish isn't necessarily a lighter or finer one; it just has a different surface quality.

A traditional sunburst top on a round-shouldered Santa Cruz dreadnought. More often, sides and back also have a sunburst, especially on maple and mahogany guitars. In this case the rosewood body has been left to show off its natural beauty. *Photo courtesy Santa Cruz Guitar Co.*

Sunburst Finishes

There's another form of ornamental finish used on tops and sometimes backs called "sunburst." In this design, a more dramatic version of the shading used on some fine violin tops, the center of the top is a rich, golden-orange hue, fading gradually to dark brown, black, or burgundy around the edges. For most devotees the classic Gibson sunburst represents the high point of this art.

Sunbursting is a difficult, time-consuming technique. It involves applying several layers of gradually darkening lacquer with an extremely delicate touch on the spray gun and a goodly amount of extra rubbing and sanding in between. Some manufacturers may reserve their less visually appealing spruce for sunbursting. This does not necessarily correlate to poorer sound quality.

By tradition, incidentally, sunbursts are visually associated with flat-top guitars used by country, old-time, and bluegrass musicians, with archtop guitars used by swing and mainstream jazz musicians, and (with a more orange-to-red graduation) with some of the Gibson Les Paul solid bodies that really scream heavy metal. New-age guitarists seem to prefer natural wood, basic white, or basic black. As for sunbursting classical guitars, why, it's simply not done!

French Polish and Spot Finishes

Oddly, the resin- and gum-based varnishes used in violin finishing don't seem to suit the acoustic properties of guitars. (A quick though oversimplified explanation of the difference between lacquer and varnish is this: you rub a varnish *into* the wood, whereas you spray a lacquer *on top of* the wood, where it dries in a thin layer through the evaporation of volatile solvents.)

An exception is a difficult form of shellac varnishing known as french polish, which, after many painstaking rubbing and sanding steps, leaves an extremely subtle gloss. It's used on some fine violins and classical guitars and a few luthiers offer it as a custom finish on steel-string guitars. Those repair people who have mastered french polishing also find it useful for spot-finishing damaged areas.

Tung oil is also sometimes used for spot finishing and restoration work, preferably on necks and headstocks rather than on tonewood. A vegetable oil in its pure form, it usually comes mixed with mineral spirits or petroleum distillates in commercial finishing preparations.

GLUES

The animal hide glues of traditional luthiery are now being supplanted by synthetic white glues that are more stable under humid conditions. Although their tolerance is higher, like animal glues they still loosen in excessive heat—the heat of a car trunk in summer, for example, or of a guitar case under the hot sun. You wouldn't want it otherwise. The main joints in the guitar should be able to be loosened with a simple application of heat so repair work, adjustments, and restorations can be made. Permanent glues are not the answer. The answer is not to leave your guitar in the trunk on a summer's day.

However, materials like epoxy resins and cyanoacrylate ("magic" or "super") glue are used by some repair people for specialized jobs—increasingly so, in fact, as more techniques are developed and applications are found. Epoxy is typically mixed with rosewood or ebony dust to build up pitted fingerboards and sometimes it's used to seat frets—a practice strongly debated within the trade. Cyanoacrylate, which is so runny that its penetrating powers exceed those of any other glue, is used for hairline cracks and crevices and other spot applications where a possible need to separate the joint in the future is not an issue. This too is a hotly debated practice.

Of the white glues, most makers and repair people favor aliphatic resin—the standard woodworkers' glue of which Tite-Bond is the best-known nationally marketed brand. Sometimes polyvinyl resin glue is used (Elmer's is the best-known brand). Polyvinyl resin is not as strong for manufacturing, but since it's less tacky (more runny), it's better for infiltrating tiny cracks and small spaces in repair work. Inferior white glues used on inexpensive guitars loosen more easily in hot, humid conditions. White glues also have their disadvantages: for example, a joint glued once with white glue may not be able to be reglued successfully once it comes apart. Many conservative traditionalists insist on hide glue for repairs simply because its able to be undone.

Resorcinol glues are the standard for holding together construction-grade plywood and presumably they're used for guitar plywood too, but because the guitar industry is so secretive about its laminates, we don't know.

PARTS OF THE GUITAR

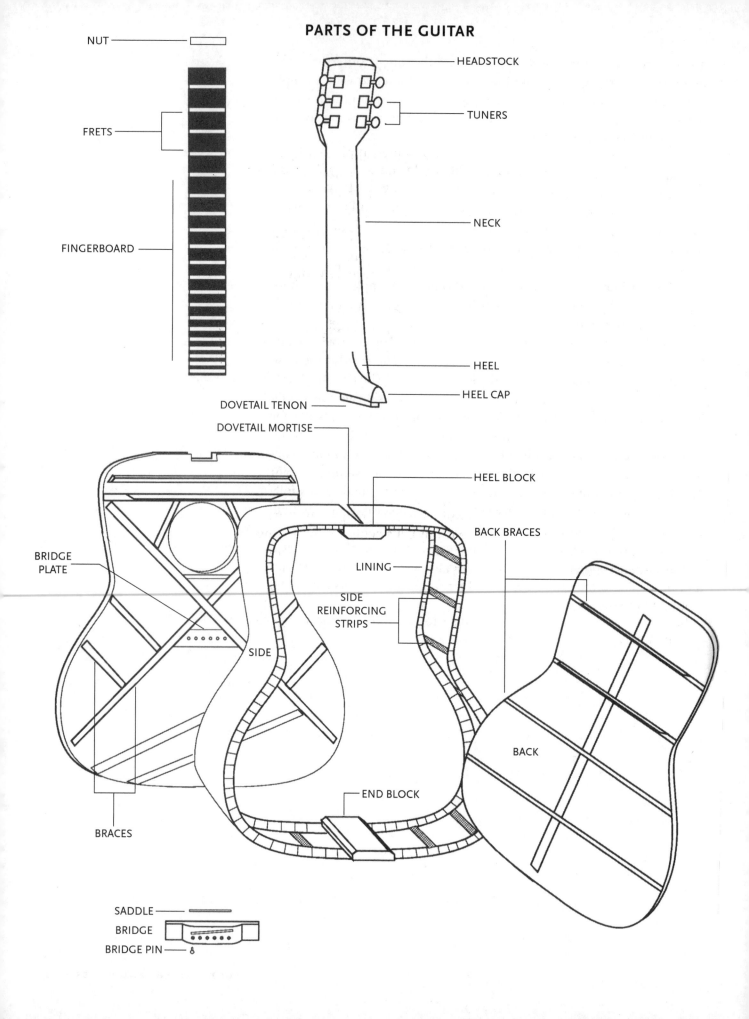

NUT

FRETS

FINGERBOARD

HEADSTOCK

TUNERS

NECK

HEEL

HEEL CAP

DOVETAIL TENON

DOVETAIL MORTISE

HEEL BLOCK

BACK BRACES

LINING

SIDE
REINFORCING
STRIPS

BRIDGE
PLATE

SIDE

BACK

BRACES

END BLOCK

SADDLE

BRIDGE

BRIDGE PIN

How Your Guitar Works

I: Where the Action Is

ACTION AND SETUP

Action Strictly Defined

The term "action" refers to the distance of the string above the fingerboard. In addition to referring to the measurable height, it also refers to the subjective feel of the string height. Action depends on:

- Nut and saddle height
- Neck straightness
- Neck set (the angle at which the neck joins the body)

Luthiers use the fret where the neck joins the body (usually the fourteenth or twelfth, depending on the model) as the standard reference point for measuring action. Normal string clearances at that fret for a steel-string acoustic guitar should be around $\frac{5}{32}$ of an inch for the sixth (low E) string and $\frac{3}{32}$ of an inch for the first (high E) string.

These figures are based on the assumption that the neck itself is unwarped and properly set and adjusted. These are starting points, subject to small adjustments for string gauge, playing style, and personal taste. When action is too high the guitar becomes uncomfortable to play. When action is too low, strings buzz and loose volume and tone quality. Classical guitar action is usually a bit higher and sometimes extra high on the bass side, electric guitar action a bit lower.

Action Loosely Defined

People also use the word *action* in a looser sense to mean the amount of perceived effort it takes to fret the strings. In this subjective sense, some other factors come into play:

- String gauge (insofar as heavier strings feel stiffer).
- Fret condition (worn-down frets require more finger pressure).
- Your technique, expectations, level of experience, and raw strength. A guitar that seems stiff to someone who plays an hour a week may seem wimpy to someone who plays six hours a day.
- Scale (string length). Strings feel stiffer when the scale is longer. (See page 99 for more information about scale.)

SETUP

The Mechanics of Setup

The sum total of nut, saddle, and truss rod adjustments that determine the action of the guitar is called "setup." A beautifully set up guitar brings out the best in the player and gives the greatest pleasure.

Setup also depends on choice of strings. Changing between extra light and medium strings, for example, affects the amount of tension on the neck (hence the need to readjust the truss rod) and may also pull up the neck a tiny bit.

Setup and Style

Some guitarists, especially beginners, have the idea that action should be so low as to be virtually imperceptible. The customer who asks to "make my action as low as possible without buzzing" is a standard joke among repair people; noted repairman Matt Umanov used to post a sign in his New York shop saying "Will everyone who wants their action as low as possible without buzzing please leave." But many experienced players actually prefer to feel the strings assert themselves a little. The instrument feels crisper to play. Beginners have their hands full just trying to get their notes to start in the right place; a good player is also in perfect control of when and how the note ends. Getting it to end definitively is easier when the strings snap cleanly back off the frets. Wimpy action doesn't give you as much control.

The kind of action you want is a matter of personal taste coupled with the demands of your particular style. The permutations of personal taste and stylistic demands are almost endless. Let's look at just a few scenarios and their rationales.

String bending, characteristic of blues, rock, and many contemporary styles, is something you'd think would be more easily accomplished with low action. After all, the fingers are using enough energy just getting the strings to bend; having to cope with high action in addition seems like too much to ask. But if you put such a deep bend on a string that it moves up into another string's space, you'll find that with high action you can get the bent string under the string whose turf is being invaded, which makes bending a lot easier. Therefore, lots of blues players favor the unlikely combination of light strings and high action. This kind of setup is a little more common on electric than acoustic guitars—acoustic guitarists don't usually use strings that are light enough to permit this kind of extreme bending.

Acoustic jazz and "new acoustic music" players of the school rooted in bluegrass tend to prefer an action similar to the one a mainstream jazz soloist would have on an archtop guitar: fairly low, very even up and down the fingerboard, and set up for medium-gauge strings. The problem is that on an archtop guitar the neck is mounted on a set back angle that makes it intrinsically easier to achieve this kind of setup. Luthiers gnash their teeth when asked to get this kind of a feel out of a flattop because it goes against the nature of the instrument. A low jazz action on an acoustic guitar tends to be always on the edge of buzzing, frets have to be dressed with finicky attention, and tolerances are so close that when a warm front blows through the next day the buzzing starts all over again. The fact that acoustic jazz guitarists tend to play with more of a heavy bluegrass touch than a light jazz touch doesn't make things any easier. Here's an idea: if you want a guitar that feels like an archtop, get an archtop. Get a modern one, with an open, X-braced sound instead of a chunky, rhythm sound.

New-age and Celtic fingerpicking players usually ask for a setup similar to the one for acoustic jazz but with lighter strings. The same teeth-gnashing problems and solutions exist. Some makes, models, and given instruments come out of the factory better disposed to this kind of setup than others, and these are the ones you should look for if you're into new-age and acoustic jazz styles. Otherwise you'll be living in a perpetual world of neck resets, changing setups, and fret dressing, your guitar will spend more time in the shop than in your hands, you'll never be a happy person, and one day you'll wake up to discover that your spouse and best friend have just drifted away, possibly with each other.

But seriously, there *is* a problem intrinsic to this kind of playing. This or any style using lots of pulled and hammered notes, and perhaps requiring light strings in order to satisfy the player's taste for vibrato and bent notes, does seem to be best expressed on guitars with low action, with ensuing disadvantages of loss of tone quality and dynamic range potential. Guitarists facing this dilemma are ideal candidates for adding a pickup to their instrument.

Ragtime guitarists and other players of complicated fingerpicking styles for the most part like the idea of a low-action guitar similar to the one new-age guitarists favor. But because many of them also play blues and similar styles requiring a more aggressive touch, they usually wind up having to go with a somewhat stiffer action.

Bluegrass and other aggressive flatpicking styles require a higher action in order to avoid string buzzing. The reason is not just because the string is set into a wider arc of motion from being struck more forcefully. It's also because good players learn that the most effective way to punch out a strongly punctuated note is to dig *into* the string, bringing the pick to rest against the next string. The direction of this pick motion causes the string to move more perpendicularly to the fingerboard, even further increasing the possibility of buzzing.

Slide guitar requires an action high enough to keep the weight of the slide from pressing the strings against the fingerboard. Of course if you play solos exclusively with the slide, the action can be as high as you like. But if you play the style of slide guitar where you wear a slide on your pinky for some notes and use the rest of your fingers for playing regular notes and chords, you'll have to accept an action that's somewhat higher than you'd ordinarily choose for fingerstyle playing alone. For this reason most serious slide players keep a second guitar with regular action for regular playing.

Beginners and most casual players, especially when they're using relatively inexpensive guitars, are for the most part best off with a relatively low, comfortable action and light-gauge strings until they reach a point in their development where other stylistic decisions might come into play. This is especially true for people whose muscles and calluses haven't yet developed. Usually just stringing the instrument more lightly than it would usually be strung will solve this problem.

THE NECK

The neck extends the strings out from the body of the guitar. At the end of the neck are the geared pegs to tune the strings. Along the top of the neck is the "fingerboard," a strip of dark hardwood in which the frets are seated. Where the neck butts the shoulders of the guitar body, it broadens out into a larger section called the "heel." Some cheaply made instruments where the neck is bolted on do not have a heel.

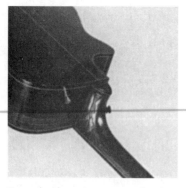

Fancy heel carving on a guitar by Harry Fleishman. *Photo by Larry Sandberg*

Neck Materials and Construction

The necks of most good steel-string guitars are made of mahogany, ideally quartersawed Honduras mahogany for maximum strength and stability. On less expensive instruments, nato, a mahogany-like wood from the South Pacific, has become a standard substitute.

Maple necks are often used on guitars with maple or other light-colored bodies. Because maple isn't quite as stable as mahogany, maple necks on better guitars are often cut lengthwise into halves or thirds and interleaved with strips of rosewood, ebony, or some other hardwood. The interleaved sections are glued together with the grain in different directions for strength and warp resistance—the same principle that adds strength to plywood and corrugated cardboard. Dark woods are chosen for visual contrast; a well-made laminated neck is pleasing to look at.

Laminated necks are not inferior. Far from it; some very fine, sturdy necks are made this way. As a rule, though, they're pretty heavy—heavy enough to upset the balance of the guitar in your lap. Therefore they feel best on large-bodied guitars where the body balances out the neck weight.

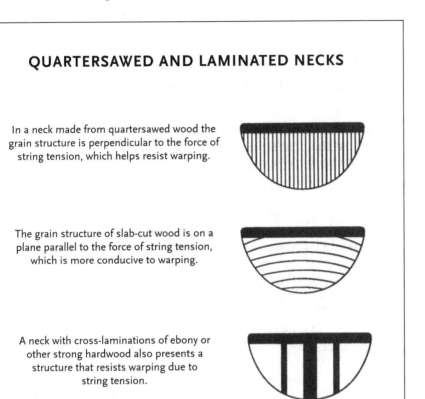

QUARTERSAWED AND LAMINATED NECKS

In a neck made from quartersawed wood the grain structure is perpendicular to the force of string tension, which helps resist warping.

The grain structure of slab-cut wood is on a plane parallel to the force of string tension, which is more conducive to warping.

A neck with cross-laminations of ebony or other strong hardwood also presents a structure that resists warping due to string tension.

On many nineteenth-century instruments, and on classical guitars to the present day, cedar may be used for the neck. Cedar works fine with nylon strings but doesn't hold up to the greater tension of steel strings as well as mahogany does. Most cedar necks have a "grafted" construction in which the headstock and heel sections of the neck "blank" (the roughly shaped piece of wood from which the neck is carved) are made of separate sections of wood glued together. It's hard to find cedar lumber large enough for a one-piece blank.

The stability of the neck wood is extremely important. Playability depends on keeping the strings a precise height above the fingerboard, so if the neck warps, the instrument becomes difficult or impossible to finger. Although a good piece of mahogany holds up amazingly well against the 150 or more pounds of string tension on most guitars, it needs all the help it can get. Therefore almost all contemporary steel-string guitar necks are built with a metal reinforcing rod, or "truss rod." (See page 82 for more information about truss rods.)

Neck Shape and Contour

The contour of the neck may be more or less rounded around the back. Most guitarists find slender necks easier to play, and call them "fast"—though other elements such as action, fingerboard width, and the type and condition of the frets also contribute to how fast a neck feels. There are also those who don't mind a stout, clubby neck, or who even prefer one. Clubby necks are stronger; there's more wood to them, after all. But now that metal truss rods are standard fixtures there's less need to rely on wood alone for strength; so, necks have gotten more slender in recent years in response to the public's preference for them.

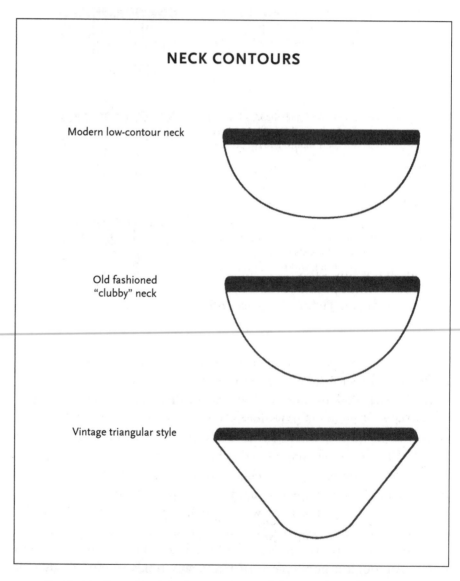

NECK CONTOURS

Modern low-contour neck

Old fashioned "clubby" neck

Vintage triangular style

Back in the nineteenth century a fair number of guitars were made with the back of the neck more triangular than rounded in shape. If your hand position is one where you play a lot with the ball of your thumb resting on the back side of the neck, as classical guitarists do, such necks can be annoying. But if you mostly loop your thumb around over the top of the fingerboard, a neck like this is even easier to play than a rounded one. There's less distance for the thumb to reach around; after all, the shortest distance between two points is a straight line. In recent years the triangular neck has been rediscovered and is making a comeback on some models. Try one if you get a chance. You may like it.

Relief

It may come as a big surprise to learn that a traditional guitar neck is not supposed to be perfectly straight. But it's true. Guitar necks should be a little warped, just like a sense of humor.

If you lay a straightedge against a guitar fingerboard, you might notice that it dips a little around the sixth fret. With a good eye, you may even be able to spot it by sighting down the neck from the head-stock toward the body. Guitar makers build this dip into their instruments to make the upper frets more easily playable and to avoid buzzing problems at the fret where the neck joins the body. The name for this feature is "relief." It might come from the fact that if you've just bought a new $2,000 guitar and noticed that the neck isn't perfectly straight, you should be relieved to know that that's the way it's supposed to be.

The line between deliberate relief and unwanted warping is a thin one, measured in sixty-fourths of an inch. For a player with a moderate touch, string height above the crown of the sixth fret (for steel-string guitars with light- to medium-gauge strings) should be about $\frac{5}{64}$ of an inch under the treble strings and $\frac{7}{64}$ of an inch under the bass strings. A heavier touch requires higher relief. Short-scale guitars require less relief than long-scale guitars. (See page 99 for more information about scale.)

Your dealer or repair shop can make fine adjustments to relief by tightening or loosening the adjustable truss rod, as discussed in the following section. Don't do this yourself. On instruments made before the days of the adjustable truss rod, or on the very few instruments currently made without them, the repair shop has to treat relief adjustments as if they were warp symptoms, by bending the neck under heat or by removing the frets and planing the fingerboard.

Occasionally you may find a player, luthier, and/or repair shop person who rejects the concept of relief and prefers an absolutely straight fingerboard.

Thanks to a new neck joint system developed by the Taylor company in the late 1990s, it may also become possible to reduce or eliminate the need for relief due to unevenness of action at the fret where the neck joins the fingerboard. (See page 88 for more information about neck set.)

The Truss Rod

Around 1920 guitar makers found that their traditional necks, designed for gut strings, warped under the much greater pressure of the newly fashionable steel strings. Even giving up cedar for stronger Honduras mahogany wasn't good enough, so manufacturers like Martin started cutting a hidden groove in the neck before the fingerboard was glued on top and laying in a long strip of ebony to add strength. Ebony was fashionable for a few years before the makers discovered that a steel reinforcing rod was even better. (However on most American instruments made during the steel-starved World War II years the rods were either left out completely or ebony was again used.)

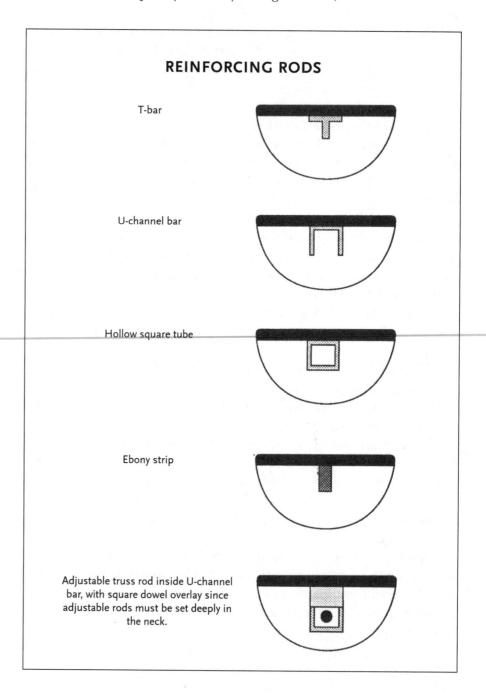

REINFORCING RODS

T-bar

U-channel bar

Hollow square tube

Ebony strip

Adjustable truss rod inside U-channel bar, with square dowel overlay since adjustable rods must be set deeply in the neck.

At first the rods were mostly T-shaped, but later on lighter hollow rectangular and U-shaped rods became standard—at least on good guitars. Cheapie guitars sometimes carried a "metal-reinforced neck" decal than meant little more than that some scrap metal, perhaps even a used hacksaw blade, was embedded in the neck.

Today you may sometimes find makers who prefer simple reinforcing rods to the mechanical truss rod design described below. Now they may use contemporary materials like titanium or graphite.

During the 1920s the Gibson company patented an improved reinforcing rod called the "truss rod" or "tension rod." Instead of merely introducing stiffening support to the neck, it created compression.

The original Gibson design had a slight, adjustable arch to it, which created tension to counteract the tension of the strings. One end of the rod was embedded in the heel so it couldn't rotate while the other end of the rod had a hex nut that stuck out of a hole in the headstock underneath a small cover plate that could be removed by loosening a few screws. Turning the hex nut increased or reduced the tension of the rod. A few unscrupulous cheapie manufacturers of past years built guitars with false truss rod covers that had nothing underneath, to convey the impression that their instruments were outfitted with the adjustable rods.

Now that the original Gibson patent has gone public the adjustable truss rod is in standard use by almost every manufacturer. Even Martin, which had argued (not without justice) for years that well-made necks don't require adjustable rods, finally swallowed its pride and went over to them in the mid-1980s when they introduced a thinner neck contour.

Truss rod design has changed over the years. Some of today's manufacturers use rods turned around from the original design. Now their stable end is mounted into the headstock while the adjusting end (usually in the form of a slot screw or hex socket) is mounted in the brace that sits directly under the end of the fingerboard. This eliminates the inconvenience, unsightliness, manufacturing complexity, and slight weakening effect of the cover plate and its hole. You can recognize guitars with a modern tension rod by peering through the sound hole to spot the adjustment screw.

The new-style rods are said to be harder to break by accidentally over-tightening than the original style was, but it's not an issue worth fussing over when you're deciding which guitar to purchase. Some modern truss rods also combine old with new concepts by mounting an adjustable rod inside a U-shaped aluminum channel rod. This is a somewhat stronger rod design but, again, it's not an important enough feature to cause you to reject a guitar that you otherwise like. Just remember that what many consider to be among the greatest guitars ever made come from the days before adjustable rods or even before nonadjustable rods. The modern truss rod is a great convenience, though, and it enables small corrections to be made by adjustment rather than by surgery.

I always thought luthier Edward V. Dick was too cautious to stick his neck(s) out like this. Note the routed-out slots for the truss rods. *Photo by Larry Shirkey, courtesy E. V. Dick*

On some twelve-string guitars, two side-by-side truss rods are used because string tension is disproportionately stronger on the bass-string side of the neck. A double rod is better in a twelve-string guitar than a single rod but, once more, it's not so important that it should be an overriding factor in making a purchasing decision.

Truss Rods and Relief

It's a common misconception that adjustable tension rods make the neck straight. Yes, having a piece of steel running through the neck is certainly going to help keep it from warping. But the adjustable rod

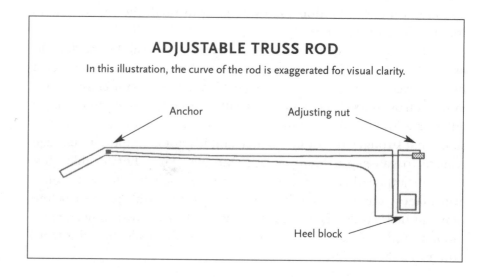

ADJUSTABLE TRUSS ROD

In this illustration, the curve of the rod is exaggerated for visual clarity.

Anchor   Adjusting nut

Heel block

isn't going to straighten the neck any more than good diet and plenty of exercise are going to make you immortal. That's because the purpose of truss rod adjustment is to regulate relief. The rod arches right under the fifth-to-seventh-fret relief area; it might take care of small action and warping problems around there, but it's no panacea for neck set and nut or saddle height problems, reverse warping, or warping that affects other areas of the neck. (A few makers use a rod that is adjustable from either end, which provides a certain amount of control over reverse warping in theory, though less in practice.)

Some makers carve a little relief into the neck before the tension rod is even tightened up. That guarantees that it will always be there. If there's too much relief built into the neck, the truss rod can be tightened to adjust it out. But, because a rod can't go backwards past the point at which it becomes slack, if there's not enough relief already built into the neck, the rod can't do anything to add it.

This truss rod tightens with a 5/16-inch hex nut driver. *Photo by Larry Sandberg*

Truss Rod Adjustment

When you tighten up a truss rod, it exerts a compressive force opposite to some of the force of the strings—about 20 pounds of torque in opposition to about 150 pounds of string tension. In order to exert this compressive force in the right direction the rod has to be seated deeply in the neck and its channel firmly glued over with a sturdy square dowel. The fingerboard that then goes on top also needs to be solid and well-glued. There must be more wood above than below the rod in order for the rod to compress the wood underneath—if the rod is too close to the fingerboard, it compresses in the other (wrong) direction. A truss rod that is not mounted deeply enough in the neck or that is mounted in a neck too flimsy to accept the compression can not do its job properly.

With most (but not all!) manufacturers' truss rods, a clockwise turn tightens the rod to reduce relief and a counterclockwise turn loosens it to induce greater relief. Some rods adjust with a nut driver (typically 5/16-inch); others with a hex wrench. You can adjust the truss rod yourself but it's not a good idea if you don't know what you're doing. Better to leave it to experienced hands. It's not always easy to judge how much of a turn is needed and you can even break the rod or strip a thread by over-tightening it.

If you must try it yourself, try no more than an eighth of a revolution of the nut at any one time and let the guitar settle in for a few hours or even days before you decide whether another eighth-turn seems necessary. Remember that this adjustment is made with the strings tuned up to normal pitch.

Also remember that of all the causes of string buzzing, improper relief is among the least likely; don't start going crazy with the truss rod to cure a buzz until you've examined all the other possibilities.

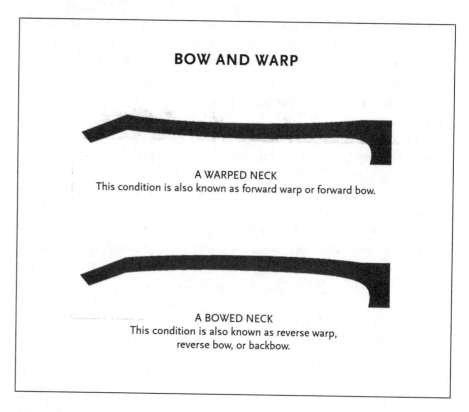

BOW AND WARP

A WARPED NECK
This condition is also known as forward warp or forward bow.

A BOWED NECK
This condition is also known as reverse warp,
reverse bow, or backbow.

WARPED NECKS

Warp and Bow

Just because a fingerboard is supposed to have some relief doesn't mean that it can't also be warped in addition to the relief. The warp could be in the same area as the relief or farther up or down the neck. Or it might be a reverse warp, where the deformation is convex rather than concave. And a neck can warp even if it has a metal reinforcing rod in it, though it's less likely.

Just like a warped sense of humor, neck warp can go in more than one direction. The term *warp* can mean any kind of distortion but it is usually taken to mean a concave one, as do the terms *forward warp* or *forward bow*. The terms *reverse warp* or *backbow* are used to indicate a convex distortion. Just plain *bow* usually means the same as forward bow, but sometimes you'll find someone who uses it to mean backbow.

Diagnosis

You can tell a bad warp just by looking. Checking string height at the fifth fret (just before the relief spot) can help you determine whether there's a subtle or incipient bow toward the middle of the neck. Here's how:

1. Put a capo on the first fret.
2. Depress the low E string (the sixth, fattest string) at the twelfth fret.

3. You should be able to insert the corner of two to four sheets of ordinary typing paper (twenty-pound bond) under the string at the fifth fret without budging it. If only one sheet scrapes its way under the string, or if it takes a lot more sheets to reach it, then the neck needs some work. Remember that very few guitars are absolutely perfect and if they are they won't stay that way forever; don't get upset as long as tolerances are within the ballpark.

The Cure

The cure for a warped neck is not a truss-rod adjustment. The truss rod exists primarily to control relief. It won't help unless the warp is in the relief area (perhaps not even then) and it won't help with a backbow except one in the relief area. The way a repair shop cures moderate warp is to place the guitar in a "straightening jig," which is a fancy way of saying that the neck gets clamped to a sturdy piece of pipe or straight lumber and left under infrared lamps for a couple of days. In more extreme cases it may be necessary to remove the frets and plane the fingerboard to compensate for the warp.

In addition to warp and backbow it's also possible for a neck to twist, or "skew" around its long axis. This happens most often on twelve-string guitars, where string tension on the bass side is disproportionately high. The treatment is fingerboard planing.

JOINING THE NECK TO THE BODY

Neck Joints

The traditional way to join the guitar neck to the body is with a dovetail tenon in the heel. (You can't see the dovetail joint because the fingerboard covers it.) The tenon fits into a mortise cut into the heel block (also called "head block"), a solid block of wood mounted inside the body directly under the fingerboard. You can see the heel block by looking through the sound hole. It's the place where many manufacturers stamp the model and serial number.

Some instruments use other straight-cut mortise-and-tenon joints rather than the angled dovetail joints; some even use necks that are bolted on through the heel block and attached by nothing more than the bolts and a butt joint. Once bolt-on necks were strictly a cheap substitution, but, since not all guitar makers feel that the dovetail is ideal, you'll also sometimes find well-made joints of other kinds on fine instruments from reputable makers. Taylor used bolt-on necks for over twenty years until they developed a new system. (See page 89 for more information.) You'll even find well-designed bolt-on necks on some fine guitars. Even on the finest guitars it's not uncommon for that 150 or so pounds of string pressure to pull up on neck joints so they have to be

Dovetail joint on a D. W. Stevens guitar. *Photo by Larry Sandberg*

dismantled and reset every twenty years or so. Some guitar makers who have accepted this fact have given up the illusion of permanency and have instead become interested in developing joints that can be more easily reset. (See page 89 for more information on neck resets.)

As for other kinds of guitars, bolt-on necks are typical on solid-body electric guitars, while a combination one-piece heel and heel block, with a groove into which the guitar's shoulders are mounted, is the standard rig for classical guitars. The dovetail joint, however, is standard on archtops. Classical guitars sometimes use an extremely large mortise-and-tenon set deeply into a large head block.

Neck Set

If you sight down the neck or lay a guitar flat on a tabletop and look at it sideways, you'll notice that the neck angles up a little from the plane of the top so that the base of the nut may be around ⅛ of an inch higher than the top. In other words, as you look down the neck from the nut toward the bridge, an imaginary line parallel to the top and extending from the base of the nut would hit the bridge about ⅛ of an inch above the soundboard.

The angle of the neck in relation to the body is called the "set" of the neck. A good set requires careful manufacturing tolerances in the neck joint. What is most disappointing about low-price guitars is the quality control of the neck set. Not too many are really bad but far too few are really right on. Too few cheap guitars are as comfortable as they could be.

The ogreish issue of neck resets has haunted the guitar industry for years. Historically, it comes with the turf that necks pull up from string pressure and many guitars need a neck reset after twenty to forty years. Ungluing and removing the neck, shimming it to set at a new angle (or perhaps removing wood from the male or female portion of the joint), and regluing it is a laborious and expensive process; in addition, fret and fingerboard work may also be necessary. Adding insult to injury, neck resets are generally not entirely satisfactory because they only affect the action up to the fret where the guitar joins the body. Any action problems on the fingerboard extension or "spatula"—the part of the fingerboard that extends over the body of the guitar—remain and might possibly even be made worse by a reset.

At the end of the 1990s the Taylor company, which is recognized in other areas as well for successful innovative thinking, came up with a new neck and fingerboard design. Basically it involves extending a reinforced section of wood from the neck itself, incorporating the fingerboard extension over the guitar body, and developing a new system of joints to accommodate this innovation. The new joint system, which involves bolting a neck heel that is mortised into what is essential a slightly inset butt joint, can be disassembled in minutes, and the neck angle can be reset by inserting spacers. As an additional advantage the fingerboard extension is now part of the neck and therefore becomes part of the neck reset, ensuring consistently even action along the entire length of the fingerboard. At this time the new system has been generally greeted with interest and admiration and it will be interesting to see how it continues to affect the industry.

Classical guitar neck set approximates that of a steel-string flattop, but on archtops the bridge is very high and the neck is set to angle down from the body rather than up. On solidbody electrics, necks are usually set parallel to the body or slightly downward.

Resetting the Neck

Because of the way the neck angles up, action rises as you go farther up the fingerboard. Action at the twelfth fret is roughly twice as high as it is at the first fret. (For the sixth string, that would be in the neighborhood of $\frac{5}{32}$ of an inch at the twelfth fret versus $\frac{2}{32}$ of an inch at the first.) Tolerances may vary to taste but a much greater discrepancy could mean that something is wrong. Another bad sign as you sight down the neck might be a sharp angling up of the fingerboard just at the point where it leaves the body (though this usually means a problem with body distortion rather than neck warping).

Bad neck set can come from a cracked heel, loose neck joint, top warping due to string tension, imperfect manufacture, or the pulling up of the entire neck (including heel) by string tension. Surgery for this problem is completely different from surgery for warping or action problems. You can't really cure a bad neck set with a straightening jig or tension rod or by adjusting nut and saddle height. The only answer is to "reset" the neck, a fairly expensive job.

A neck reset involves loosening the end of the fingerboard from the top and loosening the heel from its dovetail joint in the heel block—a painstaking process involving delicate prying work with a spatula and hot water. Then the heel is shaved or shimmed to the proper angle and glued back.

When the neck needs to be tipped back rather than forward (which is usually the case), and only a little, it's sometimes possible to remove the back (a relatively easier operation) and then shim back the heel block a little from underneath. This is called a "heel block reset" or "head block reset." Sometimes it's possible to plane or replace the fingerboard to compensate for the bad neck angle—also an easier and less expensive solution than a neck reset, though only a symptomatic one. Even so, these are all surgical operations well beyond the scope of mere adjustment.

On an inexpensive guitar a neck reset might cost more than the value of the instrument. Sometimes a repair shop can buy you time and a smidgen of comfort, and save you money, with a quick-and-dirty job of cutting down a saddle or some other setup adjustment. But it's not really a cure and the instrument still won't feel right.

FINGERBOARD AND FRETS

Fingerboard Materials

The "fingerboard" (also called the "fretboard") is the flat section of wood lying across the top of the neck into which the frets are seated. The portion of the fingerboard that lies over the body of the guitar is called the "spatula" or "fingerboard extension."

Ebony is the fingerboard wood of choice because it offers a hard, positive feel to the fingers and resists wear better than the slightly softer second choice, rosewood. Ebony is brittle and hence more prone than rosewood to cracking over the years, but experienced players tend to prefer it anyway. It's also much more expensive, so you'll only find it on top-of-the-line instruments. Lots of people are very happy with their rosewood fingerboards and sometimes rosewood is preferred cosmetically or because it may affect the resonant frequency of the neck differently than does ebony. You have to play a lot before you begin to notice the difference between the feel of ebony and rosewood. Don't kid yourself that you do—it could cost you a couple of hundred bucks you could be spending on your children instead.

Other hardwoods or even veneered plywood are used on inexpensive instruments. Walnut is marginally acceptable at a low price. Some cheap woods may be "ebonized"—died black and hardened with epoxy resin to simulate ebony. You're better off with rosewood.

Position Markers, Inlay, and Binding

Most steel-string guitar fingerboards have some sort of dot or ornamental shape called a "position marker" inlaid in back of frets five, seven, nine, twelve, and perhaps also three, fifteen, seventeen, and nineteen, in order to help the eye see where the fingers are. Sometimes "side dots" are also inlaid along the top edge of the fingerboard for the same reason. By tradition, serious classical guitars don't have dots or markers because serious classical guitarists are trained to have their eyes on the music and are supposed to know where their fingers are without having to look. Ideally this is true of any guitarist.

Some fingerboards, especially on fancy guitars, also have a strip of plastic or ivoroid cellulose nitrate "binding" along the edge. It's supposed to make the edges of the fingerboard feel smoother where the thumb rubs along the top and the base of the index finger rubs along the bottom. By tradition, classical guitar fingerboards are never bound, since in the correct classical hand position no part of the hand ever touches the edge of the fingerboard.

I've always liked the way bound fingerboards look. As to the way they feel, some of my guitars have bound fingerboards and some don't, and I've never really noticed much difference one way or the other. In fact, until I was forced to think about it at this moment of writing, I never thought about it at all. If the frets are properly smoothed off at the edge of the fingerboard to begin with, there should be no need in the first place for a binding to cover them. I suspect that the reason you sometimes see makers of otherwise cheaply made instruments go to the expense of adding a fingerboard binding is that they expect the poorly seasoned wood of their fingerboards to shrink, exposing jagged fret edges.

Twelve- and Fourteen-Fret Necks

On almost all flattop guitars these days the body begins at the fourteenth fret. On classical guitars and on most steel-string guitars through the 1920s the body began at the twelfth fret. The modern fourteen-fret fingerboard was first offered to the public in 1930 by the Martin company on a new series of guitars called the OM (Orchestra Model). It had been developed over the preceding year at the suggestion of Perry Bechtel, a famous banjo soloist who, like most other banjo players at that time of changing musical tastes, was making the transition to the guitar. Bechtel pointed out that banjo players would be more used to a somewhat narrower neck with two extra frets. (Banjo players were used to having a lot more frets accessible to them than the guitar offers.) Martin leapt at the idea, and the general public and Martin's competitors, as well as the banjoists, quickly embraced it. Few steel-strung guitars today have twelve-fret necks, though classical guitars still do.

The guitar designers created access to those extra two frets not by lengthening the neck but by shortening the upper part of the body and

This Martin D-45 shows the "snowflake" position markers and headstock inlay characteristic of the Martin 45 series plus a fingerboard and headstock bound with ivoroid plastic. *Photo courtesy C. F. Martin & Co.*

Here shown on a Santa Cruz guitar, the slotted headstock is characteristically found on small-bodied twelve-fret guitars. This convention was established by Martin guitars before the 1930s. *Photo courtesy Santa Cruz Guitar Company*

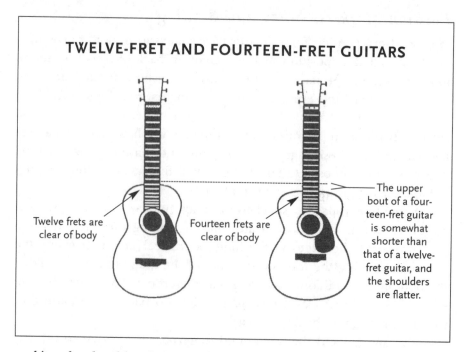

Twelve frets are clear of body

Fourteen frets are clear of body

The upper bout of a fourteen-fret guitar is somewhat shorter than that of a twelve-fret guitar, and the shoulders are flatter.

Some fans of the twelve-fret guitar appreciate the wider fingerboard; others admire the gracefully curved proportions as exemplified by this Santa Cruz Model OO. *Photo courtesy Santa Cruz Guitar Company*

making the shoulders less rounded. The total number of frets remained at twenty (varying to nineteen or twenty-one on some steel-string models, while classical guitars generally have eighteen or nineteen). A few harmless eccentrics, myself included, fancy they hear greater richness of tone coming out of twelve-fret bodies, but everyone else laughs at us. In any case, it seems perfectly clear that they would rather have easy access to those two extra frets at whatever (possibly imaginary) cost in richness of sound.

Fingerboard Width

Fingerboards vary in width from model to model. The standard for measuring width is at the nut, but on most guitars the fingerboard widens out a bit toward the spatula to a degree that varies from model to model.

Today, 1$\frac{11}{16}$ inches (the width of the nut on the standard Martin dreadnought model) is the fingerboard width most commonly offered by all manufacturers and the one most people seem to find comfortable. (Add $\frac{1}{8}$ to $\frac{1}{4}$ of an inch on most twelve-string guitars to compensate for the extra strings.) Small differences, even of $\frac{1}{16}$ of an inch, can be readily felt by experienced players.

On twelve-fret guitars, fingerboards are traditionally a bit wider, with 1$\frac{7}{8}$ inches being a pretty standard figure. This is closer to classical guitar dimensions, where the standard width is two inches.

Most people find fingerboards wider than 1$\frac{3}{4}$ inches uncomfortable for the fretting hand, especially if they mostly use the thumb-around-the-neck hand position typical of most vernacular styles rather than the thumb-on-the-back-of-the-neck style of classical playing. But suiting the fretting hand isn't what wide fingerboards are about.

They're about increasing the distance between the strings for the benefit of the picking hand, so the picking fingers have plenty of room for a broad stroke that originates in the first knuckle joint. This is the usual classical guitar stroke. It gives you the most control and the fullest tone, but most steel-string fingerpickers prefer to move from the second knuckle instead. Because this stroke takes up less space, those who use it find wider fingerboards to be of no benefit. If you're among the small number of guitarists who like to have the extra picking space, you'll find a wider fingerboard well worth the trouble—if you can find one. Since so few people care for them, few are made.

Most flatpickers find the string spread that is created by wide fingerboards quite uncomfortable under the pick because nothing but unnecessary work is accomplished by asking the flatpick to travel the extra distance between the strings.

For most guitarists, 1¹¹⁄₁₆ inches seems to be the magic compromise figure that does the greatest good for the greatest number of people in both flatpicking and fingerpicking styles. Some models with slightly narrower widths do exist, as do a reasonable number with 1¾ inches. In addition there's a psychological aspect: because fingerboard width interacts with fingerboard contour, neck thickness, and neck contour in the overall feel of the guitar, not all standard 1¹¹⁄₁₆-inches fingerboards wind up *feeling* exactly the same width. String spacing is another issue. Some makers inset the first and sixth a little farther in from the edge of the fingerboard than others, so the actual distance between strings is narrower even though the nut width is standard. Distance between the pinholes at the bridge is also a function of this aspect of string spacing.

Fingerboard Shape and Contour

Most steel-string guitars have a "contoured" fingerboard, which has a slight elliptical curve rather than a perfectly flat surface across its breadth. The degree of contour may vary somewhat from maker to maker or even from model to model. Most people find a contoured fingerboard more comfortable for the fingerings and hand positions typical of steel-string styles. Fewer steel-string guitarists like flat fingerboards, but they're found on most nylon-string guitars because they're more suitable for classical playing.

Whether you prefer a flat or contoured fingerboard, and the degree of contour you prefer, is entirely a matter of personal taste.

Replacing and Repairing Fingerboards

In time fingerboards become pitted with wear and hard playing. Ebony outlasts rosewood but unless you put in hours a day every day even your rosewood fingerboard will probably outlast you. Pits and cracks can be repaired, up to a point, with rosewood or ebony dust mixed with epoxy resin. After ten to thirty years of hard playing you might need to have a

Martin's first dreadnoughts were twelve-fret models but they quickly went to fourteen. Later Martin re-created the twelve-fret dreadnought and other companies, as illustrated by this Santa Cruz model, have also followed suit. Conventionally, twelve-fret dreadnoughts, like their smaller counterparts, have wider fingerboards. *Photo courtesy Santa Cruz Guitar Company*

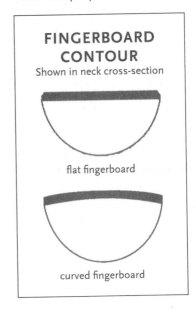

FINGERBOARD CONTOUR
Shown in neck cross-section

flat fingerboard

curved fingerboard

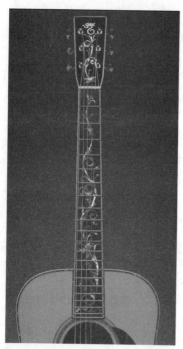

Most guitarists are happy with dot inlays to help them navigate the fingerboard; others, like classical guitarists, prefer none at all, using side dots or, perhaps, the earth's magnetic field to navigate. The fingerboard can also be a fertile area for inlay extravagance, as in this Santa Cruz dreadnought with its "vine of life" pattern. *Photo courtesy Santa Cruz Guitar Company*

fingerboard replaced. It's not a cheap job—mostly because of the time spent on the new frets that have to go in as well—but it's a routine one.

Keep your fretting-hand fingernails trimmed short and you'll reduce fingerboard wear. They shouldn't be in the least bit long anyway since they inhibit correct hand position if they are. But if good form won't motivate you maybe economy will.

FRETS

Fret Design

The "frets" are the metal bars running across the guitar's neck against which you press the strings. Frets give the notes a clear sound and make sure they're in tune.

Good frets are made of *nickel silver.* This is a metal-industry name for a hard nickel/steel alloy (sometimes also called *German silver*) that, in spite of its name, has no actual silver content. Cheaper guitars may use a softer metal that quickly wears down, such as brass.

Fretwire has two components:

- The "bead" or "crown," which is the part you actually see on your fingerboard.
- The "tang," which is the metal tongue that actually holds the fret into the fingerboard. Tangs have "studs" or "dimples," little protrusions that help grip the wood.

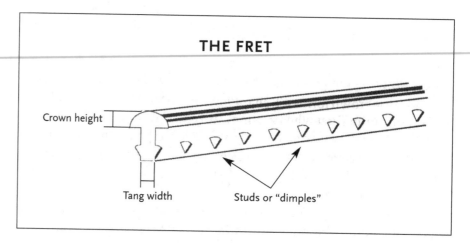

THE FRET

Crown height

Tang width   Studs or "dimples"

The tang fits into fine slots that the guitar maker saws at appropriate intervals in the fingerboard. The maker cuts the fretwire somewhat longer than the width of the fingerboard and then hammers it in. Once the fret is seated the protruding ends are nipped off. Some makers and repair people like to seat frets with epoxy glue in the grooves to hold them firmly; others are opposed to this technique because it makes the guitar harder to refret when the time comes.

Manufacturers provide fretwire gauged in many combinations of crown height and width. A medium crown width of .085 inches and height of .045 inches is common and most acoustic guitarists like it. You'll find larger (so-called "jumbo") frets (to .115 inches wide x .050 inches high) on many electric guitars and on some acoustic guitar models as well—especially those marketed for players who are used to an electric guitar feel. Which you prefer is a matter of taste. Martins and modern Gibsons have medium frets and older Gibsons low jumbo frets; old small guitars have small frets (.078 inches x .045 inches); some makers may vary fret gauge from model to model.

There are also very low "speed frets" (.110 inches x .035 inches) that are found on some electric guitars but not usually on acoustics. You might hear about these and be attracted by their name, but most guitarists find them uncomfortably low. However, repair people sometimes use them in quick-and-dirty jobs to replace individual too-high frets on instruments where all the other frets have been worn low.

In addition to having different possible combinations of crown height and width, fretwire also comes in different combinations of tang height and width independent of crown gauge. Sometimes, when a guitar is refretted, a thicker tang gauge is used because pulling out the old frets enlarges the slots. A wider tang gauge can also have the effect of bending the neck into a reverse warp because the wider tangs expand the fingerboard. This technique can be used deliberately to undo a forward warped neck.

Because the crown forms a T-shape with the tang, this kind of fretwire was known as the "T-fret" when it came into general use during the 1930s. Until then guitars were fretted with "bar frets" made of rectangular wire. T-frets are far more comfortable to play, more stable, and easier to install. Some collectors prefer to have older instruments refretted with bar frets to maintain historical accuracy but this makes little sense from a playing point of view. Unfortunately, replacing bar frets with T-frets involves refilling the original fret slots, a process so tedious (as well as cosmetically unsatisfactory) that it's usually more cost-effective to replace the entire fingerboard.

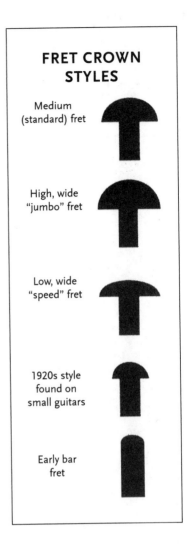

FRET CROWN STYLES

Medium (standard) fret

High, wide "jumbo" fret

Low, wide "speed" fret

1920s style found on small guitars

Early bar fret

Refretting

Frets become worn in time—especially under unwound strings. They don't wear evenly, of course, but get flattened and grooved in the spots where you play the most. If you don't play much, you'll be able to get through the rest of your life without worrying about fret wear. But if you play a lot, you'll probably find yourself asking a repair shop to dress your frets with a file and sandpaper every few years.

When frets finally get too low it's time to have them replaced. You waste finger strength pressing the string against the fingerboard, which does no good, rather than cleanly against the fret. And depressing a string against a too-low fret may bring its angle down enough that it buzzes against the next fret up the fingerboard. A temporary, quick-and-dirty solution is to file down the next fret, although that can lead to a domino effect requiring adjustment of the *next* fret up the fingerboard, and so on. When the time finally comes, it's better to get them all replaced.

Fret Placement

In order for the guitar to play in tune, the frets have to be unerringly spaced to within microscopic tolerances according to a mathematical proportion developed in ancient times by Pythagoras and refined during the time of Bach by one Andreas Werckmeister. This proportion is derived from the length of the vibrating part of the string.

As recently as twenty-five years ago, it was easy to find inexpensive instruments with badly spaced frets. But thanks to today's computer designs, standardized assembly procedures, and improved quality control, you're not likely to run into this problem on any instruments from the major manufacturers.

THE NUT

Function

The "nut" lies across the end of the fingerboard and holds the strings as they cross over from the headstock. Its six equidistant grooves hold the strings in position relative to each other. It shares the duty of regulating the height of the strings above the fingerboard with the bridge saddle (the other bearing point of the strings). It also helps transmit the vibrations of the open strings to the neck, which has its own resonant frequency that contributes to the sound of the guitar.

Materials

The nut should be dense and hard—dense to transmit sound effectively and hard to resist string wear. The traditional material for the nut and saddle on fine instruments was elephant ivory, which, of course, is now embargoed in an attempt to save the elephant from extinction. Some luthiers have stocks of pre-embargo ivory (or at least that's what they say), which should properly be reserved for restoring historical instruments.

The standard material used these days by makers of fine, hand-made instruments is bone, preferably a dense one like beef thigh bone. It sounds fine.

Synthetic materials are used on less expensive guitars and some good ones as well. Some ceramics, epoxy resin products like Micarta, and graphite materials work adequately. Cheap plastics neither sound nor hold up as well; cheap guitars use hollow molded pieces that not only do the worst possible job of transmitting sound but also eventually collapse. Brass nuts are used on some electric guitars but sound too jangly on acoustics.

Some older guitars used dark hardwood nuts, which look nice but give a softer quality to the open string tone. Most folks who own these older instruments have kept the original nuts on to preserve the historical sound of the instrument or perhaps just because it doesn't seem worth the trouble to have a new nut cut.

It's easy to get a new nut made if you need one. Some standard shapes are available precut. Suppliers sell blanks approximating the commonly used sizes and shapes and it's small work for a repair shop to cut or grind them to final size, groove them, and mount them.

If you have an instrument with an adequate synthetic nut and are happy with the way it sounds, leave it in until the strings wear it down; then get it replaced with bone. If you want to try bone sooner, go ahead—it's not that expensive to have the job done. If your instrument is good enough to be responsive to such a change, you may hear some difference or improvement. If it's not a sensitive instrument, the change won't make much difference. The best way to get a mediocre guitar to sound better is to trade it toward a better one, not to replace the nut.

If you want to match a new nut or saddle to an old guitar with bindings and other finishes that have yellowed with age, you can give a piece of bone or ivory (and perhaps some plastics) an aged appearance by letting it sit a few hours in a cup of tea. Once upon a time people also did this by blowing cigarette smoke at it, but no one with any sense smokes anymore.

Nut Height and Grooves

The ideal height of the string above the fingerboard as it comes off the nut is .007 to .009 inches measured between the string and the first fret, with the string depressed at the fourth fret. In other words, not very high.

You might be able to measure this miniscule distance with a feeler gauge, but you can barely see it. The chances are that your guitar has a first string somewhere between .010 and .012 inches in diameter. (See Chapter 8, page 154, for more details.) Perhaps you can use this as a standard of comparison for your eye to estimate if the nut is obviously too high. You might also try getting a guitar first string of known gauge and slipping it under the string. It's not exact, but it can at least tell you if the nut is *way* too high.

Telling whether the nut is cut too low is easier. With each string in turn depressed at the fourth fret, try plucking them in the area between the nut and the fourth fret. If you produce a ping that has some tone to it, you'll know that the nut isn't too low (though it may be too high). But if all you hear are buzzes or dead thuds, then it's too low.

Many factories ship their instruments with the nut grooves a bit too high. They want to eliminate any chance of the strings buzzing when a prospective customer energetically strikes the strings—nothing kills a sale faster. Dealers should make fine adjustments before the instrument gets out on the sale floor, but few bother—especially on cheaper instruments. It would not be out of line to discuss whether or not the nut should be adjusted, at no charge.

If you're handy and don't mind experimenting, you might want to try adjusting the nut grooves yourself. Do it slowly, testing in stages. If you mess up, you can always go to a repair shop (be prepared for a scornful lecture about doing work yourself and don't mention my name). Ideally the right implement for the job on the wound-string grooves is a specialized woodworking tool called a round-edge joint file. You need a set of them, each one a couple of thousandths of an inch wider than the string diameter. In the real world many guitarists adjust their own grooves with small triangular, rat-tail, or half-round files from the hardware store, and the music critics don't seem to notice. The grooves for the first and second strings should also be cut with a specialized tool: a knife-cut needle file or hobbyist's razor saw. It's a good idea to dress out the groove with a folded-over piece of fine emery paper when you're done filing. Rough edges in the nut groove lead to broken strings or strings that catch in the grooves and hinder smooth, even tuning.

Grooves should be cut into the nut on an angle parallel to the plane of the headstock. If you groove a nut parallel to the plane of the fingerboard, you'll wind up breaking a lot of strings on the sharp edge where the string drops off the nut on its way to the tuners, and you'll run a risk of buzzing, foggy tone and dubious intonation.

Ideally the string should not ride deeply in the nut—not deeper than about the full diameter of the unwound strings and half the diameter of the wound ones. If the grooves are any deeper, the strings may bind, making them harder to tune and easier to break. In real life this rule is often violated because players often do their own

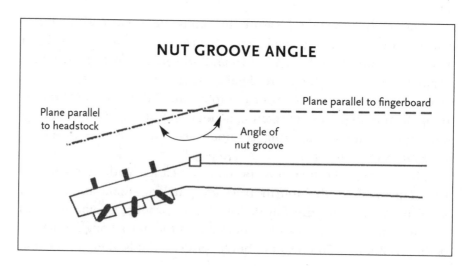

NUT GROOVE ANGLE

Plane parallel to headstock

Plane parallel to fingerboard

Angle of nut groove

quick touch-ups with a file. It seems you can get away with this up to a point. In a perfect world, if the right height would require the grooves to be too deeply cut, the repair shop would instead remove the nut (a sharp blow does the trick) and lower it by grinding down the bottom.

A nut that's too low can be shimmed up with hardwood veneer secured with aliphatic resin glue without a noticeable degradation of tone. In a perfect world, though, you'd have a new nut cut.

The function of the nut grooves is not only to hold the strings but also to space them evenly. Occasionally a factory turns out badly tooled nuts where the grooves are too widely spaced for the neck so that those for the first and sixth strings are too close to the edges of the fingerboard. This makes you accidentally shove the string over the edge when you play, especially on the first string. Some instruments have nuts where the strings are a little farther from the edge than is necessary for most people. Most players of such instruments would be more comfortable if they replaced the factory nuts with nuts that had grooves cut farther apart. Bear in mind, though, that how close you like the strings to the edge of the fingerboard is a matter of personal taste and has a lot to do with your individual fretting-hand habits.

SCALE

"Scale" is the length of the vibrating portion of the string—in other words, the distance from the point the string leaves the nut to the point at which it rests on the crest of the saddle. You might think that all guitars were built to a standard scale but that's not the case by a long shot. The guitar world is basically divided between long-scale and short-scale instruments, each of which has somewhat different playing qualities. From maker to maker there are minor variations within each of these two categories—luthiers and designers may feel that even a tenth of an inch difference makes a difference to their design.

Scale is a function of neck length, not body size. It usually works out that larger guitars have a longer scale (a larger whole tends to have larger parts) but it doesn't necessarily have to be that way. Longer necks require the frets to be spaced proportionally farther apart, so each scale length has its own mathematically derived system for fret placement. In addition to meaning "vibrating string length," the word *scale* also has the secondary meaning of the actual template that a luthier uses for positioning the frets for a given scale length.

Long and Short Scales

Long-scale instruments have a scale of about 25½ inches. (The usual long-scale range runs from the standard Martin dreadnought scale of 25.4 inches up to about 25.6 inches, favored by some custom luthiers

Fanned frets are only one of the unusual features on this guitar, though none are unusual in the work of Harry Fleishman. Note the asymmetrical design (which one could guess indicates a non-standard bracing pattern), the mixed redwood and spruce top, and the unusual bridge shape, characteristic of many of Fleishman's models. *Photo by John Youngblut, courtesy Harry Fleishman*

but found less often on factory guitars.) Most guitars made these days are long-scale instruments, even those with smaller bodies.

Short-scale instruments are approximately 24.9 inches, which was the traditional scale for smaller-bodied Martin twelve-fret guitars. However many of the classic Martin short-scale models are now no longer in standard production. The Gibson short scale is 24.75 inches and many current Gibson models are available with this scale length. Short-scale instruments, generally following either the Martin or Gibson standard, are available from other makers as well, although they are not as common in the marketplace as long-scale instruments.

Fanned Frets for Mixed Scales

Recently, many luthiers and players have become interested in instruments with non-parallel "fanned frets," which are set in a radiating pattern that is wider under the low strings than it is under the high strings. The effect of this, of course, is to create a longer scale for the lower strings. This helps punch up the sound of the low strings while keeping the highs sweeter.

Fan fret guitars are dizzying to look at whether you're playing or just watching. Oddly, fan frets become transparent to play as soon as you quit looking; most players don't notice a thing or, if they do, their nervous system sorts it out in minutes.

Longer scale gives you greater string tension and also greater volume. It's the volume factor that is responsible for the dominance of the long scale in today's market. (I suspect it's because bumping up volume with a long scale is easier and cheaper than constructing a fine top and bracing to get the same results.) However, since volume is also limited by the strength of your stroke, the acoustic qualities of the body, and the quality of the strings themselves, you can make the scale only so long before you get into the area of diminishing returns. While something around 25½ inches seems the upper limit for steel strings, modern, concert-quality classical guitars were often built to a 26-inch scale or greater during the 1980s in order to help produce enough volume to fill a concert hall. However too many guitarists found such instruments difficult and even harmful to play, and the practice has lost much favor.

The lower string tension of short-scale guitars makes them marginally softer to play and causes them to be more sensitive to vibrato and short string bends. (Many guitarists find that big bends actually *feel* easier to play with a longer scale because of the greater distance to work with between the frets.)

You might think that long-scale guitars would be harder to play than short-scale ones because the frets are a bit farther apart; but the extra stretch just doesn't seem to bother most people. Many even find the more closely spaced frets of a short-scale guitar more uncomfortable for executing cluttered chord shapes (like the basic beginner's A chord) where the fingers have to bunch up to cover several strings all at the same fret. Choosing between a long- and short-scale instrument may be an important decision but don't think that short scale is necessarily easier.

HEADSTOCK AND TUNERS

Headstock or Peghead

At the end of the neck is the flat section called the "headstock" or "peghead" (the terms are interchangeable) where the tuning machines are mounted. Most steel-strung guitars have a solid headstock through which the pegs are mounted perpendicularly. A few models, usually twelve-frets, have a classical-style "slotted headstock," where the pegs are mounted in slots cut into the headstock. The extra neck width customary on twelve-fret guitars makes the extra width of the slotted headstock more appropriate visually. However, aside from looks and tradition, there are no important structural advantages to either of the two headstock designs, nor will they affect your playing or handling of the instrument significantly.

Headstock size and shape may vary among makers. Most prefer a simple trapezoid while others use a characteristic crest or other ornamental shape. The maker's name or logo usually appears either inlaid, painted, or as a decal on the headstock. On fancy instruments there may be ornamental inlay work on the headstock.

The top of the headstock is usually covered by a veneer of ornamental wood or other material, often the same wood of which the body is made. On cheap instruments a coat of paint may be sprayed on instead.

Most headstocks are carved, along with the neck, out of one neck blank. On some instruments, even good ones, mahogany blanks may be used that, for economy's sake, are not quite wide enough for the total width of the headstock. In this case, winglike laminations of extra wood are glued on. Laminated headstocks can be expected to last the life of the guitar (or guitarist) without incident. The glue joint is about as strong as the wood, though some kinds of shearing trauma can break it. So can enlarging the peg hole for a larger brand of tuner. If this happens, it's easy enough to reglue the joint. A laminated headstock shouldn't affect a purchasing decision.

There is another kind of headstock lamination. Some makers also laminate a sheet of veneer over the top surface of the headstock to provide a cosmetic surface. Often it matches the body wood: for example, one might see a highly figured koa lamination on the headstock of a highly figured koa guitar. Black, blackwood, or very light wood laminations can also be appealing.

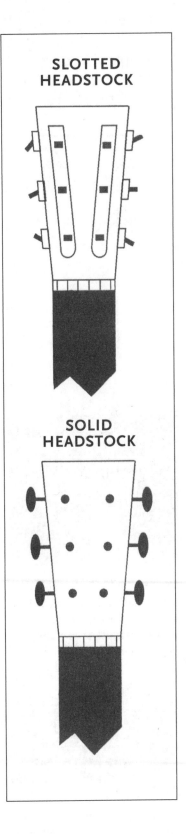

SLOTTED HEADSTOCK

SOLID HEADSTOCK

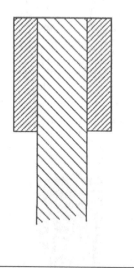

NECK BLANK WITH LAMINATED HEADSTOCK

The neck blank of this Edward V. Dick guitar has been routed out to accept the truss rod and shows an ebony headstock overlay already in place. *Photo by E. V. Dick*

Classical-guitar tuning machines are traditionally in-line, with wide bone or plastic rollers to provide more surface area for the slippery nylon strings. *Photo by Larry Sandberg*

Handstop or Volute

You'll notice that the headstock of most guitars is bent back from the neck at about a fifteen-degree angle. This is done to create downward pressure to hold the string down firmly as it crosses the nut. The point at which the headstock angles back from the neck is one of the weakest spots on the guitar, especially vulnerable if the instrument is dropped.

Some manufacturers, especially of banjos, used to carve their necks with an extra lip of wood at this point in order to create added strength. This is known as a "headstock reinforcement," "handstop," or "volute." Whether the intention is structural or ornamental, volutes add beauty to the instrument.

Tuning Machines

The gadgets that you use to tune your strings are called "tuners," "machines," "tuning machines," "machine heads," "heads," or "tuning pegs." If you ever try to tune with a stripped or jammed gear on one in the middle of a performance, you'll probably come up with a few more names. Many early guitars had violin-style "friction pegs" (wooden pegs held in place merely by their own friction against their holes), but they are no longer used except on flamenco guitars. (In the traditional flamenco playing position, with the guitar almost upright in the lap, the instrument is more difficult to balance when the headstock is weighted down with tuners.)

I'm not inclined to make too big a deal over tuning machines. Some are better than others in that they're smoother, and made of more durable metal that won't strip out over the years. In addition, tuning is easier and more precise when the machines have a greater (and therefore more sensitive) gear ratio. Some are fancier than others with more ornate knobs, chasing, filigree, or gold plating. Manufacturers consistently offer better and/or fancier tuners on their models as price brackets go up. Take what you get without worrying too much about it unless your tuners actually annoy you. Then upgrade.

Machines come in a variety of shapes. Some are individual; others (called "in-line") are mounted three to a metal strip, or "plate," with one plate for each side of the headstock. Machines for slotted or straight headstocks are configured differently and are not interchangeable. Not all machines are interchangeable. Hole spacing may vary, especially on older or foreign guitars. Some require different hole sizes or bushings. Some require complicated countersunk drilling.

Tuning machine design is generally simple. Machines have a button that turns a worm-and-screw gear that turns the shaft, or "barrel" on which the string is mounted. On straight-headstock models, the barrel is held in place on top of the peghead by a hex nut (possibly with a collar) and a washer.

While most tuners operate in a straightforward manner, some are complex. Sperzel brand locking tuners, for example, have a hand-screw that tightens down on the string to clamp it in place, making multiple winds unnecessary. They were originally designed to help stabilize the strings on electric guitars with tremolo attachments, which make the string wobble; players of non-tremolo guitars also like them because they make restringing easier and hold the tuning of new strings better.

Here's What You Need to Know About Tuners

Good tuners don't slip or have excessive play, are easy and pleasant to work, and turn evenly. If there are serious problems with any of these functions, your pleasure in your instrument will be impaired and you'll find it more difficult to get and keep your instrument in tune. But you can probably live with minor tuner imperfections. You learn to live with them as you learn to live with a tricky shift lever on your car. However, if you play in public or have to keep in tune with other people, having a good set of tuners becomes more worthwhile.

Cheap tuners are constructed to imprecise tolerances and are made of inferior metal that wears out. Unless they're so awful that they aggravate even from the beginning, just use them until they begin to go. Then replace them with a better set. You don't need top-of-the-line tuners; just a set that works comfortably. Many dealers and repair people keep old tuners on hand and you may be able to get a decent set used. You can even put them on yourself if you're handy. If they require new screw holes, drill them out first or you risk cracking the headstock. And be warned that the heads strip off the tiny screws easily. Maybe it's a job for a pro after all.

Tuners with a higher gear ratio are more sensitive, which makes fine tuning a little easier. However lots of people manage to get through life without extremely high-ratio tuners.

Unless your tuners have sealed ("self-lubricating") gears, carefully apply a little white grease to them every year or so. It's easy to apply it using the end of a toothpick. Keep on top of this; you should be able to tell when the gears feel stiff and dry. You can needlessly ruin a perfectly good set of tuners if you don't keep them lubricated. It's like not brushing your teeth. Decay occurs slowly over a number of years and you don't notice until it's too late.

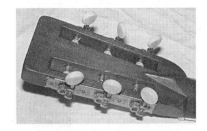

As with classical guitars, twelve-fret guitars with slotted headstocks conventionally use in-line tuners. *Photos by Larry Sandberg*

These simple, relatively inexpensive tuners are nonetheless of high-enough quality to operate smoothly and have a high-enough gear ratio to tune comfortably. They do the job just fine.

These Sperzel locking tuners are a luxury but they do help keep new strings in tune.

Enclosed tuners are self-lubricating but may add a little more weight to the headstock than simple tuners. Sometimes adding heavy tuners may improve tone. More often, however, heavier tuners will uncomfortably affect the weight balance of the instrument.

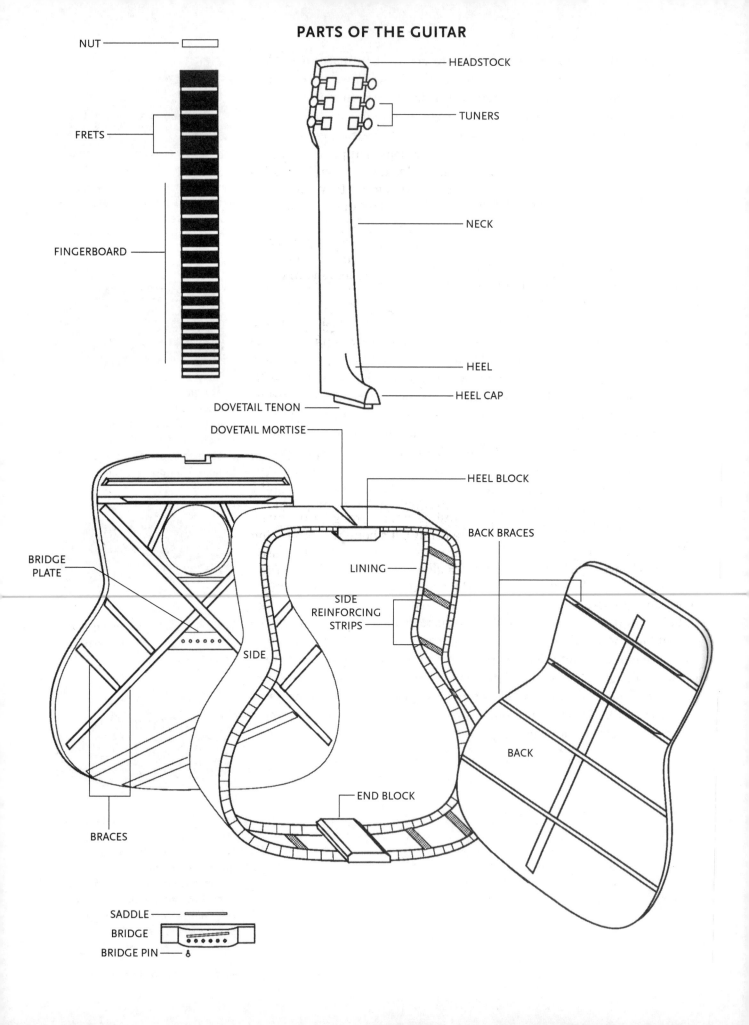

PARTS OF THE GUITAR

NUT

HEADSTOCK

TUNERS

FRETS

NECK

FINGERBOARD

HEEL

HEEL CAP

DOVETAIL TENON

DOVETAIL MORTISE

HEEL BLOCK

BACK BRACES

LINING

BRIDGE
PLATE

SIDE
REINFORCING
STRIPS

SIDE

BACK

END BLOCK

BRACES

SADDLE

BRIDGE

BRIDGE PIN

How Your Guitar Works
II: Body Language

The guitar's body is a semi-enclosed sound chamber that amplifies the sounds of the vibrating strings. The scientific name for such a body is "general resonator;" "general" because it co-vibrates with (and therefore amplifies) any frequency. A "specific resonator," on the other hand, is a body that co-vibrates with only one frequency or with a narrow range of frequencies; for example, your broken glove compartment latch that only rattles at the bottom of second gear.

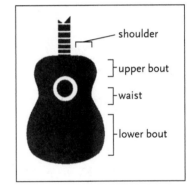

Guitarists use the word *body* in two senses: usually it means the entire chamber including top, back, and sides, but sometimes it means the back and sides alone (for example, in talking about body woods, which are different from top woods). Context usually makes the sense clear. The body is also sometimes called the "soundbox" or just the "box."

For the sake of description, luthiers have names for three separate area of the body. The two curved portions are called "bouts"; the smaller is the "upper bout" and the larger is the "lower bout." (Sometimes they're affectionately called the bust and hips.) The bouts are separated in the middle by the pinched-in "waist," which is functional: it helps you hold the guitar on your thigh. The area of the top in the upper bout below the bridge is called the "belly," and the tops of the sides on either side of the neck are called the "shoulders."

Wood type and quality are very important to the way the body works and sounds. (See Chapter 4, page 47, for more information on woods.)

THE TOP OR SOUNDBOARD

The Soul of the Guitar

The "top" or "soundboard" (sometimes also called the "face" or "table") is the voice and soul of the instrument. The quality and shaping of the top wood and of the bracing struts that support it from underneath determine sustain, volume, and presence. Only the best woods and the finest craftsmanship result in the perfect combination of rigidity and resilience that makes a guitar truly great.

The large area of the soundboard below the bridge, again, is called the top's belly. On some guitars it may arch up just a bit from the tension of the strings, so don't be disturbed if it's not absolutely flat. (This is called "bellying.") A slightly arched belly is acceptable. After you look at a few guitars you'll get a sense of how much arch is normal and how much is excessive. A severe paunch may indicate loose or broken braces.

"Playing In" a Top

Solid wood soundboards improve as the wood ages, but merely letting a guitar sit for ten or twenty years isn't good enough. Actually playing the instrument also helps make the top sound better by loosening it up. It's called "playing in" a guitar. Some instruments fresh out of the factory have inhibited, closed-in voices that begin to open up after only several hours of playing. A year makes an even bigger difference, although of course this all depends on how many hours you put in during that year. It really takes ten or twenty years for a top to mature completely, but this has to do with the chemical seasoning of the wood and finish as well as playing in.

Playing in and seasoning seem to work hand in hand. Many guitarists have observed that a well-played instrument improves more in tone than a poorly played one, and that the tone of an instrument passed on from a clumsy player to one with a fine touch also improves.

Guitars also get lonely. It seems that a guitar left unplayed for too long loses some of its vivacity and usually has to be played back in for a few hours before it sounds congenial again. Cat owners will understand perfectly.

The finer an instrument is, the more sensitive it is to these vagaries. Soundboards made poorly or of poor wood profit less from the benefits of aging and playing in and are relatively oblivious to neglect.

Laminate and Solid Wood Tops

Laminate (plywood) tops don't age at all. Because of the aging qualities and overall acoustic advantages of solid wood, manufacturers now couple solid tops to plywood bodies on all but their lowest-end models. As you get into the better guitars, the difference becomes audible, though in poorer guitars the solid tops may be more of a sales point than a perceptible asset. Design and overall quality of joining is also important, so a well-made, plywood-topped instrument could conceivably sound better than a really poor solid-topped one.

Top Materials and Building

The following discussion will recapitulate some of the basic points made in the chapter on guitar woods and further examine their ramifications. (See Chapter 4, page 47, for more information on woods.)

Spruce is the standard soundboard wood. Some players and luthiers prefer cedar and redwood; they're slightly more brilliant to begin with but may not change in character as much as spruce does as they open up. Mahogany and koa, more often body woods, have smaller and different voices than spruce when used for tops.

Solid tops are furnished to the luthier or factory in halves (preferably bookmatched) by wood suppliers or the factory's own wood products division. Some luthiers, however, do their own milling from larger planks. The halves are glued together at their center seam by the maker. In mass-produced guitars, the tops are finished to uniform specifications with as much automated work as possible. In fine guitar making, tops are worked on by hand and with hand tools, and are graduated in thickness from section to section. Tops are often graduated a bit more thickly on the bass-string side because of the greater string tension on that side.

While the bookmatched two-piece top is standard, many makers now occasionally use, with success, four-piece tops made of bookmatched cuts from larger billets consisting of two pieces glued together. This is more common on larger instruments due to the increasing rarity of spruce sections large enough to use for broad tops.

Through instinct and training, luthiers determine graduation by tapping the top and listening to it, then carve it until it is in tune with itself by eliminating unwanted components of the sound. This is called "voicing" the guitar. You can teach yourself to hear an in-tune body. Tops and backs should also be in tune with each other. Go around and gently tap the sides and backs of different guitars. If you have a decent ear, you'll learn to hear how some are better in tune than others; you can use this skill to help you judge a guitar.

The Sound Hole

The sound hole is not there to "let the sound out." Having an orifice permits the top to vibrate more freely because it relieves air pressure inside the sound chamber. A sound chamber with an orifice is known among loudspeaker designers as a "ported enclosure." Scientists call it a "Helmholtz resonator" after Hermann von Helmholtz, the nineteenth-century physicist who laid the foundations of modern acoustic science. One of Helmholtz's contributions was to demonstrate the existence of harmonics with a series of experiments involving ported enclosures. (See Chapter 3, page 37, for more information on overtones.)

Occasionally you'll see instruments with the sound hole(s) located elsewhere in the soundboard than in the middle of the waist. These are called "offset sound holes." Most often they're offset because the instru-

As an experiment, Edward V. Dick built this small sound hole in the upper bout of a guitar to see if it's sound would wrap around the player to a greater degree. It does. *Photo by Larry Shirkey, courtesy E. V. Dick*

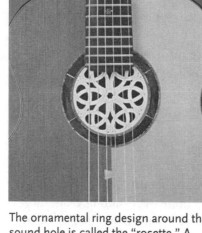

The ornamental ring design around the sound hole is called the "rosette." A carved screen over the hole itself is called a "rose." Ancient lutes frequently had roses as ornaments; here is one on a contemporary guitar by Harry Fleishman. *Photo by John Youngblut, courtesy of Harry Fleishman*

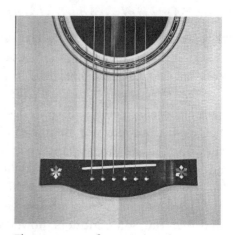

The rosette is a favorite place for a ring of abalone inlay. On this Santa Cruz model the rosette is complemented by abalone snowflakes on the feet of the bridge. *Photo courtesy Santa Cruz Guitar Co.*

A small, narrow-bodied guitar with a relatively large sound hole. This guitar would have fairly juicy-sounding high strings and would probably not have a boomy bass. *Photo courtesy Santa Cruz Guitar Co.*

ment is constructed with a nontraditional bracing pattern that requires the sound hole to be relocated, although some makers also believe that moving the sound hole so as to create the largest possible continuous vibrating surface helps bass response.

SOUND HOLE SHAPE AND SIZE

D-shaped, triangular, and elliptical sound holes are sometimes made for visual effect but more often they too are the result of some modification in the traditional bracing pattern. For example many cutaway guitars have elliptical sound holes; this is because the bracing under the cutaway bout has had to be moved down a little toward the center of the guitar, and the hole has to be made less round to accommodate it. Merely making a round hole smaller would affect the tone. All other things being equal, a larger hole creates more of a treble balance; a smaller hole reinforces the lower notes.

The Pickguard

A sheet of protective material, usually black or tortoiseshell celluloid, is commonly attached to the top below the sound hole of most steel-string guitars. This part of the top is prone to cumulative damage from picks and fingers, so a pickguard makes sense. If you happen to acquire one of the few instruments now made without one and begin to notice damage, you can always have one added later. The small, thin pickguards usually found on today's guitars don't significantly detract from a guitar's tone and volume, and whatever difference they might make is

Most pickguards are thin plastic with dark, tortoiseshell coloration; some are black or dark brown. The pickguard on this Santa Cruz Tony Rice model imitates the light translucent tortoiseshell that was found on some old instruments. *Photo courtesy Santa Cruz Guitar Co.*

amply repaid by the fact that you'll still have a top left after five years of digging picks and fingernails into it. However, heavy or oversize pickguards can make a perceptible difference in sound and don't really seem to offer any greater protection in return, so you should avoid them. Pickguard material should ideally be extremely thin; big, heavy pickguards are a thing of the past.

Pickguards on some early guitars were made of genuine tortoiseshell, which may have some marginal acoustical advantages over synthetics. But celluloid drove expensive tortoiseshell off the market decades ago and now tortoiseshell is illegal and immoral to use. Sometimes on fancy instruments you'll see a thin, hardwood pickguard that is supposed to be less detrimental to tone. I haven't had enough experience with them to comment. Guitarists who don't like the look of pickguards might consider having a transparent one installed.

Although classical guitars have no pickguards, flamenco guitars are fitted with a plastic or wood pickguard, traditionally more squared-off in shape than those on steel-string guitars, called the "tap-plate" or *golpeador* (Spanish for "striker"). Its job is to accept the percussive fingernail tapping that is part of flamenco. When classical guitarists are required to execute flamenco effects, they tap on the bridge. Archtop guitars are usually fitted with a large, heavy, celluloid pickguard mounted on screwed-in struts and spacers so it floats above the surface of the instrument. The pickguard may also serve as the mount for volume and tone controls, which then makes it unnecessary to mount them in the actual instrument. Some archtop guitar players remove the pickguard because the pickguard somewhat obstructs the f-hole.

BRACING

The insides of the guitar's top and back are reinforced by a system of struts called the "braces." Braces are usually made of spruce for the top and mahogany for the back, although other woods may also be used.

Top Bracing

The top braces do more than just reinforce the top against the pressure of the strings. They also have an acoustic function, but it's hard to define exactly what or why because acoustic engineers don't fully understand how the braces work.

From looking at the braces you'd think that they lead sound outward from the bridge into the soundboard. Some luthiers believe that this is the case and build accordingly. Others are convinced otherwise by studies that use holography and oscilloscopes to study the way the top moves, or studies using the low-tech approach of scattering graphite dust on the top and watching the way the particles dance when notes are plucked. These seem to show that the top vibrates in complex and

SOME PICKGUARD SHAPES

Standard (Martin-style) pickguard shape, here shown on a grand auditorium guitar

Traditional flamenco tap-plate, here shown on a classical-size guitar. Some steel-string makers favor this shape for ornamental wooden pickguards.

Sound-deadening oversize pickguard, shown on a dreadnought body.

surprising patterns that appear to be centered in various places depending on pitch. It's nothing at all like ripples moving outward from the bridge, nor are high and low vibrations confined to the high-string and low-string sides of the guitar. Take this and add in the many other interactions still not fully understood by luthiers and engineers—the effects of the density and flexibility or rigidity of the sides, the mass of the neck, the many variations on bracing patterns, the magic of the wood itself—and what you're left with is the mystery that makes luthiery an art rather than a science. (See Chapters 1 and 13, pages 6 and 226, for more information on bracing.)

There are three major types of traditional bracing: transverse bracing, fan-bracing, and X-bracing. Throughout the history of the instrument there have also been, and continue to be, other experimental and transitional patterns, as well as new proprietary designs that manufacturers come up with from time to time.

Fan-bracing on a classical guitar by Harry Fleishman. *Photo by John Youngblut, courtesy Harry Fleishman*

Transverse Bracing

In the earliest days of the guitar, makers used just a few braces that ran transversely across the top—either straight across or at a slight offset. This style of bracing confers no great acoustic benefits and not a great deal of strength either. Transverse bracing was used even into the 1960s by some of the cheapie American companies, but when decent X-braced Japanese instruments took over the American market in the 1970s, they pretty much wiped out the American transverse-braced instruments.

Transverse bracing is also called "straight bracing." Sometimes it's also called "cross-bracing" (since the struts go straight across the top, but this can be confusing because some people use *cross-bracing* to mean *X-bracing* because the two main struts cross to form an *X*.

Asymmetrical fan-bracing on a classical guitar by Edward V. Dick. *Photo by E. V. Dick*

Fan-Bracing

Guitar makers in the early nineteenth century had worked with three to five struts fanning out under the top's belly, but it was the great Spanish luthier Antonio Torres who, around the middle of the century, developed a system of seven main fans (plus other secondary braces) that is still the basis of classical-guitar bracing design.

Fan-bracing works well with nylon strings and their 70 pounds of tension, but it can't hold up against the 150 or so pounds of steel-string tension.

X-Bracing

X-bracing, the standard design for steel-string guitars, is named after the two main struts that cross each other to form an *X* just below the sound hole. There are also several secondary struts under the belly as

PRIMARY AND SECONDARY BRACES

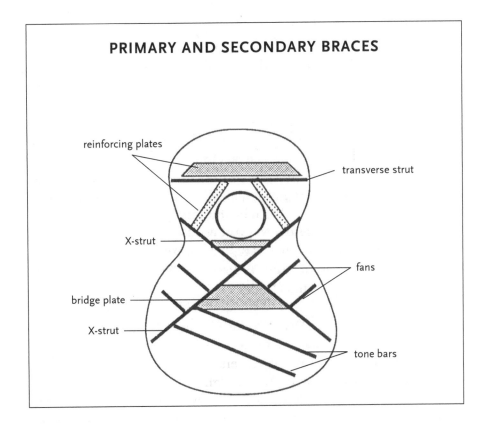

well as transverse struts and flat struts under the spatula and around the sound hole.

The X-brace was developed by C. F. Martin around the same time Torres was developing the fan-brace and was used increasingly in the Martin factory until, by the last decades of the nineteenth century, it became the sole bracing pattern on Martin guitars. It was developed decades before steel strings came into fashion but it suited them perfectly when they arrived.

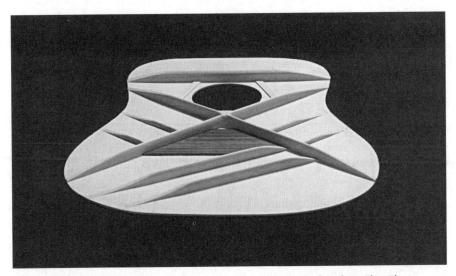

The real goods: the X-braced top of a contemporary Martin dreadnought. *Photo courtesy C. F. Martin & Co.*

Voiced and Scalloped X-Bracing

An ordinary bracing strut is a long, thin rectangle, sometimes with the top gently beveled to a crest, with tapered-down ends. On early Martin guitars the tops of the struts were shaved with a wood chisel into parabolic curves so that they resembled the shape of a suspension bridge. Shaving the struts made them lighter and let them flex more so the top could move more freely. However, the tops also arched up ("bellied") in back of the bridge, especially when steel strings came into general use in the 1920s. The tops were *supposed* to belly, at least a little, but the public perceived the bellying as a fault. Eventually Martin got tired of customer complaints and in 1944 discontinued shaved braces in order to create more support for the top and reduce bellying. Five years earlier Martin had moved the crossing point of the X about an inch farther away from the sound hole and closer to the bridge, also to add greater support under the belly.

Scalloped bracing—along with the "high brace position," as it's known—gave most early Martin guitars a distinctive sound. Its cachet derives from the very real difference it makes in most of those instruments. In the 1960s and 1970s it became fashionable (maybe in places it still is) for owners of modern Martins to have their struts shaved by a repair shop skilled in the job. Martin wasn't crazy about the idea and, quite reasonably, refused to honor warranties on custom-scalloped instruments. In any case, word was getting around that scalloped was better than unscalloped (or at least it was supposed to be better, and was certainly hipper), and in the mid-1970s Martin reintroduced scalloped bracing on selected models. (The original high brace position is now also again available on selected models.) Now many manufacturers offer these features. On good guitars it makes a difference, though whether it's one that suits your personal taste is another story. On less well-made guitars it may be a meaningless feature—nothing more than a marketing ploy.

In a fine instrument, both the soundboard and the braces are "voiced"—a sensitive process of listening to how the wood sounds when tapped and gently shaving with a sharp chisel to bring it perfectly into tune with itself—by the luthier. However on mass-produced instruments the braces may be preshaved, which cancels out much of the value of scalloping.

Other bracing features also contribute to how the guitar sounds. Short, stubby, squarish braces are traditional on some models but many luthiers now believe—with support from naval and architectural engineering studies—that tall, thin braces impart the greatest strength while permitting the top to move most freely.

In contemporary guitar marketing, scalloped bracing may be at times nothing more than a buzzword. What's important, after all, is that the top should move, and if the top isn't good then fooling with the braces is meaningless. So after you read the sales specs, use your ears.

If you read sales literature, you'll see some other terms that mean about the same thing as scalloping—or that almost do. "Shaved" and

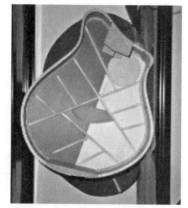

Harry Fleishman's take on the X-brace. Note the asymmetrical bracing and the offset sound hole just below the cutaway.
Photo by Larry Sandberg

"parabolic" usually mean scalloped in the traditional manner, but this isn't always true. "Tapered" usually means simply that the brace ends are tapered down. "Voiced" implies that the top and braces have been finely tuned by hand-shaving, whether the shaving is a scalloped shape or not.

Kasha and Other Bracing Systems

A physicist named Michael Kasha has influenced several contemporary luthiers by proposing radically new bracing theories based on the principle (which is somewhat oversimplified here) that every desired harmonic component of the guitar's tone must find some section of the instrument in which to vibrate.

In Kasha-style or Kasha-influenced bracing, the struts are arranged in a circular pattern around the bridge with the idea of evenly and effectively distributing vibrations to all areas of the guitar. The design also partitions the top into numerous small areas that reinforce vibrations of the various harmonics. Kasha-braced guitars can also usually be recognized by an off-center sound hole and a bridge that is wider on the bass side. (However, more traditionally braced guitars may appear this way as well.) The sound hole is positioned off-center both to accommodate the bracing and to provide a larger unbroken surface area to vibrate. The bridge is wider on the bass side to more effectively support low-frequency vibrations; sometimes the bridge is even designed in two pieces to permit the bass and treble sides to transmit vibrations independently.

I have had the opportunity to play a couple of experimental, Kasha-inspired guitars. My sense was of power, extremely even balance, and a certain impersonality. A friend who has also played Kasha-braced instruments describes them as "terrifyingly efficient" in terms of the balance of volume and tonal qualities on all strings throughout the instrument's range. However, he, too, was left somewhat cold in spite of the instruments' indisputable assets. Great guitars, like great personalities, often have foibles and weaknesses, and eliminating them destroys an ingredient in their character. This is one of the reasons so many serious guitarists own more than one instrument.

Strongly Kasha-derived instruments are produced by only a few luthiers, mostly in the realm of classical guitars. Sociologically, they are cult instruments that have not achieved mainstream appeal or impact, though Gibson did carry on a short and superficial flirtation with Kasha principles during the 1970s. That almost no one has had a chance to try a Kasha-braced guitar, and that no major performer uses one, doesn't help. However, Kasha's principles have encouraged many more luthiers to try asymmetrical and other nontraditional bracing patterns, leading to many interesting and successful developments.

Among commercial makers, several have come up with their own systems; Ovation, for example, uses several bracing patterns including

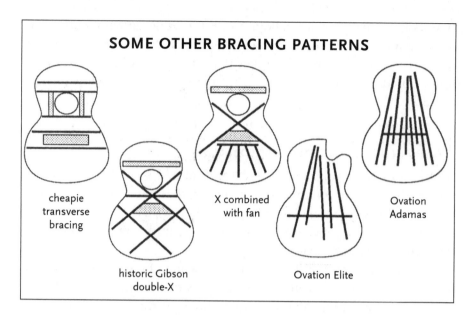

SOME OTHER BRACING PATTERNS

cheapie transverse bracing

historic Gibson double-X

X combined with fan

Ovation Elite

Ovation Adamas

an A-shape as well as a reworked version of the fan-brace for its Adamas series of graphite-fiber-topped steel-string guitars. The response of the Adamas instruments is, to my ear, similar to that of Kasha-style instruments in some ways. In addition many luthiers have their own variations on the traditional X-brace.

Damaged Braces

Top and back braces can split or come loose due to climatic shrinking or sometimes just from a blow that leaves no sign of external damage. Loose or split braces may cause buzzes and rattles that sometimes seem to be coming from the strings rather than from inside the guitar.

An experienced person may detect brace damage simply by tapping the guitar and listening. Sometimes damage can also be seen with an inspection mirror or felt by reaching inside the guitar.

Brace repair may sometimes require taking off the back. Over the past twenty years special clamps and jacks have been designed to eliminate this as much as possible, thus making brace work cost-effective even on relatively inexpensive instruments.

THE BRIDGE

Function and Structure

The "bridge" provides an anchoring point for the strings. It also transmits the vibrations of the strings to the top of the guitar; therefore, what it's made of affects the sound of the instrument.

The actual bearing point of the string is the "saddle," a strip of bone or similar material that rests in a groove in the bridge. The bridge also works in partnership with the "bridge plate," a wide, flat strut located inside the body, directly under the bridge, and a little below the point where the X-braces cross.

The bridge should be glued directly to bare wood. On cheapie guitars the bridge may be glued over the finish, in which case it won't stay there long. Cheapie makers may bolt down the bridge in addition to gluing. Bolting doesn't work in the long run because the bridge pulls away from the wood anyway, even if the bolts keep it from actually coming off the guitar. In addition, the bolting system is acoustically inferior. Makers have used bolted bridges at occasional aberrant points in their histories.

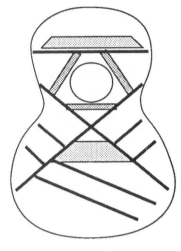

Bridge plate
(shaded area below the "X")

The Bridge Plate

It's not the bridge that actually holds the strings onto the guitar. Under the bridge is a flat brace of dense hardwood—maple and rosewood are best—that reinforces both strength and acoustic transmission. When you insert the ball at the end of the string through the pinhole in the bridge, it pulls up against the bridge plate. The purpose of the pin in the bridge hole is not to hold the string down, but simply to keep the ball jammed under the bridge plate.

When a soundboard begins to warp due to climate changes, one possible treatment is to straighten it in a press and then put in a larger bridge plate to help strengthen the area and more widely diffuse the string tension. Purists, however, will avoid doing this with historic instruments, but will instead try to re-create the original bridge plate.

The size and quality of the bridge plate somewhat affect the instrument's balance, volume, and sustain, and a cheap plywood plate may produce unwanted elements in the tone. Over time (say, two to four decades' worth, or less for a plate of inferior wood) the ball ends of the string can chew up the plate and it will need to be replaced. If, on an older guitar, the strings are too shallowly seated in the bridge holes so that the winding from the ball end rides up, it's a sign that the plate may need to be replaced.

The rosewood bridge plate is clearly visible between the lighter-colored spruce braces on this guitar by Edward V. Dick. Note also the neck joint, head block, and end block. *Photo by E. V. Dick*

Bridge Woods

On most steel-strung guitars, the bridge and fingerboard are made of the same wood for the sake of appearance—though on cheap instruments they may only *seem* to be made of the same wood. Ebony is the wood of choice but it's expensive and you'll only find it on top-of-the-line models. Rosewood is a bit softer and marginally less brilliant in tone than ebony. On a few top-grade guitars the maker may use a rosewood bridge because ebony is not as well-suited for the particular instrument. Ebony is considered too harsh-sounding for classical guitars in general and rosewood is preferred for those instruments.

On less expensive instruments, ebonized walnut or other hardwoods may be used. They're not as good as rosewood but they're acceptable if the compromise is reflected in the price.

Martin and some other makers used ivory bridges on a few models through the nineteenth century and into the beginning of the twentieth. They sound brighter than ebony and are very beautiful.

At the other extreme are the plastic and extruded nylon bridges that some manufacturers—even Gibson, at a low point—tried on cheap models during the 1970s. Avoid them; they're no good at all. Sometimes you can spot a guitar with an inferior bridge that can be improved by investing in a bridge replacement.

Bridge Shapes

The usual guitar bridge shape is the "belly bridge," so called because it resembles a rectangle with a paunch. (This has nothing to do with the part of the top called the belly.) The paunch is there to provide greater surface area for gluing and for diffusing string tension and vibrations. On Martins and on almost everybody else's bridges, the belly points toward the end of the body. By tradition, Gibson mounts its bridges with the belly pointing toward the sound hole. Belly bridges came into fashion in the early 1930s, probably as a way of dealing with the heavier gauges of steel strings then becoming popular.

Most bridges in the days before the belly bridge were simple rectangles, but there were ornate variations. The classic Martin "pyramid bridge" was rectangular with a small pyramid carved on each foot. Some Larson Brothers bridges gracefully tapered into a long triangle at

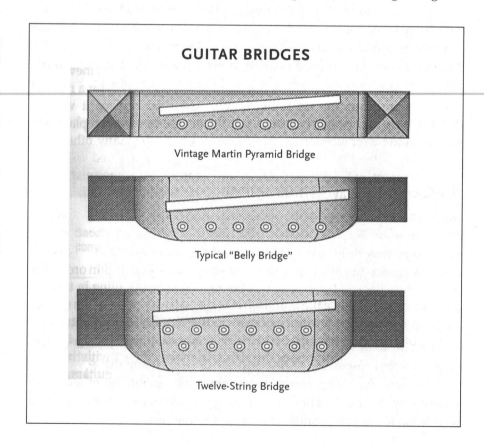

GUITAR BRIDGES

Vintage Martin Pyramid Bridge

Typical "Belly Bridge"

Twelve-String Bridge

A traditional belly bridge in rosewood on an Epiphone Bluesmaster guitar. *Photo by Larry Sandberg*

Pyramid bridge on an old Martin. *Photo by Larry Sandberg*

each end. On its J-200 model, Gibson still uses the ornate mustache bridge, so called because its feet are shaped like the elaborate, waxed mustachios of a Gay Nineties dandy. Today you'll still find ornamentally carved bridges on some custom models as well as some bridges flared out on the bass side by those luthiers who subscribe to the theory that this increases acoustic efficiency in the bass. On flashy models there may also be inlay work in the bridge feet. (These are not to be confused with the "ornamental" inlay dots that cover bolt holes on cheapie bridges.)

Fingerpicking guitar champion Rollie Brown playing a Gibson J-200 with its distinctive "mustachio bridge." *Photo by Larry Sandberg*

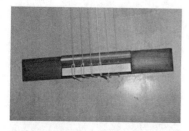

A classical-guitar bridge. *Photo by Larry Sandberg*

All these bridges are varieties of the "pin bridge," designed with holes through which the string ends are seated and then held in place against the bridge plate with a pin. C. F. Martin was committed to the pin bridge from the beginning of his career. It seems likely that he was impelled to develop his X-brace design at least in part to accommodate the pinholes, since fan bracing leaves no room for them. Like the X-brace itself, the pin bridge was invented in the days of gut strings but made great sense for steel strings once they came along.

By contrast, classical guitars have a "loop bridge" in which small holes are drilled though a raised section of the bridge in back of the saddle. The strings are then looped through these holes so that, unlike steel-string guitars, it is the bridge rather than the bridge plate that holds the strings. Put a set of steel strings on a classical guitar and the bridge won't stay mated to the body for long.

Archtop and Maccaferri guitars are constructed on the violin principle: a raised bridge holds the strings up off the top but the strings run over the bridge and are mounted in a tailpiece bracket attached to the end of the guitar. At one time you could also find tailpieces used on cheap flattop guitars to save the maker the trouble of constructing an adequate bridge; I don't think anyone's building that poorly anymore.

Bridge Pins

The composition of the bridge pins as well as of the saddle may affect tone. In my experience, ebony or rose pins (to match the bridge) sound better than the plastic pins that are used in many guitars. Upgrade cost is minimal. Some people have tried brass pins to brighten tone; others swear that ivory is best. Non-embargoed, fossil ivory is generally used for bridge pins, nuts, and saddles when the player must have ivory. Some old guitars still have their original ivory fittings.

THE SADDLE

Function, Structure, and Materials

The strings rest on the "saddle," a strip of bone or other dense material seated in a groove in the bridge. The saddle may be shimmed up, ground down, or replaced by a taller or shorter one to help compensate for changes in action caused by humidity changes, warping, and the natural settling in of the guitar.

Saddles are made of the same materials as nuts: ivory on fine historical instruments, dense bone on today's best instruments, and synthetics on other instruments. (See Chapter 5, page 96, for more information about the nut.) Some cheapie guitars of earlier times, and perhaps of the present as well, used a piece of fretwire for a saddle, which made them sound tinny and strident.

The top of the saddle should be smoothly curved. A sharp edge along the top might cause strings to break too easily where they cross it. Grooves should not be cut into flattop and classical guitar saddles, though they are customarily used on archtop and electric guitars. Sometimes it may be necessary to groove the saddles on twelve-string guitars in order to make sure that the pairs of strings seat correctly. This adjustment may also need to be made to any guitar if the bridge pins are not perfectly in position.

Adjustable Saddles

During the 1960s a few manufacturers came out with adjustable saddles that could be raised or lowered by screw mechanisms at either end. Adjustable saddles are standard on electric and archtop guitars. But on flattop guitars they're a disaster. They kill volume, dull the tone, and inevitably buzz and rattle. Fortunately it's not a prohibitively large job for a repair shop to pull out the adjusting mechanism and replace it with a wooden plug and properly seated saddle or, perhaps, to replace the bridge. Some decent instruments from this period—many otherwise respectable Gibsons, for example—can be greatly improved with this operation. You will still find adjustable saddles on some misguided instruments. Try to avoid them or, if the guitar is otherwise satisfactory, get them replaced.

Compensation

The saddle, and hence the bridge, must be perfectly placed in order for the guitar to play in tune. (The quality of singing or playing in tune is called "intonation.") Since the twelfth fret is the halfway point of the string, the saddle should be located as far from the twelfth fret as the twelfth fret is from the nut.

But it's not that simple, because all six strings are not equal in diameter and composition. This means that steel strings have actual vibrating lengths, which are slightly different from their measured lengths so that each string needs its own separate adjustment, or "compensation." The greatest difference of all is between the two unwound strings and the four wound strings. If this phenomenon is not compensated for the guitar will not play in tune across the entire length of the fingerboard.

Compensation is accomplished by adjusting the shape and angle of the saddle within the bridge. Take a look at the way the saddle groove is cut into the bridge. On almost all modern guitars the groove is cut on an angle so the end of the saddle under the low strings is about 3/64 of an inch farther back from the neck than the end under the high strings. This is called "offset." An offset saddle provides sufficiently good intonation for most people's ears but even more sensitive adjustments can bring the instrument's intonation closer to perfection.

This is the saddle of a guitar from the late 1920s, before guitar makers realized they needed to offset the saddles. In this case luthier Jon Lundberg carved a compensated saddle to help solve the problem. Look carefully and you'll see how the second string is set back, and how the crest of the saddle angles slightly forward from the sixth to the third strings. Even better is a saddle that is compensated like this and offset as well. *Photo by Larry Sandberg*

In this bridge on a guitar by Harry Fleishman, a separate saddle piece is used for each string. Notice how the pieces move slightly forward from the sixth to third strings and back again for the second. *Photo by Larry Sandberg*

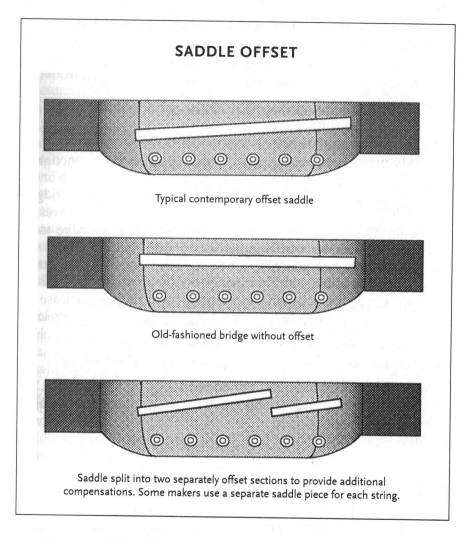

SADDLE OFFSET

Typical contemporary offset saddle

Old-fashioned bridge without offset

Saddle split into two separately offset sections to provide additional compensations. Some makers use a separate saddle piece for each string.

Because of the differences between wound and unwound strings, the most accurate degree of compensation is achieved by separately off-setting the two high strings and then starting a new offset for the four lowest strings.

For instruments with an unwound third string (generally only electric guitars) the separate offsets would be between strings 1–3 and 4–6. If you're one of those blues fanatics who prefer an unwound third string (even on an acoustic guitar), in order to make string bending more dramatic, you're going to run into some pretty audible intonation problems. You might want to consult a repair shop if your saddle is not specially compensated for an unwound third string.

Some instruments have two to six separate saddle pieces seated in a staggered offset arrangement; however, even a single-piece saddle can be filed or ground into this shape. If your guitar has only offset, or is an older instrument with no offset at all, you can have your saddle compensated by an experienced repair shop if you care to. It's probably not worth it on a cheapie guitar; poorly made instruments usually don't sound that deliciously in tune anyway even if the specs are right. You're better off saving your money for a better guitar than putting it into upgrading an inferior one.

If you happen to inhabit the world of pure mathematical truth, the amount of compensation on your guitar should ideally be adjusted to within at least a sixty-fourth of an inch to precisely suit your individual action and string-gauge setup. Even changing from one gauge of strings to another could throw off the specs. But in this real world of toil and trouble, few if any people actually get a new saddle cut just because they change string gauge. There's a point at which you can't really hear much difference and for most people that point is around a thirty-second of an inch. In any case experienced players often fine tune while they're playing by bending the strings slightly, even on notes within a chord. Some probably do it without even knowing it.

KEEPING YOUR TEMPER

The issue of intonation is so alarming that, by contemporary standards of tuning, nothing is ever really in tune anyway! This apparent existential dilemma is actually a compromise worked out around 1700 by a musical theorist named Andreas Werckmeister and promulgated by Johann Sebastian Bach in some of his most important works.

It all goes back to that unfortunate discrepancy that exists between the Ideal World of numbers and ideas, and the Real World of imperfect things, which most of us inhabit. According to the number theory governing intonation, a fretboard (or any musical scale) that's laid out perfectly in one key will be imperfect in other keys—increasingly imperfect as keys become further removed from one another. Players of "variable pitch" instruments (wind instruments, fretless string instruments, and the voice) can compensate by varying air pressure or moving their fingers slightly. Players of "fixed pitch" instruments (like the piano, harp, harpsichord, organ, or any fretted instrument) cannot. Theoretically, their "temperament" (intonation system) can never be in tune in all keys. This was OK back in the days of minstrels and harpers and other primitive vaudevillians who were more interested in booze and wenches than in playing in different keys. It was even OK in the days of the great Renaissance choral composers, because their singers could easily compensate with their voices. Then again, that's *why* the great composers of the Renaissance were choral composers.

But for J. S. Bach, who was so impelled to celebrate the glory of God in music that he had to use every key to do it, a temperament that was unequal in every key was a drag. Some form of compromise was necessary. Plato and Pythagoras, inhabitants of the Ideal World, might never have compromised. But though Bach's imagination rose to the heavens, his feet were set solidly on the ground.

Bach used Werckmeister's compromise system, called "even temperament," in which the scale is equally out of tune in every key, but only a little. So little, in fact, that our spirits have been lifted, without hindrance, by Bach's music for the *Well-Tempered Keyboard* for over three hundred years.

There's a little test you can run to see how accurately each string intonates. Lightly touch the string directly over the twelfth fret without depressing it; then pluck it and, at the moment of plucking, release the fretting finger. This produces a clear, bell-like tone called a "harmonic." (It may take you a few tries to get the hang of it.) Then fret and pluck the note at the twelfth fret and see if the fretted note is exactly the same in pitch as the harmonic. Do this with all the strings one by one. Ideally the harmonic and fretted notes should be exactly the same.

You can also test twelfth-fret intonation with an electronic guitar tuner. Put the string exactly in tune, so that the meter on your tuner centers out perfectly on that note. Now play the twelfth-fret note. It too should be perfectly in tune.

In real life many respectable guitars are not quite perfect. Finding small degrees of imperfection by testing with a tuner shouldn't upset you. It could come from a slightly pulled-up neck or a faulty string or even the gradual drying out of an older guitar rather than from faulty compensation. It's something that should concern you only at the point that you begin to hear it in your playing. Many acoustic guitarists never play the kind of up-the-neck chords that sound a little out of tune if the compensation isn't quite perfect.

Nylon strings don't require compensation. Electric guitars do but many of them have massive saddles with adjusting mechanisms for each individual string. Such mechanisms are sound-deadening on acoustic guitars.

THREE-PIECE AND TWO-PIECE BACKS

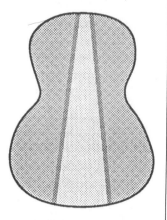

Three piece back joined with two marquetry strips. Ideally, the two outer sections should be bookmatched.

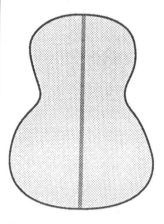

Two-piece back joined with marquetry center strip.

BACK AND SIDES

The traditional woods for back and sides have been rosewood, mahogany, and maple. Each has its own distinctive sound qualities: rosewood is brilliant, maple brightly astringent, and mahogany sweet. (See Chapter 4 for more information about the characteristics of these and other less commonly used woods.) For maximum projection the back and sides of the guitar need to reflect sound rather than absorb it. The wood must be stiff yet must also have resilience and tone-coloring qualities as well.

Raw material for backs and sides is supplied by wood merchants in pre-cut "sets" consisting of the back pieces and two sides. In the best-quality sets, the back halves and side pieces are each bookmatched. (Three-piece backs with two bookmatched wings and one large center section are becoming more common as the remaining tropical hardwood trees large enough to provide wood for two-piece backs become rarer.) Good-grade sets may be matched visually by the supplier but in fine guitar making the back and sides should be acoustically matched as well. (As with tops, the luthier does this by tapping the wood.) Ideally the back and sides should both come from the same tree but such sets are rarer and more expensive.

Nowadays most guitars have laminate backs and sides with veneers of mahogany, maple, rosewood, or some other hardwood. Because plywood can be readily steamed and pressed, a few makers offer instruments with slightly arched plywood backs designed to "focus" the sound as in the carved backs of archtop guitars.

Back Bracing and Side Reinforcement

Guitar backs are also braced with a combination of struts, some low and flat and others high and thin. Traditionally the purpose of back bracing has been purely structural: to help hold the body stiff so that it serves as a resonating chamber. Some contemporary luthiers have experimented with other bracing designs including X-bracing similar to that of the top. The purpose of such bracing is to turn the back into a sort of second soundboard reinforcing the top's sound-producing function.

On many good solid-wood instruments built along traditional lines, the sides are given added strength and rigidity by strips of cloth soaked in glue. Sides, being made of bent wood and particularly exposed to knocks, are vulnerable. Plywood sides, being less prone to cracking, are not usually treated this way.

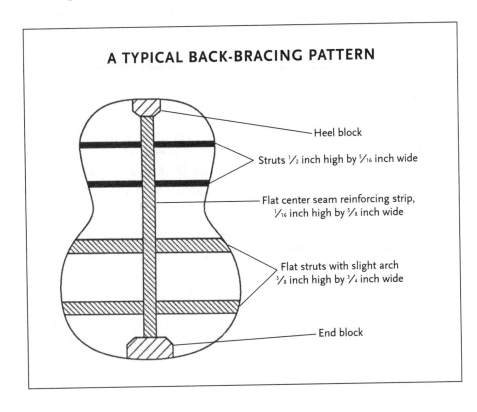

A TYPICAL BACK-BRACING PATTERN

- Heel block
- Struts 1/2 inch high by 5/16 inch wide
- Flat center seam reinforcing strip, 1/16 inch high by 5/8 inch wide
- Flat struts with slight arch 3/8 inch high by 3/4 inch wide
- End block

Unusual back bracing on a Fleishman guitar. Instead of using the standard cross-braces, this instrument uses a floating X-brace on the back. Notice how the center portions of the braces are raised from the back. This permits the back to vibrate more than usual and to form an acoustical link with the top but, in order for this technique to work best, you have to angle the guitar as you play rather than holding the back tightly against your body. *Photo by John Youngblut, courtesy Harry Fleishman*

Linings, Bindings, and Blocks

The back, sides, and top are less than ⅛ of an inch thick, so there is not a lot of surface area for the glue joint where they meet at their edges. Therefore, the insides of the joints are supported at the sides by additional ribbons of wood called "linings," which are notched (the woodworking term is "kerfed") in order to make them easier to bend to the shape of the sides. Cedar and other woods are used for linings.

On the outside of the guitar the joints are reinforced by thin strips of "binding" material, usually celluloid plastic, but sometimes an ornamental wood. Bindings may be simple or have decorative patterns. The structural value of bindings is small, however, and their decorative value is incidental. Their most important job is to seal the edges of the back and sides against moisture penetration because wood sucks up atmospheric humidity mostly through the edge grain. On cheap guitars the "bindings" may be painted on.

Additional reinforcement is given to the two sides where they join at the top and bottom by the heel block (or head block) and end block, respectively. The heel block also provides the location for the mortise of the dovetail joint that joins the neck to the body and may also provide support for a strap button. The other end of the strap is attached to the "end pin" mounted in the end block.

SIZE AND SHAPE

This section describes the major guitar sizes and shapes and explains their nomenclature. (See Chapter 7 for additional information on how size and shape affect you as a player.)

APPROXIMATE STANDARD GUITAR SIZES
Body length is for fourteen-fret models (except classical).
twelve-fret guitars usually have slightly longer bodies.

SIZE NOMENCLATURE	MARTIN SIZE PREFIX	BODY LENGTH (IN.)	UPPER BOUT WIDTH (IN.)	LOWER BOUT WIDTH (IN.)	MAX. DEPTH (IN.)
Concert	O ("oh")	18⅜	10	13½	4¼
Grand Concert	OO ("double-oh")	18⅞	10⅞	14⁵/₁₆	4⅛
Classical		19⅛	11	14½	4⅛+
Auditorium	OOO ("triple-oh")	19⅜	11¼	15	4⅛
Grand Auditorium	OOOO (formerly M)	20⅛	11¹¹/₁₆	16	4⅛
Jumbo*	J	20⅛ +	11¹¹/₁₆ +	16 +	4⅞
Dreadnought	D	20	11½	15⅝	4⅞

*Gibson also uses the term *jumbo* for its dreadnought-size guitars. In general speech, however, *jumbo* usually refers to instruments of the size in the table. Dimensions of jumbo-size guitars vary more greatly from maker to maker than do dimensions of other body sizes.

The preceding table gives an approximation of the standard guitar sizes along with the standard industry designations ("grand concert," "dreadnought," and so on.) Martin's size prefixes are also given. Because Martin was the dominant player in the formative years of the American guitar, its size designations have entered common usage. Thus, it's common to hear people in the music industry speak of a "double-oh" or "triple-oh" or D-size guitar even when the instrument is not a Martin—and even if that instrument's maker calls it by some other model designation.

Of course actual sizes and proportions may vary somewhat from maker to maker and there are various oddball sizes as well. Instruments in the jumbo range are especially subject to variation from maker to maker. Many concert or auditorium-size "electro-acoustic" models with built-in pickups are designed primarily for amplified use, so they're built with shallow bodies (about three inches deep) closer to the feel of a solidbody electric guitar.

COMPARATIVE GUITAR SIZES

Concert-size body (inside) and large jumbo

Dreadnought (inside) and large jumbo

Concert-size body (inside) and dreadnought

In addition to the standard models listed here, there are also a small number of ¾- and ⅞-size models made for kids, which are smaller overall including neck and fingerboard dimensions. Travel guitars are similarly miniaturized guitars.

The concert size was standard around the time of the Civil War, but over the years public taste has more and more shifted toward the louder, deeper sound that comes from larger-bodied guitars. All things being equal, larger guitars tend to be louder and more bass-heavy. However, because loudness also comes from the soundboard's ability to vibrate, some old, small guitars with extremely vibrant tops are amazingly loud—even loud enough to overwhelm good contemporary dreadnoughts. The ability to build such instruments is now almost lost; certainly the will to build them has been. It's easier to get loudness from size than from wood quality and painstaking care. In any case, contemporary taste is mostly for bassy instruments and the public perceives bigger as better in general. Makers are not going to make what no one wants to buy, and dealers are not going to stock them. As a result, small guitars, especially good ones, are harder to find.

Shape

You'll find some oddities of shape now and then, especially in the work of experimentally minded luthiers, but there are really only two basic guitar shapes in general use today: the dreadnought and the ordinary, non-dreadnought shape that has no particular name but usually looks suspiciously like a standard historical Martin. Each of these in turn has two main variations. Among dreadnoughts, most follow the square-shouldered Martin design, but a few follow the rounder-shouldered design of some (not all) of the Gibson jumbos. Among non-dread-nought guitars, most are fourteen-fret, square-shouldered models; the few twelve-fret models available have rounder shoulders.

The dreadnought shape, which quickly became popular after Martin introduced it as a standard production model in the early 1930s, is extremely broad-waisted. This maximizes its cubic volume and therefore tends to maximize bass frequencies and overall acoustic volume. (See Chapter 13, page 230, for more information about dreadnoughts.) Dreadnoughts are also large, deep guitars overall. There's no particular reason why the broad waist can't be used on smaller instruments as well and it's been done, but it's usually used only with large instruments.

Body depth is important in bringing out bass notes. Traditionally, dreadnoughts have been deeper and most smaller-bodied guitars shal-

---

BASIC GUITAR SHAPES

The twelve-fret, fourteen-fret, and dreadnought silhouettes are the three basic guitar shapes in common use. Each of these shapes may come in smaller or larger sizes.

TWELVE-FRET GRAND CONCERT GUITAR
Note the round shoulders. A classical guitar is almost the same size and shape, though a bit broader in the upper bout.

FOURTEEN-FRET AUDITORIUM GUITAR
Note the broader upper bout and flatter shoulders.

STANDARD DREADNOUGHT GUITAR
Note the narrower waist and more oblong proportions.

---

lower, with one classic exception being the Gibson Nick Lucas model originally introduced in the 1920s and now reintroduced by Gibson and copied by other makers. In recent years guitar makers have experimented with deepening smaller-than-dreadnought body sizes in other models as well. Lowden has made interesting grand auditorium guitars almost as deep as an acoustic bass. Martin offers its jumbo models in two body depths.

The basic body shape parameters are these:

- Smaller and shallower
- Larger and shallower
- Smaller and deeper
- Larger and deeper

Each combination of these variables affects the qualities of low and high notes, and the relationship between the high and low note, differently.

CUTAWAY GUITARS

Some guitars also have a *cutaway* upper bout in which a large area is simply removed in order to permit easy access to the upper frets. Pointy cutaways are called "Florentine" cutaways; rounded ones are called "Venetian." The difference is solely cosmetic. "Double cutaways," in which portions are removed from both sides of the bout, are often found on electric guitars but hardly ever on acoustics. Taking out some of the bout degrades tone and volume to a certain extent—generally to too great an extent with a double cutaway.

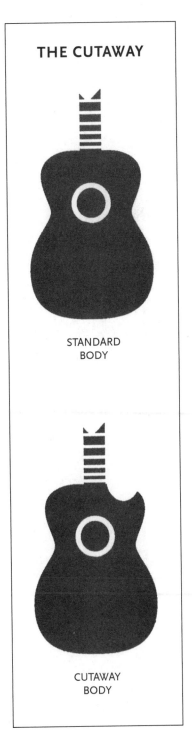

THE CUTAWAY

STANDARD BODY

CUTAWAY BODY

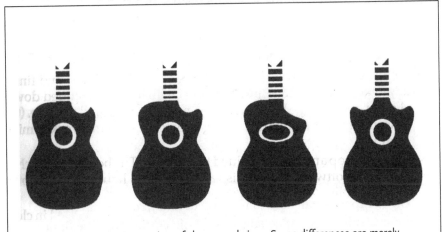

Cutaways come in a variety of shapes and sizes. Some differences are merely cosmetic; others permit varying degrees of access to the upper frets. Sometimes a cutaway causes the bracing struts to be moved down, requiring an elliptical sound hole to make room for the struts in their new location. The double cutaway is found fairly often on electric guitars but rarely on acoustics.

PUTTING THE GUITAR TOGETHER

Procedures vary from maker to maker, but these are the major steps a large high-quality manufacturer might take. Of course each manufacturer has its own version of this procedure and might not necessarily conduct its operations in exactly this order. All operations, major and minor, can add up to over two hundred steps. Note that pre-assembly milling operations (the cutting to shape of the various pieces of wood) are not included here. Currently, much of this work is being done by robotic cutting, carving, and shaping machines.

A high-end maker, of course, works more slowly and carefully on its quality models than a midrange mass marketer does, and with less automation. Some makers—Martin, Larrivée, and Taylor are good examples—make models that cover a fairly wide range of price and quality and, as one would expect, their less expensive models are produced . . . less expensively.

Partially completed high-quality instruments are set aside to stabilize between major operations; so, the steps below may take place over a period of about three months, depending on the manufacturer. Again, this depends on the quality range of individual models. Mid-priced, mass-produced instruments are made far more quickly, using more automated operations, and with simpler finishing stages. For example, there might be fewer lacquer coats, final shaping of necks and braces might be done less carefully or by machine, interior sanding might be less smooth, and so on.

Here are the steps:

1. Side and back pieces are selected and visually matched. Back halves are assembled and braced. The sides are soaked in water and bent to shape by hand over hot, cylindrical shaping irons and then checked against molding jigs. (In cheaper plywood guitars the wood is steam-pressed rather than worked by hand.)

2. The end block and heel block are glued into place to support the sides as they are joined together. Linings are glued into place. These components have been previously milled, perhaps robotically. One traditional method is to use ordinary wooden clothespins as clamps; mechanical clamps may also be used, as can clamping jigs for faster production.

3. Meanwhile, the rough halves of the top are assembled and finely contoured. The sound hole is cut out and the bracing glued down. Fine shaving of the braces is done once they are glued in place. (On cheaper guitars, bracing is precut and handwork is minimal.) Some of this work, especially sound hole cutting, may be done robotically.

4. Now the top and back are glued to the sides. The body, sandwiched between softwood boards, is left for several hours in a clamping jig resembling a press until the glue sets.

5. The binding is hand-glued around the edges and clamped.

6. In traditional construction the neck blanks (mahogany billets milled to approximate shape) are finely shaped by hand using carving tools, files, rasps, sandpaper, and an almost-obsolete woodworking tool called a draw knife. Now it is usually done by computer-controlled robotic machines, ensuring uniformity (good) and robbing instruments of their individual character (bad, but not so bad when you consider that not all necks were good).

7. In traditional manufacturing, a dovetail joint is cut into the body's heel block. The tenon at the end of the neck heel is individually shaped to fit the heel block mortise and the neck and joint are fitted together (but not glued). The set of the neck angle is then checked against a measuring jig.

    In traditional manufacturing this is all handwork, so an individual neck fits only the guitar for which it is made. Some manufacturers now robotically machine the two halves of the joint to uniform specs or use a different style of joint. Again, this is not necessarily a bad thing because neck joints may need to be disassembled for repair and modern neck-joining techniques may make neck repairs or replacements easier.

    The neck and body, though not yet married, will travel together throughout the rest of the assembly process.

8. The truss rod is mounted into a groove cut into the neck below where the fingerboard will be mounted. Then the fingerboard (with frets slots already cut) is glued on top and the frets are mounted and finished. The entire neck/fingerboard construction is given a final trim and inspected; then the frets are hammered into their slots.

9. Next, the neck and body are scraped and sanded smooth and, where applicable, wood filler is rubbed into the pores before the wood is stained—the first step in the finishing process. Then the still-separate neck and body are sprayed with seven to ten coats of lacquer finish. Each coat, when dry, is finely sanded so that the final thickness of the finish is .007 inches. When the finish is dry the bodies and necks are buffed with a wax compound. Fine finishing is an expensive process so finishing an instrument less finely is an effective way to keep costs down on lower-priced models.

10. The neck and bridge are glued into place and left for the glue to set. The self-adhesive pickguard is mounted. Then saddle and tuning hardware are mounted and the instrument is strung up and ready for final visual and playing inspection and adjustments before shipping.

⑦ Suiting Yourself

MAKING A GOOD MARRIAGE WITH YOUR GUITAR

Chapters 5 and 6 may be about how your guitar works, but it's really you who does the work. The guitar just sits there until you play it. When you do play, it will be with a flatpick, fingerpicks, bare fingers, or some combination thereof. You're going to use them to pluck the strings somewhere more or less over the sound hole, or maybe down closer to the bridge. You will have put on some strings that are relatively light or heavy. Your style of playing is going to be relatively loud or soft. It may involve strumming chords, picking out individual notes, or some combination of both. You may need to be heard in a kitchen, a living room, an auditorium, a barroom, or a subway station. You may be a soloist, a vocal accompanist, or part of a band. And exactly which notes you play and how you want them to sound will be a function of the style of music you play: bluegrass, blues, folk, pop, or whatever.

These are your choices, but your guitar also has a will of its own. Depending on its size, shape, wood, and bracing pattern, your guitar may be more or less well suited to express your own will. A mismatch will lead to a frustrating battle of wills—a battle that your guitar will win, since it's more intransigent than you are. This chapter offers some suggestions to help match your will to your guitar's.

The more you play different guitars, the more you'll discover that they have personalities all their own. Some have an all-around competence: they do what they're told, but they have no fire or spiritual brilliance that makes them unique. Great guitars have character. Like great historical and artistic figures, they may have flaws as well as brilliance. You learn to live with, and within, the instrument's weak and strong points. It makes life more interesting. Players who like instruments like this are usually the ones who keep two or three around. Players who prefer all-around competence can get what they need from just one instrument.

Celtic guitarist Eileen Niehouse.
Photo by Larry Sandberg

As a partisan of small guitars, I welcomed the return of small-bodied instruments like this Santa Cruz parlor model during the last decade of the twentieth century. It seems that more people are willing to discover the intimacy and clarity of smaller instruments all the time. *Photo courtesy Santa Cruz Guitar Company*

THE IDEAL GUITAR DOES NOT EXIST

A guitar is a bundle of compromises that would put even the U.S. Congress to shame. It generally sounds better the more lightly it's built; but, if you build it too lightly it will warp or pull apart. The body wood on a good instrument is only around $\frac{3}{32}$ of an inch thick, which is barely enough to hold it together. A guitar sounds better with lots of mass in the neck and headstock; but, if a maker actually puts extra mass there (and, yes, it's been done—with lead weights!), then it won't balance comfortably in your lap. Unlike a violin or an archtop guitar, where string pressure compresses the instrument together, the flattop guitar is built with explosive string tension that wants to tear it apart—and someday it will.

Even if the ideal guitar did exist it might not be ideal for you. The highest ideals of guitar making are qualities like balance, separation, and dynamic range. These are the qualities that a virtuoso soloist demands, yet they may not satisfy other needs. It's not so much that a fine solo guitar would be overkill for strumming rhythm in a country band; it would flat out be the wrong tool for the job. So you have to know who you are or at least who you want to be in order to find the guitar that's ideal for you.

In each of the following sections we'll take a look at the guitar from many perspectives, one style at a time. For example, you'll learn why a dreadnought shape might be exactly the shape you need for the style of music you want to play and why a dreadnought shape may be a poor choice in terms of your comfort in handling the instrument. Balancing out these pros and cons is entirely up to you.

The ideal guitar may not exist but neither does the ideal guitarist; it all balances out in the end.

GUITARS DIFFER DIFFERENTLY

Never forget that guitars of the same model are not always identical in sound and quality. Dreadnought sound differs from jumbo guitar sound in typical ways; the Martin sound differs from the Santa Cruz, Gibson, and Taylor sounds in typical ways; rosewood sound differs from maple sound in typical ways. But not all rosewood Martin dreadnoughts or maple Gibson J-200s, even of the same period, even with successive serial numbers, sound exactly the same either.

Everything boils down to the individual instrument. Fine guitars have more distinct personalities than inexpensive, mass-produced models; but these too have their differences. Even among fine models from fine manufacturers you have to watch out for the occasional dog. Dogs aren't that common, though, so for the most part you'll be listening for fine points of balance and tone quality between individual instruments—differences in the realms of taste and suitability. Among lower-end, mass-produced instruments there's greater sameness, but even so it pays to be on the lookout for differences here as well. At this level, don't look so much for fine points as for gross differences: Is this guitar dead or alive? Is it comfortable to fret the strings or not? Do the high strings sound full or tinny?

SUITING YOUR BODY

Size and Shape Make a Difference

Most people just assume that the popular dreadnought shape is the one to get, since bigger is supposed to be better. Many wind up being happy with their dreadnoughts but others find that the dreadnought shape is just too large for them to be comfortable with. You may find that a big guitar isn't comfortable if you're a small person overall or have short arms—although some small people seem to be able to make themselves comfortable with guitars anyway.

Even the larger jumbos, some of which may have even broader lower bouts than a dreadnought, may be more comfortable because the waist is deeper so that the instrument sits lower in the lap. Less broad and less deep jumbos may be more comfortable still.

Although the even smaller sizes are less popular these days and are harder to find, there's a lot to be said for them. Not only are they comfy for smaller people, but they're often just more downright congenial for just about every size of person. They're much friendlier to hold and often give you a much more satisfying sense of listening to yourself; the big guitars seem to project their sound more outward to the audience than to the ears of the player. There's much to be said for the friendliness of small guitars, especially if you're playing mostly for yourself.

Some people's body types just don't seem to work well with some guitar body types. Big busts or broad middles or short torsos or pudgy thighs can be an uncomfortable match for large, narrow-waisted guitars, though even here you can't generalize: for some, it's just not an issue. Arm length may be a deciding factor. Using a strap even while seated may help an instrument of any size lie comfortably against a large person.

CUTAWAYS

Do you need a cutaway? Probably not. Most acoustic guitarists find they can get all of the music they need and want out of the first fourteen frets. Twelve, in fact. Cutaways are special devices for specialized lead guitarists whose styles demand them. You should probably keep away from them unless you know you're going to need one, or unless the guitar you're in love with just happens to have a cutaway anyway.

A cutaway may take away more than it gives you. Building a cutaway is a big job that can easily bring an instrument into a new price bracket. Especially for beginners, the extra money may be better spent on a better-made, better-sounding, better-playing instrument instead.

The deep cutaway on this Santa Cruz FS model permits easier access to the upper frets. *Photo courtesy Santa Cruz Guitar Co.*

There's an additional irony in the way cutaways give you a poor return for your dollar on beginner-quality instruments. Inexpensive guitars are the ones most likely to suffer from weak-sounding high notes and stiff action on the highest frets. Therefore, when you buy an inexpensive guitar with a cutaway, all you're getting for the extra money you're shelling out is access to the least satisfying, least congenial area of the fingerboard. The sound of the highest frets also tends to be weak on large-bodied guitars, even some better-quality ones. If you really have high-note lead guitar in mind, you might be best off with an electro-acoustic instrument or an instrument—not necessarily an expensive model—that will sound good when you put a pickup in it. (See Chapter 9 for more information about amplifying your acoustic guitar.)

Left-Handed Guitars

If you're a lefty, you've got three choices, with the choice being entirely up to you. This is not really a decision that anyone can make for you, though you should certainly get as much advice as you can from your teacher if you have one and other left-handed guitarists.

1. You can play the guitar the way righties do. Among the left-handed people who play this way are Artie Traum, Dave van Ronk, Christine Lavin, and Nils Lofgren. I'm sure that there are even more closet lefties who play right-handed. A good many of them probably feel that they have a definite advantage over right-handed guitarists, since in most player's styles it's the fretting hand that works the hardest.

2. You can play a left-handed guitar. This is a guitar on which it's possible to reverse the order of the strings so that the low strings are still on top (toward the ceiling) when you hold it with the neck pointing right. You need a special lefty guitar to do this because guitars are braced more strongly on the bass side to compensate for the extra tension of the heavier bass strings. Left-handed guitars also have the pickguard mounted on the opposite side of the sound hole. When you purchase a left-handed guitar it's important to confirm that the instrument is actually braced in reverse, rather than just having the superficial pickguard change.

   This much said, it must be noted that it's also true that some people just take a righty guitar and string it upside down and get away with it, at least for a while. If you must do this, at least use the lightest strings you can.

3. You can play a regular guitar upside-down. That is to say, hold a regular guitar left-handed (with the neck pointed right), but don't re-string it. This means that not just the guitar but everything else too will be turned upside-down; so, as far as your picking-hand work goes, you're in a completely different universe from the overwhelming majority of guitarists. You will have to develop a set of accommo-

dations unique to your instrument. You'll find it more difficult to learn from and share with other guitarists and, while you may be able to develop some original stylings, you may also find it difficult or impossible to play some of the things that guitarists are normally expected to be able to play. Most of the people who play this way are self-taught musicians who grew up in primitive or isolated environments. Elizabeth Cotton, the wonderful guitarist who wrote the fingerpicking standard "Freight Train," was one.

Whatever course you choose, be prepared to stick with it. Once you learn to play one way you'll find it nearly impossible to switch.

Many of the major and some of the cheapie guitar companies make left-handed guitars, though they're not always easy to find. A search of the Web, or perhaps of the back pages of the guitar magazines, will lead you to shops that specialize in left-handed instruments.

Guitars for Kids

You're not going to help little kids learn to play by putting grown-up-size guitars into their hands. They need a ½-, ¾-, or ⅞-size guitar with a body not just small enough to hold comfortably but with a fingerboard width and scale suitable for small hands. There are a few such steel- and nylon-string instruments currently available, though few of good quality. As a result, most people wind up getting low-grade, offshore-produced instruments that, for most kids, work well enough.

For younger kids especially, nylon-string instruments have the added advantage of being easier on the fingers. They'll do for beginning music lessons and school events and it's likely that, by the time they're ready to grow into steel strings, they'll also be ready to grow into a larger guitar.

Most kid-size guitars are cheap—some very much so. Music stores like to buy the very cheap ones and rent them out, and this is usually the best way to go when your kid is starting out. However, you get what you pay for. If your kid turns out to have real talent, then you should certainly work with his or her teacher to find a good-quality instrument. Talent needs to be given every possible opportunity to flourish. Good-quality modern instruments are available at fair prices and some of the undersize vintage Martin and Gibson guitars are wonderful instruments and priced according to their size.

SUITING YOUR EYE

Ornamentation

Most forms of guitar ornamentation have functional origins. Bindings seal the edges of the top joints. Headstock inlays are used to proclaim the maker's identity. Fingerboard inlays provide visual clues to help the fingers navigate up and down the frets.

Though there are plenty of simple guitars—and beautiful ones at that—there are few absolutely plain ones without even a visually satisfying binding or rosette. I'd just as soon have a simple looking guitar that glowed with the inner light of its wood and nothing else. It's too bad the Shakers didn't make guitars. However, many makers reserve their best woods for the top-of-the-line instruments that wind up getting a lot of inlay work. As a result I've had to compromise on owning at least one ornate guitar just because it sounds so good. I'd rather it had less stuff all over it.

But ornamentation can be very pleasing to those who enjoy it and admire the skills of fine woodworking and inlay carving. In particular, the craft of cutting and engraving mother-of-pearl and abalone has its own set of aesthetic conventions going back hundreds of years. (If you really want to get into carving and inlay you might like fancy banjos, where the legacy of ornamentation is much richer, even more so than with guitars.)

Some luthiers also enjoy woodcarving as well as inlay work. Since carving the body is unwise from a structural and acoustic point of view, the neck heel and the headstock are basically the only areas where ornamental carving can be indulged in. The headstock shape, whether ornate or simple, is one area where many luthiers seek to establish a characteristic design—in fact, headstock design is legally recognized as a trademark. Ornate neck heels are, by tradition, more commonly associated with banjos than guitars, but from time to time—and almost always as the result of a custom request—a luthier will ornament the heel area with relief carving.

If you have all the money in the world, you can even commission custom carving and inlay work. Some luthiers love to do ornamental work on their instruments, others do aftermarket work, and most of the high-quality factories have custom shops offering various ornamentation options. If you're on a limited budget, though, it makes much more sense to make sound and playing features your first priority and forget about the fancy stuff.

Let's look at some more typical forms of ornamentation.

HEADSTOCK AND NECK INLAY

Both abalone and mother-of-pearl are used on fine guitars and plastic imitations thereof are used on cheaper ones. Folks generally call mother-of-pearl "MOP" or "pearl" for short, and sometimes the term is used loosely enough to include abalone shell as well. The term *pearl guitar* usually refers to an instrument richly decorated with abalone purfling and MOP inlays.

Pearl or pearloid plastic is typically used for position markers and decorative headstock inlay, which can be quite extravagant. (Conventional patterns include: leafy designs called "flowerpots"; griffins;

eagles; nubile, masthead-like feminine figures in various stages of undress; snakes; lizards; and whatever else turns you on.) Some makers treat the headstock inlay as a standard logo; others vary it from instrument to instrument.

The position markers are usually pearl, pearloid plastic, or some other light-colored material such as a white hardwood, for maximum contrast with the dark fingerboard. Simple circles are typical, though small diamond-shaped inlays of the sort used on many early Martins are also common. Sometimes the twelfth fret gets a double or especially large inlay, and some instruments use giant blocks of glowing abalone or other material instead of small markers.

Another convention, though not as common on guitars as on banjos, is the ornate leafy vine or "tree of life" inlay running up and down the entire fingerboard. And a final possibility is to have your own name inlaid across the fingerboard. It does wonders for getting your guitar back if it's stolen but (unless you're a certified celebrity) it may make your guitar pretty hard to sell. Still, it won't get you into as much trouble later on in life as having "Fifi" with a heart and arrow tattooed on your left arm will.

The most extravagant fingerboards and head plates (headstock overlays) ever made are those of the iridescent pearloid plastic known affectionately as "mother-of-toilet-seat" (sometimes abbreviated MOT in descriptive catalogs). In its heyday it was used even more extravagantly

In addition to its unusual, asymmetric sound holes and mixed spruce and redwood top, this ornate instrument from Harry Fleishman features an original floral variation on the traditional "tree of life" fingerboard inlay that is echoed in the floral inlay around the sound holes. *Photo by John Youngblut, courtesy Harry Fleishman.*

on banjos than on guitars, likely enough inset with fake glass rubies and emeralds. Gibson was the worst culprit (or best example, depending on your taste), particularly in the 1930s—people probably needed something to cheer them up during the Depression. This stuff really shines under the spotlights, folks, and if I'm not mistaken, the Gibson factory's custom shop will still do it for you it you want it done. And it goes just great with fezzes, plumes, and shiny cloaks and tunics.

BINDING, PURFLING, AND ROSETTES

Various plastics and hardwoods may be used for the bindings, including the grainy-looking, off-white nitrocellulose or cellulose acetate known as ivoroid. Many makers use plastic binding in a solid color on their least expensive models, and with increasingly complicated alternating light and dark stripes on their more expensive models, as status symbols.

The extra strips of inlay inside the edges of the binding are called "purfling." The most famous purfling designs are the inlaid abalone strips on 40-series Martin guitars and the legendary "herringbone" purfling pattern used by Martin on its better guitars from the nineteenth century up until 1944. The prestige of "herringbone Martins" has less to do with the herringbone itself and much more to do with the location and scalloping of the bracing design that was also discontinued in 1944; however, since it's a lot easier to put on herringbone purfling than it is to do labor-intensive handwork on braces, you'll see herringbone purfling on all sorts of guitars at all sorts of quality levels these days. (Even Martin has responded to the public's lust for herringbone by imitating itself: the herringbone purfling and the scalloped bracing as well are now once more available on some models.)

Headstocks of D. W. Stevens archtop guitars. The highly ornate headstock depends on an intricate shape as well as a traditional "flowerpot" inlay to achieve an almost tropical proliferation of lushness. On the simpler headstock shape, the simple ivoroid binding and the inlay of the maker's name, though not readily perceived as ornamentation, nonetheless create an aesthetic value of their own. *Photos by D. W. Stevens and Larry Sandberg*

Wood binding and a delicate pattern of purfling and inlay on a D. W. Stevens guitar. *Photo by D. W. Stevens*

Abalone purfling around the top, fingerboard, and sound hole complement the mother-of-pearl, snowflake fingerboard inlays on this late 1920s Martin 00-42. *Photo by Larry Sandberg*

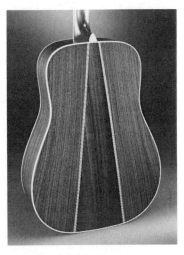

Marquetry strips separate the sections of this three-piece back on a Martin D-35. *Photo courtesy C. F. Martin & Co.*

Sometimes, particularly around the sound hole and down the center of the back, you'll see ornate marquetry strips of multicolored dyed wood. These are actually thin sections cut from larger blocks of glued-together wood strips. The sound hole inlay, whether of marquetry or any other material, is called the rosette.

Finish

If you're a professional, or even a wannabe, you have to think of suiting your audience's eyes as well as your own. The fashion these days among most stage musicians, especially those who front a band, is not so much inlay as colored finishes. For a while white was big, then black was in, and now, for the new millennium, black remains strong but blues and greens are also popular; as are translucent colored finishes that show the wood grain through the color.

If you decide you want a cheaper instrument with a colored finish, remember that you'll probably be sacrificing sound to get it. Some colored finishes are heavy enough to be acoustically detrimental; in addition, you may reasonably expect most makers to reserve their worst-looking wood, which also has some likelihood of being their worst-sounding wood, for opaque finishing. However colored finish can be applied quite as finely as any other and is done so on better-quality guitars.

If you're a strumming singer standing in front of a band, then looks may be as important as sound and a colored guitar may be just the one for you—especially if it matches your outfit or your hat.

The famous, pre-war, Martin herringbone purfling pattern, here recreated on a contemporary 000-28 Eric Clapton model. *Photo courtesy C. F. Martin & Co.*

SUITING YOUR STYLE

The sound qualities that make one sort of guitar more suitable for one style than another become more pronounced as the qualities of the wood and craftsmanship improve. The most inexpensive instruments are less distinctive so the following generalizations are less applicable in lower price brackets. And remember—they *are* generalizations.

General Playing and Casual Styles

For all-around playing, self-accompanying country music, and other contemporary styles, most players do well with an auditorium- or jumbo-sized guitar or with a well-balanced dreadnought. The jumbos are particularly good for strumming chords; dreadnoughts are good for strumming chords with articulated bass notes and bass runs; auditorium or smaller sizes are good for fingerpicking. Smaller jumbos and grand auditorium guitars make reasonably good compromises for people who both flatpick and fingerpick. However it's also possible to find individual dreadnoughts that are well-balanced enough for fingerpicking, even though this isn't what dreadnoughts are really all about.

Most casual players who are going to play a variety of songs and styles around the house wind up walking out of the music store with a dreadnought. But if versatility is your goal, consider the advantages of smaller guitars for comfort, a more balanced sound, and overall congeniality. Guitars in the auditorium-size range are fairly easy to come by in a number of styles and price brackets. Even smaller guitars—those in the concert-size and grand concert-size range—are harder to find hanging there for you to try out in stores, though they certainly are being made, and in a reasonable span of price ranges. Since the smaller models are less popular and therefore harder to move, you can sometimes find slightly more advantageous deals on used ones if you're lucky. In any case your best bet for versatility is a well-balanced instrument rather than a boomy, bass-heavy one.

Bluegrass and Old-Time Music

For punchy bluegrass playing, fiddle tunes, and old-time stringband music, a strong-sounding dreadnought is what most players prefer. You'll have to make your own decision whether you prefer a more balanced instrument or one that really booms in the bass, depending on how you play; in any case, cutting power is what you're looking for.

For an authentic period sound in old-time stringband music, you'll want a smaller, less cutting guitar. An important thing to consider is whether there's a mandolin in the band. If so, a guitar with too thick of a sound in the high strings—exactly the kind of sound you generally do want if you're a solo guitarist—is going to create too much clutter. This is because in rhythm strumming you'll be hitting those notes

The preferred guitar for bluegrass is the dreadnought shape, in this case a Gallagher model, with its rumbling bass and cutting treble. *Photo courtesy J. W. Gallagher & Co.*

Old-timers playing old-time music on old instruments at the Chester Country (Pennsylvania) Old Fiddlers Picnic. *Photo by Larry Sandberg*

exactly when the mandolin goes "thwock" and competing to fill the same space in the ensemble.

Blues

You can play blues on anything, even a dreadnought, but the most authentic sounds come from instruments with strong, thick-sounding trebles. This usually means a smaller-bodied guitar made perhaps of mahogany rather than rosewood. Many accomplished country blues stylists who go for a period sound eschew the sound of Martins and Martin-derived guitars from contemporary makers and prefer Gibsons and minor-brand guitars of the 1930s and 1940s. If you fingerpick more than flatpick, consider a fingerboard somewhat wider than the standard 1¹¹⁄₁₆ inches for flatpicking.

Contemporary Fingerpicking

Many exponents of complex picking styles such as ragtime, new-age, new acoustic, and contemporary Celtic music prefer a clean, brilliant, well-separated sound most likely to come from a guitar of about auditorium size or smaller, with a somewhat wide fingerboard to help separate the strings so the picking hand has room to do its best.

A small-bodied mahogany guitar with a large sound hole, like this Gibson L-1, offers the kind of thumpy low notes and syrupy highs that many blues players like. Note the magnetic pickup, in this case a Sunrise model, mounted in the sound hole. *Photo by Larry Sandberg*

Acoustic Jazz

For acoustic jazz and post-bluegrass new acoustic music, most players prefer extremely well-balanced dreadnought or jumbo guitars, perhaps with a cutaway for playing single-string solos high up the neck.

SUITING YOUR SUITCASE: TRAVEL GUITARS

Several companies make small-bodied guitars for travel although, with increasingly stringent carry-on restrictions, even these may wind up in the plane's cargo compartment. Even so, they're also easier to carry around and easier to play in a car. (Not while you're driving, please! Cell phones are bad enough.)

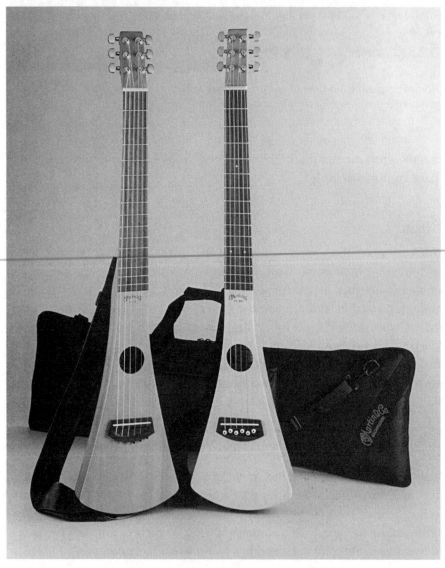

Steel- and nylon-string versions of the Martin Backpacker guitar. *Photo courtesy C. F. Martin & Co.*

Some are simply small guitars, essentially like kids' guitars. Others are unique. At this writing, Taylors generally have the most satisfying sound but a slightly shorter neck and are intended to be pitched slightly higher. The Martin Backpacker models have a full-size fingerboard but tiny bodies; you either like their small sound or you don't. Or you can use a pickup—but that means having an amp. The Tacoma Papoose model is the most distinctive: very small but pitched high and with a sound quality all its own. It's sometimes used as a "piccolo guitar" on recording sessions. Other brands, in a spectrum of price and quality ranges, also exist. By definition, don't expect a booming low register from any of them. Also consider whether your travel plans are such that you require a hard case and, if so, which brands have hard cases available.

Alternatively, you might consider traveling by air with a cheap, expendable guitar or with a decent instrument in a molded fiberglass case or trunklike, metal-clad flight case. You might even think of leaving your guitar at home on vacation. Segovia (along with several other famous musicians) is famous for saying, "When I don't practice for a day I know it; when I don't practice for two days, my instrument knows it; and when I don't practice for three days, my audience knows it." Fine. But most of us don't play at that level to begin with and don't have audiences. I've often left my instrument at home for two-week travel vacations. Segovia's right: it's no good for your fingers at all. But mentally, it's refreshing to get away for two weeks and to come back with new ideas and renewed spirit.

SUITING YOUR POCKETBOOK

Here are a few suggestions about what to look for in each price range. Remember that street prices are often considerably lower than list prices.

The following advice is what I say to my own students based on those instruments I've used or sampled over the years. Some of my students ignore my advice and wind up with instruments that satisfy them, and sometimes me, anyway. There are many exceptions to these generalizations. Listen to me and then follow your heart.

Follow inflation too. These price categories, loose and approximate at best, will undoubtedly need to be readjusted the further we move into the new century.

Under $300

With time, patience, and the right local resources, you might get a decent used guitar at this price. Most of the new instruments available in this price range are not very good so if this is all you have to spend, by all means get a used one if you can. Sometimes you'll find a music store that makes a point of stocking adequate used guitars for people to buy as their first instrument.

At this price, go for playability first and settle for the best sound you can find among the playable instruments. Since larger (dreadnought and jumbo) guitars are currently in fashion, it's sometimes possible to pick up a decent smaller Japanese or Taiwanese guitar from the 1960s or 1970s at a reasonable price. Unfortunately, in this price range there's a tendency to find adequate-sounding guitars that have pulled a little too far out of whack to be easy to play anymore. And trying to learn on a hard-to-play instrument is even more off-putting than trying to learn on one with unsatisfying sound.

Most instruments in this price range can't be expected to hold up very well over the long run and won't give you much satisfaction once you get beyond the basics of playing, so figure that you'll want to move on to a better guitar after a year or so and start planning ahead now. If you possibly can, budget money for a better guitar from the outset or rent your starter guitar instead of buying a cheapie. Some stores allow you to put all or some of your rental fees toward purchasing a guitar when the time for deeper commitment comes along.

There's no getting away from the fact that it takes a certain amount of finesse to get an acoustic guitar to sound good, and finesse translates into dollars. For around two hundred bucks you can go out and buy an electric guitar that will allow you to get off to an unimpeded start. (Of course, you're going to have to spend another seventy-five or so bucks on a practice amp.) This isn't usually the case with acoustics. For under $200, you'll be lucky if you wind up with an acoustic guitar that sounds the least bit satisfying and that doesn't fight your efforts to play it. With patience and the assistance of a teacher or experienced player, you could luck out. Take all the help you can get. Playability is iffy in this range and an experienced guitarist can help you hear. Sometimes the playability issues can be resolved with five or ten minutes of easy adjustment work. Perhaps the music store will be cooperative on this issue; perhaps not. And perhaps reasonably so, if the job is going to eat up more of the profit on a cheap instrument than a store can afford.

You might also consider starting off with a nylon-strung guitar. It's easier to find cheap playable and listenable nylon-strung than steel-strung guitars. The problem is that you just don't know whether you'll be one of the people who loves or hates the wider fingerboard conventional on nylon-strung guitars.

At this price point you're going to wind up with a laminate-top guitar that's manufactured offshore. As a starting point, look in the $250 price range at instruments from Epiphone, Fender, Ibanez, Sigma, Washburn, and Yamaha. Having learned from these models in this price range, start comparison shopping with cheaper brands and models. Some music stores sell cheap new guitars for as low as $99. They're not very good, and they only make sense if you want a temporary instrument to test how serious you are about learning. But then you get caught in that same old double bind: the less satisfying the instrument, the less likely you are to succeed.

$300 to $450

There's a pretty big difference between instruments at the bottom and top of this range. While playability is iffy on cheaper guitars, you can expect reasonable playability in this range and can begin to find solid wood tops. Start your search in this price range by looking at brand names like Epiphone, Fender, Ibanez, Larrivée, Sigma, Washburn, and Yamaha; then go on to see what other instruments in the local market seem comparable.

$450 to $750

At this point you're still in the realm of laminate bodies but should expect solid tops and respectable playability. You can also expect to get an instrument that will satisfy you for a while, perhaps one good enough to hang onto as a knockaround guitar even after you get good enough to buy a much better instrument and be spoiled by it.

The starting-point brand names in this range include Epiphone, Gretsch, Ibanez, Seagull, Tacoma, Washburn, and Yamaha. Several brand names associated with high-end guitars also belong here. Through most of the 1990s, this price range belonged exclusively to off-shore guitars. Now companies like Guild, Larrivée, and Martin, aided no doubt by CNC technologies and other manufacturing methods developed offshore, have found a way to get into the market at this price point.

Once you look at these brands, remember to take a look at what else is around before you make your purchasing decision.

In this price bracket you can also start to find respectable acoustic-electric guitars from offshore manufacturers.

$750 to $1,000

This is an odd price bracket. Many, though not all, of the instruments in this bracket are not really a whole notch better in quality than those in the next lowest bracket. This is the bracket that begins to see the transition from top-of-the-line laminate-body instruments (including especially electro-acoustics) to low-on-the-line all-solid-wood instruments.

To find the best instrument for you, take as your starting point brands such as Guild, Larrivée, Martin, Simon & Patrick, Tacoma, Takamine, Taylor, and Washburn.

In this price range you can also begin to do well with used solid wood guitars of better quality than new laminate guitars.

$1,000 to $2,000

There are still some top-of-the-line laminate guitars in this price range, especially those from companies like Takamine and Washburn, with good electronics built in. But if you can afford to go shopping in this bracket, you're generally better off with a solid wood guitar.

In this range you'll find many good-sounding instruments to choose from. At the lower end, instruments from Tacoma represent good value for the money. Guild also makes good instruments at the lower end of this range. Several of the major high-end players, including Larrivée, Lowden, Martin, and Taylor, are represented here, though not by their top-of-the-line instruments.

You can get a good guitar in this range, especially as you approach the top, and with patience and good ears you may be able to find one that sounds better than one that goes for more. But remember that this kind of money can get you a terrific used guitar as well.

Over $2,000

You should be able to get a first-rate guitar in this range. Breedlove, Collings, Goodall, Larrivée, Lowden, Martin, Santa Cruz, and Taylor are the major large- and small-factory players in this market. There are also a number of limited-production shops, like Franklin and Schoenberg, active at this level. A good number of models—especially those with exceptionally fine woods and labor-intensive ornamentation and handiwork—run into the range well above $4,000. While there's no reason to stint if you can afford to please yourself, you don't have to pay that much to get a really good guitar.

Instruments from custom luthiers and limited-production shops generally start as low as $2,500 and can go up into five figures depending on the amount of handwork and the prestige of the luthier. In some cases prestige may not correlate on an even curve with the quality of the individual instrument or even overall quality, nor does quality of handiwork always correlate with quality of sound. But this is true of factory instruments as well.

You can also get wonderful used guitars, including fine vintage instruments, for this kind of money. Remember, though, that in the vintage market you're paying for perceived rarity and other qualities unrelated to the soundness and sound quality of the instrument, so you have to know your stuff. There are a lot of new guitars around that are better than many vintage instruments.

8 Strings

STRING BASICS

Your guitar has six strings, numbered 1 to 6 starting with the one closest to the floor as you hold the guitar. In other words, the string that is thinnest and highest in pitch is the first string. If in doubt, check the labels on your package of new strings. And if you don't have a set of new strings around, get one today. It's not wise to be without extra strings.

The convention in numbering strings is to start with the highest, but the convention in reeling off the note names of the strings is to start with the lowest. (I don't know why this is the case. If you think it's done deliberately to confuse you, maybe you're right. I can't think of any other reason.) In standard tuning, the guitar strings are tuned E-A-D-G-B-E from low to high, strings 6 to 1. Therefore you can call the second lowest string either the A string or the fifth string, as you please. The sixth and first strings are distinguished as *low* E and *high* E.

One end of the string has a loop wound around a little metal widget called a "ball," even though it isn't. It's more like a barrel, if anything, and sometimes people actually call it a barrel instead.

The function of the ball is to hold the string in place underneath the bridge. Therefore, guitar strings are reasonably enough called "ball-end" strings—reasonable, that is, if you accept that the thing that's not a ball is a ball. Fortunately, our political leaders have us well-enough trained to accept these things without question. There are also strings called "loop-end" that are for banjos and mandolins. Loop-end strings, strangely enough, actually have loops on the end.

Strings come in different materials and in different gauges (diameters). The kind of strings most people have on their acoustic guitars, want to have on their guitars, and that you'll most likely find on your own first guitar when you bring it home, have first and second strings of plain stainless steel wires, and third to sixth strings with a core of steel wire overwound with fine bronze or brass wire. Therefore they're called the "wound" strings. (The technical name for them is "roundwound.") The lower strings are wound because they need to have more mass in order to vibrate slowly enough to produce their lower pitches. If you made strings with that much mass out of a solid piece of wire, they would have to be so thick that they would loose their elasticity and be unable to vibrate properly. Winding becomes necessary on steel guitar strings once the string diameter gets larger than about .021 inches.

FROM CATGUT TO STAINLESS STEEL

People loosely use the term *catgut* to refer to musical instrument strings, but Morris and Garfield have nothing to worry about. Instrument strings in the old days were typically made of sheepgut, as are some violin strings in the present day. No one is even sure where the term *catgut* came from. Historians suggest derivations from words like *kit* (an ancient form of mini-violin) and *catlin* (a term in ship-rigging, the technology of which influenced early string makers). Others speculate that Catigny, the French town that was an early center of the string industry guilds, had something to do with it.

Gut strings were originally made by the same craft guilds that made strings for tennis and badminton racquets. Perhaps this explains why the words "Stop that racquet!" are so often applied to beginning players of string instruments.

Technology for making wire strings has existed since the late Middle Ages, when it was discovered that one can reduce the diameter of super-heated, high-carbon iron rods by drawing them through a series of thinner and thinner holes in a die.

Metal wire was used in early days on the harpsichord and some lute- and mandolin-family instruments like the *chitarra battente* and cittern, but gut was used for the more lightly built guitar. During the nineteenth century, however, gut-string technology improved and manufacturers were able to produce more powerful strings with greater tension than before. It seems possible that the development of the X-brace by the C. F. Martin Company during this period was a response to this emerging string technology. (See Chapter 13, page 226, for more information on this topic.) In the end the gut-string manufacturers undid themselves, for as guitars grew larger and stronger, partially in response to the availability of the more powerful gut strings, it became possible to use metal strings as well.

Guitarists may have begun to use steel strings as early as the 1880s. Some early modern guitars, like those Orville Gibson made around the turn of the century, seem to have been just heavy enough for this purpose. The Martin company didn't start uniformly bracing its guitars for steel strings until the late 1920s, although their guitars had tended to become more robust over the preceding few decades. Classical guitarists continued to use gut strings until the late 1940s, when Albert Augustine introduced nylon strings made with the new technologies developed by DuPont during World War II. Steel strings just don't give classical guitarists what they need in the way of tone and handling and they sound too thin, jangly, and tinny.

Today's steel strings are still made by drawing metal through a series of ever-decreasing holes in dies. Wire for the unwound first and second strings is drawn through circular dies, but wire that will be used as a core for the wound strings is now generally drawn through a final hexagonal die, the better to create a gripping surface for the winding. (Such strings are called "hex-wound" or "hex-core.") Then the core is placed in a lathelike machine that rotates it while a wrapping of even finer wire is wound tightly around it.

PICKING YOUR STRINGS

Now that you know enough about strings to get confused, you're entitled (by the standards of contemporary society) to call yourself an expert. But before you start giving advice to others you'd better figure out what kind of strings you want for yourself.

The only way to decide what sort of string you want to use is by experimenting. The information in the rest of this chapter should help you make some informed decisions about the range of your experiments. In short, your decision will be based on the following factors:

String gauge: This is the diameter of the string, and it is the main factor in determining how hard you have to press down.

Kind or material: What the string is made out of and its design play an important part in how it sounds and, to a lesser extent, in how it feels under your fingers.

Your guitar: Personal taste aside, some instruments just work better with some kinds or gauges of strings than others.

Brand: This is the least important factor, since most manufacturers sell similar products, and most brands come from marketing companies who sell differently labeled but otherwise identical products from the same few factories.

If you absolutely need to have someone give you a starting point, here it is. Unless your guitar is delicate enough to require extra-light or compound strings, start off with light gauge (.012 to .053) 80/20 bronze, and then cycle through other kinds for a couple of years until you settle on what you like. If you're new at the guitar, it will be a while before you can hear or play well enough to tell the difference, anyway. You'll also discover that a fresh set of strings—no matter which kind or brand—almost always sounds better than the ancient, grungy set you just took off, so you'll have to teach your ear to compensate for that as well.

Assume it could take a couple of years before your ear learns to sort out what you like best. And once you have decided, don't be afraid to change your mind every so often. You're allowed to. It's called artistic growth.

WHAT ARE STRINGS MADE OF?

The strings that we loosely call "steel strings" fall into two main groups: bronze-wound strings for acoustic guitars and nickel-wound strings for electric guitars. There are also compromise kinds called "compound" strings that feel halfway between nylon and steel, and "copper-coated steel" that are halfway between bronze and nickel. Other kinds of strings, like the nylon strings used on classical guitars, aren't suited for vernacular music as a rule. One brand of strings comes coated with PolyWeb, a Gore-Tex–like material.

Bronze-Wound Strings

The strings most people use on acoustic flattop guitars are generally called "bronze" in the music industry, even though many are actually brass. (Bronze is an alloy of copper and tin, while brass is an alloy of copper and zinc.)

Some brands label their strings according to the composition of the alloy. 80/20 strings are ±80 percent copper and ±20 percent zinc. The brighter-sounding 60/40 strings are ±60 percent copper and ±40 percent zinc. "Phosphor bronze" strings are true bronze (±90 percent copper and ±10 percent tin) with an added fraction of phosphorous that seems to lengthen the life of the string. They're usually a little more expensive but their slightly longer life makes them cost-effective.

How you hear strings is a matter of taste, so to speak, but there's a pretty good consensus that phosphor bronze strings sound softest and warmest, 80/20s are somewhere in the middle, and 60/40s are the brightest and coldest. (Most brands with the word *bright* in them are 60/40s.) In the case of brands that don't tell you the alloy, you'll just have to use your ears to tell you whether you like them or not, without being prejudiced by metallurgical data.

Coated Strings

Elixir brand strings, a division of the W. L. Gore company that brings us Gore-Tex, sells bronze strings coated with its PolyWeb material. If you like very bright strings, keep away, but if you like a warm, somewhat dull sound, you might like them even more than phosphors. Though they start off on the dull and warm side, they pretty much stay at exactly the same level until they finally die. The coating reduces (but does not eliminate) squeaks and inhibits the kind of string corrosion that especially plagues people with very acidic perspiration. They're easier to wipe clean and they last a lot longer, possibly even long enough to make their steep price cost-effective. If you think you might like them, you should certainly try them.

Copper-coated steel strings are a completely different kind of beast, now rendered largely unnecessary due to technological changes. These were designed for acoustic guitars with old-fashioned magnetic pickups that were optimized for the kind of nickel-wound steel strings used on electric guitars. These pickups are not efficient at picking up bronze-wound acoustic strings because of the strings' low magnetic content. The copper (around 30 percent of the string mass) lends warmth and authority to the acoustic tone, while the remaining 70 percent steel is enough to activate magnetic pickups. But they're compromise strings. On an acoustic instrument their sound doesn't suit most people as well as the sound of bronze strings, while on an electric instrument their sound is not as pleasing as the sound of nickel-wound strings. Nowadays these strings are largely unnecessary because contemporary magnetic pickups of the sort made especially for acoustic guitars are optimized to pick up acoustic bronze-wound strings effectively.

Nickel-Wound Strings

These strings are for electric guitars. They're pretty much the same as acoustic guitar strings except that the windings are made of a nickel-iron alloy or nickel-plated steel. This is because the magnetic pickups used on true electric guitars are designed to pick up the vibrations of the magnetic field of the string; you therefore have to use strings with magnetic properties. If you have a magnetic pickup on your acoustic guitar, you'll have to use nickel- or copper-plated strings to get the pickup to work properly. (See Chapter 9 for more information on pickups.) Most guitarists feel that nickel strings are not as resonant as bronze when used on an unamplified acoustic guitar, though every so often you'll run across someone who prefers them on an acoustic guitar anyway.

Nickel-wound strings last somewhat longer than bronze before they fray or go really dead, which will save you some money over a period of years. But because they're made of harder metal they'll also wear your frets down faster, which over a period of years will cost you some money.

Compound ("Silk and Steel") Strings

In a compound string set, the first and second strings are regular steel, a little lighter than those in a regular light-gauge set. The difference comes in the lower strings, which are wound over a much thinner metal core than usual. Additional microfilaments of nylon (or, in days past, silk) floss are added to the core to give the string enough mass to function and a lower string tension. The result is a moderate-tension, easy-to-play string, usually with a sweet, warm tone and soft volume. The bass strings usually have a little less separation than those in a bronze set, though this also depends on the guitar. Don't expect to actually find any silk in a set of strings labeled "silk and steel."

Compound strings are sometimes good for a beginner's first set because they're gentler on fingertips that haven't grown calluses yet. They can sound excellent on twelve-strings, where they produce a pleasingly airy sound in addition to having the advantage, especially crucial on twelve-strings, of lower string tension on the bridge. They are the string of choice for delicately built guitars, early Martins, and similar instruments, but they still exert far too much force to use safely on classical guitars. A set of compound strings running in gauge from .011 to .049 generally exerts about as much tension as a set of "extra-light" regular strings running from about .010 to .047; they feel about as soft to fret, feel slightly more robust under the picking hand, and sound warmer and duller.

Gauges of compound strings may vary significantly from brand to brand, just as they do with regular strings. Most brands of compound strings actually exert a tad more string tension than extra-light round-wounds. But even so, many players prefer the touch and sound of compound strings to extra-lights on small or fragile guitars. It depends entirely on the guitar and on personal taste. Using a set of extra-lights, but replacing the first and second strings (usually .011 and .014) with .012 and .016, is also an alternative worth trying as long as the guitar can stand it.

Flatwound and Groundwound Strings

WINDING AND SQUEAKING
Beside the PolyWeb coating described above, there are several ways of treating the windings of both bronze- and nickel-wound strings to make them feel smoother and cut down on string squeaking. However the best way to cut down on squeaking is to learn to run your fingers more lightly along the strings. The most useful way to navigate on the fingerboard is to maintain some contact with a string to guide your fingers, so for most players a certain amount of squeaking is inevitable.

Music stores also carry a spray-on lubricant called Finger-Ease that some guitarists like.

FLATWOUND STRINGS
Flatwound strings are wound with flat wire ribbon. They have an extremely well-centered but very dull sound that's not very popular among acoustic guitarists, though the few who do like them really like them. The flatwound concept works somewhat better with electric guitar strings, especially on instruments not made to be played acoustically, and very well on the electric bass and members of the violin family, so they're more popular on those instruments.

By nature, flatwound strings are a bit less flexible than regular strings. Few brands market guitar flatwounds and many retailers don't even bother to carry them.

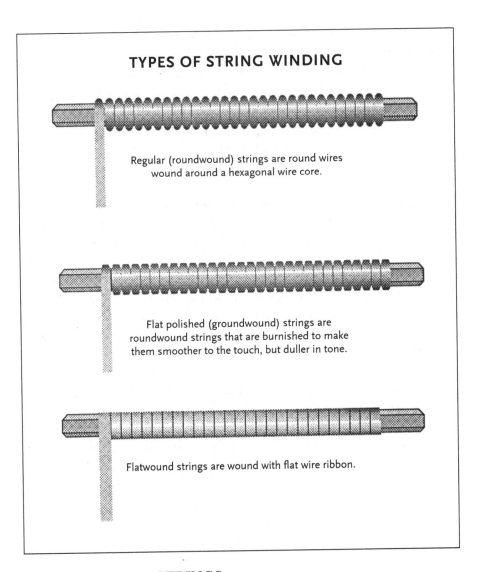

TYPES OF STRING WINDING

Regular (roundwound) strings are round wires wound around a hexagonal wire core.

Flat polished (groundwound) strings are roundwound strings that are burnished to make them smoother to the touch, but duller in tone.

Flatwound strings are wound with flat wire ribbon.

GROUNDWOUND STRINGS

There's also a compromise string variously called "groundwound," "half round," "polished," or "flat polished," where the outside of a regular round winding is polished down to created a smoother, flatter surface. Like flatwounds, they're more popular among bass players than among guitarists. Most guitarists find them a sonic no-man's-land that offer none of the clear advantages of regular or flatwound strings and all the disadvantages.

Remember that regularly wound guitar strings are called "round-wound" to distinguish them from all these other types. But in normal talk, when you just say "strings," everyone assumes that you mean roundwounds. Do not confuse roundwounds with groundwounds, ground round, or tofu.

Nylon Strings

In a nylon-string set the first through third strings are nylon monofila-ment (like fishing line), while the lowest three are a multifilament nylon floss core wound with copper, silver-plated copper, bronze, or another metal. Nylon strings are intended for classical guitars, which are built much more lightly than folk guitars. Nylons don't put out enough energy to drive the top of a folk guitar effectively and almost always sound so weak on a guitar intended for steel strings that it's not worth putting them on, even as an experiment. However, many nineteenth-century Martins and similar guitars were originally built for gut strings and are too delicate to accept even compound strings, so you must put nylons on them.

Classical-guitar bridges don't have pins. Instead of seating the end of the string under the bridge plate, you run a nylon string through a hole in the bridge parallel to the soundboard and then wrap it around itself and turn it under itself on the edge of the bridge. Once the string is tightened, tension holds the wrap securely in place. A few string makers offer ball-end nylon strings for those who are too wimpy to learn to wrap the string properly. Using them is considered uncool by the cool people who know how to wrap their strings. They also don't last long, since they tend to break off at the ball. Because of differences in pliability and friction, most players prefer to wrap the unwound strings around themselves two or three times, but the wound strings need only one wrap.

Like steel strings, nylons are available (though in a more limited variety) in different gauges and winding materials. An oddity in the nylon-string world is the wound third string. (The French company Savarez even makes a wound second string.) Wound third strings are good for giving some vitality to cheaper classical guitars, which tend to have weak-sounding third strings. (A robust-sounding third string is what separates the men from the boys as far as classical guitars go.) They also work well on old nineteenth-century guitars that have to be strung with nylon, because they make the guitar play a little more like a steel-string instrument.

People still refer to nylon strings colloquially as "gut," even though almost half a century has passed since nylon drove gut off the market. When I was a kid, I once found a set of real gut guitar strings and tried them out. Don't bother.

STRING GAUGE AND TENSION

Gauging String Gauge

Although some players approach string gauge with an attitude bordering on mysticism, there's really no mystery about it. It's cut and dry and strictly quantitative: gauge is the diameter of the string as measured in thousandths of an inch. The "heavier" the gauge, the thicker the string is and the more tension it exerts. You also have to work harder to depress a heavier-gauge string against the fret. As a rule, heavier-gauge strings generate more energy and therefore drive the top more strongly. In other words, they're louder.

As a beginner you may not believe that differences of one or two thousandths of an inch make much of a difference, but—on the high strings especially—experienced players can detect such differences instantly and find them essential in determining their sound and style. If you manage to sample a variety of string gauges over the next year or two, you'll learn to tell the differences yourself without even trying.

The string industry sells guitar strings in sets usually named "ultra-light," "superlight," "extra-light," "light," "medium," and "heavy." The exact gauges of each string within a set usually vary slightly from brand to brand. For example, one brand's "light" set might offer a slightly lighter-gauge third string than most other brands, so that particular brand might appeal to you if you play a lot of blues and want a third string that's easier to bend.

Ultralight and Superlight

Sets starting around .008 and .009 are generally used only by electric guitarists who like to do a lot of string bending. They don't put out enough energy to drive the top of an acoustic guitar past a thin whisper. However, sometimes someone will use them on an acoustic guitar for a special effect. Of course if you use a pickup on your guitar it's a different story—especially if it's a magnetic pickup that works by detecting string vibrations alone, rather than body vibrations, as transducer pickups do.

Extra-Light Gauge

Extra-lights, starting around .010 or .011, are good for delicately built guitars and for some blues and contemporary styles that require a lot of string bending and vibrato. (The lighter the string, the more responsive it is to these techniques.) They're a bit too light for most of the student-grade instruments on the market these days but if you're just starting to play you might want to use extra-lights for around a month, until you build up some calluses, and then move to lights.

Compound Strings

Compound or "silk and steel" strings (see page 151) have roughly the same degree of tension as a set of extra-lights, but sound considerably warmer and less brilliant. They come in slightly different gauges from brand to brand; some may feel a bit tighter or a bit looser than extra-lights depending on gauge. Most start at .010 or .011.

Light Gauge

Light-gauge strings, starting at .012, are probably the best strings for you, and certainly the best starting point unless you have a delicate instrument that absolutely must have lighter strings. They offer the best compromise between the volume and robust tone production that come from heavier strings and the ease of playing and sensitivity to bending and vibrato that come from lighter strings. To most people they feel very natural picked by a flatpick, fingerpicks, or bare fingers, resisting the stroke neither too much nor too little.

Medium Gauge

Mediums, which start at .013, are for people who play hard with a flat-pick or fingerpicks, don't need to bend strings much, and have sturdy instruments that can withstand their string tension and effectively diffuse the amount of energy they put out. If you play a lot, you can learn to bend medium strings, but most people find it too hard and painful and not idiomatic enough in sound.

Some instruments seem to lose rather that gain volume when they are strung with mediums instead of lights. For some reason certain cheap, heavily built plywood-top guitars also seem to behave this way.

The stiff feel of medium strings goes very well with a stiff flatpick because the strings let the pick come off quickly to help with fast playing. A lighter string gives under the pick, distracting its motion.

Medium strings are generally favored by bluegrass musicians and heavy strummers who use dreadnought and jumbo-size guitars. They take some getting used to but for some styles and guitars they do the job much better than lights.

Heavy Gauge

Most flattop guitars can't tolerate the tension of heavies starting at .014; in fact, using them voids the warranty on most new instruments. They sometimes were used on big band acoustic archtop rhythm guitars, which are built like the Pyramids and require a huge amount of energy to get the top moving. Some resophonic guitar players also use them, though most prefer mediums. Heavy-gauge strings are so unfashionable, and justly so, that they're hard to find.

MEASURING STRING GAUGE

The tool that's used to measure string gauge—or the breadth of any small object—is called a "micrometer." Many guitar stores and repair shops keep one around, even though a good all-metal model, with accuracy to a thousandth of an inch, is pricey. (The less costly plastic models made for other crafts are only accurate to a hundredth of an inch—not a fine enough tolerance for measuring guitar strings.) If you get hold of one of these gadgets and go around measuring guitar strings, you'll sometimes find that a string is not exactly the diameter it says on the package. So if from time to time a string feels heavier or lighter than you think it should, it may not be fantasy.

TYPICAL STRING GAUGE AND TENSION

Because exact gauges vary slightly from brand to brand, the table below gives the gauges of a mythical "average" set and the approximate total string tension of that set assuming it's strung on a normal, long-scale guitar (±25.4 inches). On a short-scale guitar (±24.9 inches), tension would be a tad lower.

In comparison to the tension figures below, tension on nylon-strung guitars is usually in the neighborhood of seventy-five pounds. Tension on twelve-string guitars ranges from about 205 to 250 pounds, depending on gauge and scale.

TYPICAL STRING SETS
in thousands of an inch.
Exact specifications vary slightly according to manufacturer.

	first	second	third	fourth	fifth	sixth	approx. tension (lbs.)
Elec. Ultralight	.009	.012	.016	.024	.032	.042	105
Compound	.011	.014	.023	.028	.038	.047	130
Extra-light	.010	.014	.022	.030	.039	.048	125
Light	.012	.016	.025	.032	.044	.053	150
Medium	.013	.017	.026	.035	.046	.056	175
Heavy	.014	.018	.027	.038	.048	.059	200

Terms like "light" and "extra-light" have become increasingly meaningless because many string marketers discriminate between acoustic and electric guitar standards when labeling their products. "Extra-light" referring to electric strings might mean a set starting at .011 inches, but with acoustic guitar strings is likely to mean a set starting at .012. Therefore it's become increasingly common among guitarists to skip the name game completely and refer to sets of strings as, say, "nine-to-forty-twos" or "twelve to fifty-threes." And, since the first, last, and to a lesser extent in-between gauges tend to be similar from brand to brand, people even say "nines" or "twelves."

A few string packagers offer strings in "mixed" or "custom" sets that feel or sound better on some guitars or for some purposes. One such example is the set sometimes called "bluegrass," or "heavy top/light bottom," where the low strings are like mediums (or lights) and the high strings are like lights (or extra-lights). The purpose of such a set is to let you punch out low notes without having the high strings sound too strong or too individual when you strum. Another popular configuration has more-or-less mediums (or lights) on strings 6, 2, and 1 and lights (or extra-lights) on strings 5, 4, and 3. To some players such a set feels more even from string to string because, in fact, the tension of the individual strings tends to be more relatively even. Whether you're attracted to a mixed-gauge set for reasons of sound or feel, the only way to tell whether it's for you is to try it.

MAKING UP YOUR OWN STRING SET

Not all manufacturers gauge their prepackaged sets exactly alike. If among them all you still can't find a set you like, or if you just want to experiment a little, you'll find that most dealers also sell strings individually so you can mix and match to make up your own custom set. (Because buying strings one at a time is generally more expensive than buying sets, it may be cheaper to just buy a whole set and then discard and replace one or two strings. Sometimes dealers will give you a little back in trade for the leftovers.)

As a rule, electric guitarists are more into making up custom sets than acoustic guitarists. Among the super-light strings used by electric lead guitarists, small differences in gauge feel much more pronounced than they do among acoustic guitar sets. (The lighter the gauge, the larger the percentage difference a thousandth of an inch makes.) Many electric guitarists, and some acoustic players as well, get extremely finicky about string gauge—often with good reason, even though they appear silly about it sometimes. But it's also a great area for one-upsmanship and prima donna affectation, if you're into that.

Prepackaged gauged sets generally make sense. If you start mixing in grossly disproportionate custom strings, they will no longer feel and sound balanced with each other on most guitars. Unless your instrument responds unusually, if you mix, for example, an extra-light fourth string into an otherwise light-gauge set, you'll probably find that: (1) you get disoriented whenever you pick the fourth string because it gives much more than the others do; (2) its tone color is out of place; and (3) it's not as loud as the others. Of course if your instrument does respond unusually, custom string gauging is the answer.

On many electric guitars you can adjust the pickups for relative loudness on each individual string, so the volume problem can be easily solved. Not so on acoustics, except when using some, but not all, brands of magnetic pickups.

Nonetheless, each guitar and each player's touch is unique, and sometimes accommodations have to be made. One very common need is for a slightly lighter third string, to make the bluesy sounds you get when you "bend" the string by pushing up on it easier. Some people even go so far as to use an unwound third, which is great for bending but requires that you recompensate your saddle. (And even with a recut saddle it's still very difficult to keep an unwound third playing in tune. Unwound thirds are more commonly used on electric guitars, many of which have adjustable saddles.)

Individual strings are also handy for people who need to replace only one string or who find, as many do, that they like to replace the unwound strings more frequently than the wounds. (They seem to die faster and to feel dirty faster, too.) If you play so loud that you break strings (Elvis was good at that in his younger days), or if you leave your strings on so long that they become fatigued, then I don't have much sympathy for you.

STRINGS AND SETUP

Ideally, a guitar's action is set up for a given string gauge. For example, a guitar set up with low action would buzz more with hard playing when strung with light strings than with mediums. But the choice of lighter-gauge strings in the first place suggests that the player doesn't intend to do much loud playing. If volume is your priority, then a big guitar with medium strings and action on the high side is the usual way to get it.

STRING BRANDS

String makers start with raw drawn wire obtained from the same vendors that supply wire for pianos, electrical and communications cable, fencing, bailing, construction, and so on. The guitar string companies wind the strings, add anticorrosive chemicals, wrap in the metal ball ends that hold the strings under the bridge, cut the strings to length, package them, and ship them out. Because the string companies are not the original makers of the actual wire, they are known in the music industry not as string makers but as "string winders." If you call them that you'll sound either hip or incomprehensible, depending on whom you're talking to. But then that's what talking hip is all about.

There are only a few string-winding companies. As a rule they market their own brands and also supply strings to other packagers who sell them under different brand names. Generally you don't know who the winder is. Most brands offer a similar variety of string types (brass, bronze, compound, etc.), though different brands may have slight differences of gauge specifications for the individual strings within each set. Some brands with widely differing list prices ultimately come from the same string winder—in other words, they're the same strings.

There isn't much point in recommending any specific string brand. Try them yourself and make up your own mind—no one else can do it for you. Unless you're in a small town where your retailer has no competition, you should be paying something like 50 percent to at most 80 percent of a manufacturer's list price for your strings. Many retailers offer good string discounts to help increase their walk-in trade. Others happily discount orders of a half-dozen or a dozen sets. Strings will keep for a long time and a little tarnish won't hurt them.

When you go string shopping, you'll notice that some brands market string sets according to style: "blues" strings, "bluegrass" strings, and so on. Some are created to meet the specifications of a famous player who endorsed the set. All this means is that the individual gauges of the strings have been customized to meet somebody's set of expectations about what is ideal for that particular style.

BAD VIBES, HEAVY METAL FATIGUE, AND OTHER TOUGH BREAKS IN THE LIFE OF A STRING

What happens when strings get old? It's not a pretty picture.

- The winding wears and breaks at the point where the string contacts the frets. Unwound strings become thinner where they rub against the frets. The string's molecular structure changes under tension and metal fatigue sets in.
- The string becomes corroded with perspiration acid, tarnished with airborne impurities, and rusted from ambient humidity.
- Dirt, finger oils, and dead skin tissue coat the string.
- All of the above factors result in uneven mass throughout the string length, causing "dead frets" (not the fret's fault) and erratic intonation. You can add significant life to your strings by making sure your hands are clean before you play and giving your strings and neck a quick wipedown with a clean rag when you're done.

Why do strings break? Sometimes they just wear out or get struck too hard. But, if you find that you keep breaking the same string in the same place, look carefully at your guitar at the point where the string breaks. Often the problem is caused by a nut or bridge saddle that is improperly shaped, a nut that is improperly grooved, or a bridge pin-hole on an older guitar that has worn away, causing the string to cross the bridge at too sharp an angle. If you suspect that any of these string-bearing points could be the cause of excessive string breakage, check with your repair shop. A minor dressing, adjustment, or replacement could cure the problem.

WHEN TO REPLACE STRINGS

Unless you're replacing a single broken string on a newish set, don't wait to replace your strings individually as they break. Trust me: you'll be happier that way. Otherwise your strings will all be out of sound balance with each other and you'll go crazy trying to remember which string you replaced when. (Unless, of course, you keep such data on your computer log, in which case you're crazy to begin with.)

How often should you change strings? It depends on how much you play, on how hard you play, on how abusive your body chemistry is to strings, on the kind of strings you use, and on your personal taste. Some people get weeks and months out of a set of strings. Some deposit a heavy layer of sweat and dead skin tissue on a set of strings within minutes. Still others have a knack for causing strings to tarnish without affecting their sound. Though most people prefer the sound of strings that have been played in for several hours, some professionals have a signature sound that depends on the jangly brightness of brand-new strings. They pay for their sins by having to change them every time they play, and sometimes for every new take in the recording studio.

Generally speaking, change strings when any of these things happens:

- They won't stay in tune or they sound out of tune when you play.
- They sound obviously dull. Or you find yourself playing harder and harder in order to draw a lively sound from them (this means that they sound *un*-obviously dull).
- They've been on for a while and one of them breaks.
- They feel dirty. (Sometimes a quick wipedown will get you through a few more days or weeks. I like to use a rag moistened in rubbing alcohol, being careful not to drip any onto the fingerboard or body.)
- The windings fray or develop obviously worn spots.

When it comes time to change strings, take them all off at once only if you're planning to clean and oil your fingerboard. (See Chapter 12, page 199, for more information on taking care of your guitar.) Otherwise you might as well replace them one at a time; it's easier to tune up your new strings against the older strings and it's slightly better to keep your guitar at constant tension. Except when shipping a guitar, keep the strings up to pitch, even when you won't be playing it for a while. Guitars are made to stay up to pitch.

9 Pickups and Amplification

AMPLIFIED VERSUS NATURAL SOUND

Each musical instrument has its own unique blend of vibrations. (See Chapter 3 for more information about guitar sound.) Pre-electric instrument-building traditions were all designed to produce an instrument whose vibrations mix together in the air a few inches or feet in front of the performer, reaching the audience as a tasty acoustical stew of tones and overtones blended together from the various resonating surfaces and chambers of the instrument. When you introduce a pickup or even a very closely placed microphone, you skew these factors and the instrument sounds different. If you're a grouchy old guy like me who grew up in ancient times when the sound of amplified or recorded music was considered the exception rather than the norm, you may hear amplified or recorded sound as untrue to the original acoustic sound—though it may be true to itself after its own fashion.

If you're younger (or just more open-minded), then you may perceive electronically altered sound as normal. Certainly it can represent a whole new world of possibilities. Whatever the case, it's certainly true that few people have ever had the opportunity to listen to a fine guitarist playing a fine acoustic guitar in an intimate setting with no amplification. Even so-called "live" performances in small halls and coffeehouse-type venues are amplified—and a good thing, too. You can hear them better and the performer can perform more easily and with greater dynamic range.

The great value of pickups is that they free performers from the microphone, offering advantages in terms of posture and stage movement as well as clarity of sound in the audio mix with voices and other instruments. They also introduce the possibility for creative use of electronic modification of sound, or "sound processing." (See page 177 for more information on this topic.) Many professionals who use add-on or built-in pickups and electronics regard them as necessary (or convenient) evils in performing situations but don't much care for them privately. Some still feel this way. When you're used to a fine guitar, it's just more satisfying to listen to your own instrument purring softly against your rib cage. The performer you see on stage with an electro-acoustic, laminate guitar is very likely to regard that instrument as a tool for the road to be discarded for a new one every few years, and to own a fine, all-wood guitar to play at home and in the studio.

So, it's important to recognize that you can't put a pickup inside an acoustic guitar, run it through an amplifier or recording console, and still have it sound exactly like an acoustic guitar in a living room. Oh, the manufacturers say their equipment does it, but it doesn't. Don't kid yourself. Some of today's pickups sound very natural indeed but they still have a sound of their own. Once you accept this you'll be in a better position to judge which pickup you prefer, to enjoy it for what it is, and to use its sound effectively.

It's also important to bear in mind that most audiences will accept the sound of an amplified acoustic guitar as being natural and may in fact prefer it that way—just as many performers do. The "natural" sound of the acoustic guitar that people have become used to hearing on CD is actually the sound of a (typically) closely miked guitar to which additional sparkle has been added by the magic of the recording studio. Why lament this? Instead, go with the electron flow and make the best of it by making your guitar sound its best electronically.

TRANSDUCERS

Introduction to Transduction

"Transducer" is the technical term for any kind of gizmo that converts one kind of energy (like sound) into another (like electricity). Even the ordinary microphone into which you say "testing, testing" is a kind of transducer, and so is the dilithium chamber on the starship *Enterprise* (I *think*). In the more down-to-earth realm of guitars, there are three main types of transducers: contact pickups; magnetic pickups; and minimicrophones. All are mounted inside the body or sound hole of the guitar and these days almost all are provided with a wire that leads to a connecting jack built into the endpin.

You can buy a guitar with a built-in pickup or add one to the acoustic guitar you already own. Depending on the kind and brand of pickup you get, it might be a job for a repair shop or it might be something you can do yourself. If you're adding a pickup to a guitar you already own, you'll probably have to have the endpin hole reamed out to accommodate the larger-sized jack. Then you plug a connecting cable into the endpin jack, run it to your amp or sound system, crank it up, and *get down*.

Contact Pickups

Contact pickups are transducers mounted in direct contact with the guitar's wood. They work by sensing the wood's vibrations.

A few decades ago you would occasionally find "dynamic" transducers used on guitars. In a dynamic transducer, the vibrations set in motion a diaphragm that moves a coil inside a magnetic field to create the electrical signal. Basically, it's a contact microphone. In a "piezoelectric" transducer, a crystal does the same job. Piezoelectric transducers are the key elements in the seismic sensors used to measure earthquakes. Piezo pickups (as they're called for short) have a much wider frequency sensitivity and, if properly engineered and mounted, minimize the annoying bass boominess that is typical of dynamic pickups. For these reasons, piezos have just about wiped dynamic pickups out of the marketplace.

Pronunciation, by the way, varies. Many say "PIE-zo," as in apple, cherry, or coconut cream. Others, knowing that the device is named after the physicist Enrico Piezo, say "pee-AY-zo." One of these pronunciations, you may be sure, is the correct one.

In common parlance, the term "transducer pickup" is used to mean only piezoelectric transducers even though, having read the previous semantic discussion, we know that it properly refers to a wider variety of devices.

Most piezo pickups are strips that mount in the bridge groove under the saddle. They need to be professionally installed because a hole for their wire must be drilled through the bridge and bridge plate in such a way as to avoid any braces, and the saddle height needs to be readjusted.

A few pickup brands—McIntyre is probably the best known—mount with putty or adhesive inside the body of the guitar, usually on or near the bridge plate.

Pickups, Preamps, and Impedance

With most piezo pickups you'll find you get better sound if you use a preamplifier. Make sure you get one with an impedance level precisely suited to that particular brand of pickup. "Impedance" is the level of electrical resistance that the circuitry of the preamp or amp offers to the signal from the pickup, measured in units called *ohms*. Like economics, impedance is a theoretical area that remains a mystery to most people. It's confusing because the specified impedances of two devices don't necessarily have to be the same in order for them to work together. Far from it, in fact. Think of it as something like marriage.

The exact figures (in ohms) that are required to match two pieces of equipment may vary individually from one piece to another, so study the manufacturer's specs carefully and test the system before purchase. A system in which all the elements do not balance will produce disappointing sound, usually by killing the low notes and making the high ones tinny.

Many would-be electrophysicists are stumped by the difference between resistance and impedance. Impedance may be taken to mean the resistance offered by an entire circuit, processes and all. My friend Harry Fleishman has an even better definition. Impedance, he reminds us, is what the government does. Resistance is what the people do.

Most contact pickups are mounted on, in, or near the bridge, where the vibrations are strongest. Some brands are available in the form of actual bridge saddles; others are strips that mount under the saddle. You'll have to experiment to see which brand of pickup and which placement location give you the sound you like best. Of course most people necessarily do their experimenting by listening to different pickups installed on other peoples' guitars. Some do-it-yourself pickups come with putty for semi-permanent mounting; you can move the pickup around to experiment. Bear in mind that the putty could have a muting effect on tone; however, sometimes that effect is beneficial because internally mounted contact pickups tend to be brittle-sounding.

If you're having a repair shop install the pickup you can delegate the responsibility for where to mount it to them. Most repair people have strong, mutually exclusive opinions about where best to mount pickups and their taste may differ from yours as well as from each others'. Some favor installing two pickups on either side of the bridge for better balance and control of tone.

For after-market, add-on contact pickups, you'll do well to begin by looking at products from L. R. Baggs, Fishman, McIntyre, and Seymour Duncan, as well as the Fishman or Dana Bourgeois systems that combine a contact pickup with a microphone. Most contact pickups sound strident by themselves and need a preamplifier to modify the sound, or "signal" as it's called in this context, as well as to strengthen it. On some models you run your "signal path" through an external pickup; on others the pickup may be mounted inside the guitar. (See page 170 for information about signal paths.) Some internal pickups just sit inside the guitar with their battery compartment and barely reachable on-off switch; most turn themselves on automatically when you plug in your cable. Other pickups are actually mounted in the upper bout with convenient, externally reachable volume and tone controls. Generally the more mass you have mounted in your guitar, the more detrimental it is to tone and volume. As a result the pickups with the biggest, most intrusive preamps are typically found in laminate guitars or all-wood guitars of, at best, journeyman quality. It's best not to add a lot of electronic gadgetry to a really fine guitar.

The advantage of piezo pickups is their relative ease of installation and, in the basic models, simplicity and lack of invasiveness. Their disadvantage is a frequently clunky, echoey sound quality and sometimes inaccurate reproduction of guitar sound. These were much greater problems in the past than with today's pickups, and judicious use of preamplification goes a long way toward eliminating those problems

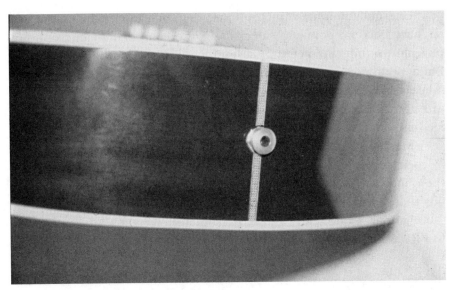

An endpin jack. *Photo by Larry Sandberg*

that remain. As with any pickup, there's a tendency to cause feedback; this, however, is a problem intrinsic to all amplified acoustic guitars.

Generally, any pickup is wired to a jack mounted in the guitar's "endpin," the pin at the bottom of the guitar to which you attach your strap. Endpin jacks are larger than the standard endpin and require reaming or drilling best done by a professional repair shop. Because so many guitarists now attach aftermarket pickups to their instruments, manufacturers are beginning to ship guitars with oversize endpins that do not require drilling out for jack mounting.

Internal Mini-Microphones

Another way to amplify your guitar is to mount a small microphone somewhere in the sound hole of your guitar. Mikes differ from contact pickups in that they sense not the movement of the guitar's wood but rather the sound pressure levels of the surrounding air as it is set in motion by the vibrating wood. Mikes potentially give you the most natural sound but also offer you the greatest sensitivity to feedback, which is a hassle to be avoided. As with contact pickups, you'll have to experiment to see exactly where you want to place the device to get the sound you want.

Some mini-mikes of a sort popular in recent decades clip right onto the edge of the sound hole. (It may be because they're specifically designed for this purpose or because they were originally intended to clip onto a newscaster's lapel.) If yours doesn't, rig some sort of mount yourself out of duct tape and bailing wire, or have an experienced repair shop construct a wooden mounting bracket for you. Twenty or even ten years ago, people were achieving a relative degree of success this way with inexpensive Radio Shack lapel mikes; but now specialized, high-quality products have made makeshift solutions outdated.

A sound hole–mounted magnetic pickup, in this case, a Fishman model. *Photo by Larry Sandberg*

Internally mounted microphones designed especially for the guitar have become popular, especially in the combination microphone-plus-pickup units marketed by several manufacturers; the Fishman and Dana Bourgeois models being among the most popular and readily available. These systems offer the opportunity to blend the microphone with the pickup sound to a greater or lesser degree in order to control feedback and nuances of tone.

Most miniature microphones are able to be so tiny because some of their preamp components have been left out of the pickup unit; these may be mounted elsewhere on the guitar or included in a small box that sits at your feet or clips onto your belt.

Various models are available from different manufacturers and you'll have to experiment to see which you like best.

Magnetic Pickups

Magnetic pickups are the kind of pickups used on electric guitars. The energy that they pick up and convert into an electrical signal is not sound vibration, as it is with the other types of transducer, but is rather the oscillation of the magnetic field of the vibrating string. However, just as on electric guitars, the tonal qualities of the guitar body feed back into the vibrations of the string, controlling to some degree how the instrument sounds even magnetically.

Magnetic pickups for acoustic guitars are designed to be mounted across the sound hole. For this reason, they are also called "sound hole pickups." Because they are by nature removable, sound hole pickups usually come with a cable that leads outward from the sound hole and connects with your amplifier or sound system. For permanent installation, the cable can be cut short and fed, just as with a transducer or internal microphone, to the endpin jack. For semi-permanent installation, a jack and plug can be wired in-line between the pickup and the endpin jack, enabling the pickup to be removed without having to remove all the wiring.

Magnetic pickups are usually aftermarket additions. Magnetic pickups installed by the manufacturer are rare in guitar history and are available on only a few commercially available models (like the Epiphone J-160E). In this case, the pickup is located at the base of the fingerboard just above the sound hole.

Until fairly recently you had to use electric guitar strings with magnetic pickups because acoustic guitar strings lacked sufficient magnetic properties to work on earlier magnetic pickups. (Sorry, a vibrant personality and good haircut are not enough.) But today's pickups are much improved. They are optimized to balance out the lesser magnetic qualities of bronze-wound acoustic guitar strings, with quite favorable results. However with some brands, especially when mounted on instruments that have this propensity, the first and especially second strings are disproportionally loud. In fact this happens often enough that it's one of the main drawbacks of magnetic pickups.

Why choose a magnetic pickup? Some purists eschew them, on the grounds that they're (horrors!) electric. Well, they're no more or less electric than any other form of transducer.

At their best, magnetic pickups can be bright and clear with a strong, crisp bass. And, although some models sound more "electric" than others, the best magnetic pickups can also sound very "acoustic." A lot depends on the amp. (See page 171 for more information about amplifiers.)

It's also possible to combine a magnetic pickup with a microphone or contact transducer, as in the Highlander or Dana Bourgeoise systems, or to install a magnetic pickup that incorporates a microphone, like one of the Fishman models.

At their worst, magnetic pickups are as bad as any other kind. You can certainly get them to sound bad if you work at it. And the tendency of some magnetic pickups to exaggerate the unwound strings is very real, especially with the cheaper, most conveniently mass-marketed brands. Those relatively few models with adjustable "pole pieces" offer the best control of this problem. Pole pieces are little magnetized screws that screw up out of the central magnet, essentially permitting you to vary the proximity of the magnet to individual strings.

But the main problem with sound hole pickups, and the main reason so many guitarists are reluctant to purchase them, is that they are . . . sound hole pickups. By mounting across the sound hole, they can affect tone, especially bass response, and reduce volume considerably—so using a sound hole pickup is not a decision to be taken lightly. Some models, such as those by Fishman, are so small that they minimize the problem. Another professional-level model, the limited-production Sunrise with its huge, heavy magnet and large pole pieces, takes a big bite out of the acoustic sound of your guitar but amply repays you when plugged in.

Incidentally, magnetic pickups don't work with nylon strings by definition. Therefore, only contact transducers or internal microphones can be used with classical guitars.

For what it's worth, I use sound hole pickups on my utility instruments and like them a lot. They actually make these instruments sound better as plugged-in guitars than they do as acoustic guitars. But you should keep them pretty much out of your acoustically favorite guitars, though.

Why Plug In?

We've already looked at the advantages of plugged-in guitars for achieving onstage freedom from instrument mikes, allowing you to work the vocal mike without distraction, and permitting you to enter the seductive realm of sound processing. (See page 177 for more information on this topic.)

Plugging in also allows you to play more softly. How can that be? In a purely acoustic environment, the only way to get louder is to beat harder on the guitar. Forget about any quality of delicacy you might be trying to achieve. Forget about nuances of dynamics. But with amplification, you can touch the instrument softly and still be heard.

In a larger sense, this aspect of plugging in allows the acoustic guitar to achieve full partnership with instruments like drums, pianos, and electric guitars that formerly overwhelmed it. Standing in front of a microphone with a guitar did not, as a rule, do the job. This partnership was once available only in the recording studio or with stage amplification run by the most professional engineers, with the best equipment, under the best of circumstances. And any seasoned performer can tell you how often *that* happens.

Now it can happen to anyone. Acoustic guitars have become an important part of garage and stadium bands alike, as they never were—as they never could be—before. It's all thanks to pickups. Just remember that there's another side to this coin, and that is that the intimacy and fellowship of playing purely acoustic music are ruined, and swiftly, once you plug in. Fortunately, you can have it both ways. Just pull the plug.

The Great Signal Chain of Being

Acoustically unexceptional guitars can be made to sound quite good plugged in. When you plug in, your guitar is no longer simply a musical instrument. The entire "signal chain," as it's called, is your instrument: the guitar, the preamp and any other sound processing devices, and the amplifier itself. The guitar is merely, in engineering parlance, the "driver" for the rest of the signal chain.

This in a way cheapens the almost holy qualities that go into making a great acoustic guitar. Possibly it does so to your advantage. Considered merely as a driver, the acoustic guitar doesn't have to be great anymore. It merely has to be adequate: adequate enough to drive the rest of the signal chain into giving you a sound you want. Oddly, it's been my experience that, in order to do this, a guitar doesn't have to be good or great. Rather, the combination of driver and electronics has to be good or great—and sometimes what that means, in practical terms, is that the guitar merely has to be good enough.

It still may be that only a truly great guitar can make a truly great driver. But the right second-rate guitar can, as a driver, achieve results pretty close to first class. It's a compromise, of course, but real life is full of compromises. In a real-life scenario, you sound better if you are in complete control of the signal chain, and using a compromise driver, than if you brought a fine guitar into a venue with second-rate microphones, a sound system that was sub-state-of-the-art in 1978, and a sound person experienced only with electric guitars, if with any. This frees you from any need to put a great guitar into the baggage compartment of an airplane, or into the trunk of a car on a sweltering or sub-zero day.

Aftermarket or Factory Installation?

Many guitars are available at all price and quality levels except the very lowest with factory-installed electronics. In fact, some very good instruments come with electronics built in, but if you really care about getting the best acoustic sound, it might be the best course to stick to a purely acoustic instrument and add nonintrusive electronics. Or add none at all, and instead buy a second instrument to play plugged in. Bearing in mind the concept of the guitar as driver, you may find that an instrument of lower price and quality than your primary instrument makes you perfectly happy for playing plugged in. Many of the instruments marketed with pre-installed electronics—and they're generally of the contact-pickup-with-preamp variety—fit this description and may fit your bill completely.

ELECTRO-ACOUSTIC GUITARS

In some instruments, called "electro-acoustic" guitars, one or another combination of volume/tone control, equalizer, or preamp is usually built into the guitar along with the pickup. Electro-acoustics are sometimes designed on the assumption that they will be used with the pickups all the time, so many models don't have as much unamplified volume, or as full an unamplified tone, as a true acoustic guitar, and may be shallower than purely acoustic guitars, in order to make them more congenial to players used to the thin bodies of electric guitars. Many players find shallow-bodied instruments more comfortable to stand with, as well. If you like acoustic guitars, you probably won't like them, but if you're used to electric guitars, you might like them very much. Yamaha currently has several models of shallow, electro-acoustic instruments on the market, but thin-bodied, electronically equipped instruments are also available from Alvarez, Ibanez, Ovation, Tacoma, Takamine, Washburn, and other makers as well.

AMPLIFIERS AND SOUND SYSTEMS

Remember the concept we introduced earlier of driver and signal chain—a plugged-in guitar is only half an instrument. Your amplifier or PA system is the other half. If you want your acoustic guitar to still sound like an acoustic guitar when you plug it in, don't plug it into an electric guitar amp. You need to plug it into a specially dedicated, acoustic guitar amplifier or into a public address, or PA, system. Here's why.

Electric Guitar Amplifiers

Electric guitars have the characteristic sound they do mostly because of their amplifiers. Electric guitar amps are optimized to color their sound in certain very specific ways, mostly by boosting middle frequencies and by deliberately introducing a certain amount of distortion. Plug an acoustic guitar into one and, naturally enough, you'll get the sound of an acoustic guitar with its sound colored in certain very specific ways, mostly by boosting middle frequencies and by deliberately introducing a certain amount of distortion. You might even like this sound, and use it to your advantage. Fair enough. But it's not the sound of an acoustic guitar.

Oddly, though, some electric guitar amps seem to work better with classical guitars than acoustic guitar amps do. Acoustic guitar amps are optimized for the brightness of steel strings and tend to make nylon-strung guitars sound cheap and squeaky. Electric guitar amps that are capable of producing a warm jazz tone, like vintage Gibson jazz amps, their modern copies, and Polytone amps, may be the best choice for classical guitarists. Some models of bass amp and keyboard amp might also satisfy you.

On-Stage Sound Systems

Get on stage and plug your guitar into the house PA or play through a microphone, and your guitar will sound like itself as long as the sound person can twist the dials competently. Why? Because a good PA is designed only to reinforce the sound; to make it louder without coloring it or distorting it at all. For using microphones with the human voice or the natural sound of any acoustic instrument, the best amplifier is the kind of sound system that people still call a PA or public address system, even though today's music-oriented professional systems are much more sophisticated than what a high-school principal uses to make a speech in the gym. For professional "sound reinforcement," as concert-quality amplification is called, microphones and pickups for each performer are fed into a master console where they are equalized and mixed, just as they would be in a recording studio. Acoustic guitar pickups are designed primarily to feed into a voice amp console along with voice and instrument mikes, rather than into a guitar amp. Running a guitar pickup directly into the mixing console is called "direct input," or DI for short.

If you choose to use a preamp or sound processing equipment, it enters the signal chain ahead of the DI. Don't be surprised if your pickup doesn't seem to sound as good as what you hear coming over a professional sound reinforcement system at a stage show. A road guitarist in a major act may use much more than a small interface box between the guitar pickup and the sound system—hundreds or even thousands of dollars' worth of sound processing equipment, in fact. Then add a professional sound system worth more than you make in years, operated by a professional technician, and it's no wonder that you don't sound like that at home.

Also remember that the usual professional setup many pros prefer is to have the acoustic guitar miked and DI'd at the same time, giving the sound technician two separate signals to work with. (As a variation on this, you'll also sometimes see a guitar player working with a combination of a mike feeding into the sound console and a pickup running into an onstage guitar amplifier used as a stage monitor, and which might also be miked. Doc Watson often works like this. Neither of these setups are the kind of thing anyone is likely to run in their living room.

At this time there is one personal PA system on the market that is worthy of the attention of acoustic guitarists, especially those who sing and who work with a partner. It is the Fender Passport system, which packs up into a neat, portable package. There are two sizes, the larger considerably more powerful than the other and much less portable because of its size and weight, but with advantages in power and features. The smaller model is fine for, say, a coffeehouse listening room but would frustrate you in a noisy bar. It's lightweight, convenient, small enough to set up in your home rehearsal room, and worth considering for any amateur or semi-pro who doesn't have to compete with noisy crowds. A great advantage is that several musicians may use a single system. Either unit is worth considering by schools, churches, and others who might need a portable PA. Also keep your eyes open for similar systems. It's hard to imagine that other manufacturers won't come out with worthwhile competing products.

When you plug into an onstage sound system, you are usually given a device called a DI (or direct input) box to plug into. The DI box converts the high impedance of your guitar pickup to a low impedance signal that can travel a longer distance over the cable to the engineer's sound console at the back of the house without degrading. Most DIs are "passive"; they simple convert impedance without affecting sound. Some are "active," containing amplification and perhaps tone-altering circuitry. Generally speaking it's the performer's responsibility to provide a cable to plug into the DI and the house engineer's responsibility to provide the box itself; some performers carry their own boxes anyway. It's good to ask.

Acoustic Guitar Amps

The decade preceding the millennium saw the rise of a new kind of guitar amp: the acoustic guitar amp. Unlike the electric guitar amp, its circuitry is designed to produce clean, undistorted sound—very much like a PA, in fact, except that most models introduce a slight degree of coloration by optimizing the strummy, jangly frequencies that characterize the steel-strung flattop sound. Fortunately for those who prefer the warmer aspects of the steel-strung guitar, it's possible to cut down the inherent jangliness of most acoustic guitar amps by using their tone controls.

Acoustic Guitar Amp Power and Volume

When you go shopping for an acoustic guitar amp, there are several features you should look for. One is raw power. It seems to be a psychoacoustic fact that you can get away with a relatively less powerful electric guitar amp than you can with a PA or acoustic guitar amp. Less powerful amps begin to distort more readily as you crank up the volume. This is exactly what most electric guitar users want. To maintain a clean sound at higher volume levels, you need more power. If you're used to running a twenty-two-watt electric guitar amp and try to run a thirty-watt acoustic guitar amp at the same volume level, you may be unhappy with the clarity of your sound.

This is why so many of the acoustic guitar amps on the market are relatively more powerful than their electric guitar counterparts. They need that power to stay clean. In addition, acoustic guitar amps are generally "solid-state"—that is to say, they use transistors rather than tubes. Tubes have a warmer, thicker-sounding, more distorting quality that electric guitarists generally prefer. Transistors are cleaner. Acoustic guitar amps are generally totally enclosed, rather than having open backs like many electric guitar amps, for similar sonic reasons.

Having warned you about increased power requirements, you should also be aware that they may not be necessary for your needs. If your goal is to stay at home, have fun with your friends, enjoy amplification more for its sound processing possibilities than for volume, and perhaps perform in respectful, intimate settings or even classrooms and school gyms, then a small amp may be just fine. The kinds of power and circuitry that give you clean sound at high volumes cost exponentially more the more volume you require, and there's no point in paying for what you don't need. Keeping size and weight down are also points to consider. I'd recommend keeping away from bigger, heavier amps unless you absolutely need one professionally. Buying an amp you can't carry up a flight of stairs, or that won't fit in the trunk of your car, or that doesn't fit neatly into a corner of your room at home, is something you might end up regretting.

Microphones and Other Inputs

Most acoustic guitar amps are equipped with several different input jacks and many have two channels. A channel is an independent signal chain in which you can control tone, volume, and other parameters independently of other channels. On a two-channel amp, for example, you can plug in two different instruments, or separate vocal and instrument microphones, and control the volume and tone of each individually.

When each channel has a separate volume control for its own pre-amplifier, these controls may be called either "volume" or "gain." In addition, there is usually a third volume control that governs the total output of the post-preamp power amplifier section of the circuitry. This is usually called "master volume," or sometimes just "volume."

In addition, many amps have more than one input for each channel. The purpose of multiple inputs per channel is not to allow the use of multiple instruments but rather to match the impedance, power output, or plug type of the input device. For example, many amps have separate guitar inputs: one for a raw guitar pickup, another for a pickup with a preamplifier.

Very often the second channel of the acoustic guitar preamplifier is dedicated, by its plug type and impedance characteristics, to a microphone. Generally the manufacturer has conceived of this microphone as being an internal guitar microphone rather than a vocal microphone and has optimized the frequency handling of the circuitry accordingly. However, with adequate built-in equalization, or with the addition of an outboard equalizer, it's possible to fake the microphone channel into working satisfactorily with a vocal mike, thereby converting your acoustic guitar amp into a miniature PA that you or a vocalist can sing with.

With somewhat degraded but still acceptable results, you may be able to get your acoustic guitar amp to handle several musicians by introducing an outboard mixer into the signal chain before the amp input.

Another pair of in-and-out plugs may be present on your amp belonging to an "effects loop." This circuit enables you to attach sound effects and sound processing devices directly to your amp's circuitry instead of inserting them into the signal chain outboard. This reduces the noise level and improves the quality and manageability of some devices and eliminates the problem of the impedance of a given device not matching the amplifier's inputs. However, some devices sound and work better when connected in front of the amplifier pickup. Others sound better when used outboard.

Equalization

"Equalization" is another feature to look for in an acoustic guitar amp. Equalization—called "EQ" for short—is the act of adjusting a specific frequency range to the volume level relative to that of other frequency ranges. The bass and treble tone controls on your stereo are equalizers; they allow you control the volume of low and high frequencies relative to each other. Because you have two parameters, bass and treble, these tone controls would be called a "two-band" equalizer. If you have a mid-range control as well, then you have "three-band" EQ. Acoustic guitars are fussy about how they sound when played through an amp. You should have at least three bands of equalization, and you probably won't find a product with fewer; four or five are better but, for a guitar, over seven can get finicky and confusing in practice. With four and more bands of EQ, the controls are usually labeled numerically by frequency in terms of cycles per second (Hertz or Hz) or hundreds of cycles per second (Kilohertz or K or Khz). The measurement is named after the pioneer physicist Heinrich Rudolf Hertz.

Don't let Heinrich intimidate you. A number like 100 Hz simply means bass; around 400 Hz is midrange. Eight hundred Hz to 1 Khz is a section of the upper midrange that the human ear tends to perceive as creating a froggy-sounding, muddy clutter, a condition further exaggerated by the characteristics of transducer pickups; most players prefer to turn this range down ("notch it" or "roll it off") a lot. Frequencies around 3.5 Khz and above represent not so much the sound of the string itself as they do the various elements of sparkle that make steel strings sound like steel strings; so, being able to control them is very important for making the guitar sound strummy and alive or, alternatively, for controlling the potentially annoying jangliness of amplified steel strings. On some devices, the EQ controls in this frequency range may be labeled "presence" or "brilliance."

On instruments with insufficient equalization controls it's possible to add an outboard equalizer. Pricey, professional rack-mount equipment is available, but many players prefer to use an inexpensive pedal unit of the sort available from BOSS or DOD. These can also serve as a preamp and are very popular; many performers prefer to put one in their signal chain between the guitar and a house PA system so they can share some of the control of their sound instead of giving it over entirely to the sound person. You can also use an outboard EQ to make an electric guitar amp sound a little more like an acoustic guitar amp—but not entirely so.

Some amplifiers have a separate contour or tone shaping control that enables you to go to a preset equalization pattern determined by the manufacturer. Thus, for example, on many Trace Elliott models you can set all your EQ controls at neutral and, instead of adjusting them laboriously by ear to suit your taste, you can pull on a knob in order to arrive immediately at a setting that the manufacturer has guessed will please you. If they guessed wrong, you're still free to make EQ adjustments as you wish.

Notch Filters and Parametric Equalizers

Another useful feature to look for is a "notch filter." Some makers label it simply the "antifeedback control." Acoustic guitars are especially prone to feedback because the various frequencies that come out of amplifiers and PA loudspeakers enjoy finding a home in the guitar's air chamber. Sometimes, like unwanted guests, they become unruly: an outside frequency that matches the resonant frequency of the guitar's top and air chamber will set it in motion, creating feedback.

A notch filter is like a specialized EQ control that you can control in order to reduce only the narrow frequency band that causes feedback. A switch turns it on; then you use a knob to change the notch frequency until you find and "notch out" the one that causes feedback.

Having a notch filter on your acoustic guitar amp is a good thing; you'll find it comes in handy sometimes. However, notch filters are also available in the feature set of many outboard sound processing devices, especially those dedicated to acoustic guitars. To some extent you can also use an outboard equalizer with at least six or seven bands as a notch filter, though with less satisfactory results; the bandwidth is wider than that of a notch filter, so it can take too many frequencies away from your sound.

There is also a device similar to a notch filter called a "parametric equalizer." With it you can control not only the frequencies you notch, but also the width of the range of frequencies, or "bandwidth," that gets notched, giving you finer control. By narrowing bandwidth, which audio engineers call "Q," you can make the effect of the notch filter less audible in your sound, if the feedback permits. Or, if the feedback frequencies cover a wider bandwidth, you can broaden the Q accordingly. Parametric EQs let you exaggerate, or "boost," as well as notch, or "roll off," the frequency range you choose. An outboard "dual parametric equalizer" even allows you to boost or roll off two separate frequency ranges.

Parametric equalizers are useful tools for controlling the clarity and feedback of bands working in large venues and for getting certain effects in the studio. They are generally considered to belong to the arsenal of the sound engineer, not the individual musician. They do a specialized job, are tricky to use, and require considerable practical experience. You are unlikely to need one.

Reverb

Many acoustic guitar amps come with the seductive "reverberation," or echo, effect—"reverb" for short. Echo can add a mysterious warmth to a performance, especially when used with the voice, or can add dramatic, but often wearing, effects when turned up. Reverb is seductive and, like seduction, can cause you to lose your clarity. At first you think you can't live without it; later you find that you can unless you're among those guitarists who choose to make it part of their sound.

It's good to have reverb built into your amp, but if you don't you can add an outboard unit that will likely give you greater variety and higher quality at a relatively low cost.

SOUND PROCESSING DEVICES

There's more to "picking up" than the pickup itself. Most players find that the sound of a bare pickup alone just isn't good enough. Some pickups put out a fairly weak electrical signal and the amplifier, when cranked up to boost it, adds noise of its own. Therefore it's common to use a "preamplifier" ("preamp" for short) between the pickup and the amplifier or console.

In addition, pickups may produce a sound that is unbalanced, tinny, or lifeless. ("Balance" refers to the dominance or subordination of certain frequencies within the total sound.) Therefore it's also common to add an equalizer, tone control, or other sound processing device between the pickup and the amplifier or console. (Equalizers are essentially glorified tone controls that let you boost or suppress selected frequency ranges.)

Some guitars with built-in pickups also come with built-in volume and tone controls, and possibly a built-in, multi-band equalizer and preamp as well. If you're adding a pickup to an ordinary guitar, you can purchase these gadgets assembled in a small box, called a "pickup interface," that sits on the floor at your feet or, in some cases, may clamp onto your belt or hang from a strap over your shoulder as well. Many pickup manufacturers offer a matched interface box for their pickup, or you can buy one separately. You can try to get by without one, but they'll usually make you sound better and also put more control of the way you sound into your own hands, instead of leaving you at the mercy of whoever is operating the sound system.

Sound processing devices are more complicated in that they give you sound effects like glimmering chorus, shimmering phase shift, glowering fuzz tones, and so on that add show and glow to your sound. Many duplicate—often with greater variety—devices like echo and notch filter that may already be available in a guitar preamp and sound system. Some are dedicated to acoustic guitars and have effects especially suitable for acoustic playing but, if you're also an electric guitarist, you might be perfectly happy using your electric guitar device with your acoustic as well. Many come equipped with headphone jacks so you can rock out in your private corner without having to crank up an amp.

Sound processors, also known as effects boxes, usually come in foot-pedal or small box form, but the most complex ones are designed to be mounted on professional sound equipment racks. Effective, enjoyable devices can be had at street prices around $200 or less from makers like BOSS, Korg, and Zoom, as well as other companies. Whether you learn to use effects effectively or affectedly is entirely up to you.

10 Used, Vintage, and Modern Guitars

LOOKING FOR MR. GOODFRET

A lot of professional musicians own used instruments. It's easier for them to come by a good used instrument than it is for amateur players. Pros hang around music stores and other musicians and are in touch with what's available. They know what to look for and how to evaluate an instrument without having to do research and make comparisons. They buy and sell instruments among themselves. And because they already have what they need, they can afford to sit tight until something they like comes along at a good price.

For amateurs, it's harder. You can wait forever before what you want appears in the classifieds. You may feel (correctly) insecure about your ability to spot anything wrong with an instrument. You probably won't have the advantage of immediate sound and feel comparisons of hundreds of good guitars you've encountered in your life. If you make the rounds of thrift stores, flea markets, and garage sales, the prospects are even more dismal. Sometimes you can luck out, but not often. What you usually find is unplayable junk on which ignorant sellers have put too high a price because someone told them that old guitars are valuable. Even pawnshops, once good hunting grounds, have turned barren. Most pawnbrokers know that good old guitars can be valuable but wouldn't recognize a good guitar if they saw one, so they overprice everything out of fear, and their policies are reinforced when some know-nothing comes along and meets their price. Some also stock junky new instruments to sell to people who think they're getting a good deal just because they're buying from a pawnshop. They're not.

Finally, be suspicious of good instruments being sold at an absurdly low price. They could be hot. It happens all the time. Use your head and don't get greedy.

But buying a used instrument is a great way to save money. If the classifieds don't help, try to get a used guitar from a dealer or other reputable trader. Some teachers and working musicians deal instruments on the side. Some dealers don't like to sell used instruments because profit margins are higher on new goods. But some always have a few used instruments around that they've taken in on trade and a few even enjoy the public service of keeping around a bunch of beat-up, adequately playable junkers for quick turnover at low prices. Some of them are off-brands that aren't worth buying new, but if you can find a playable used model for under a hundred bucks to get you through the first six months of testing your commitment, they make sense at that price. You're still not getting a very good guitar, but at least you're getting what you pay for.

Looking for a used guitar in a higher price range makes sense when you want features that have been discontinued. For example, many of the small-bodied Martins, Gibsons, and Guilds are no longer in standard production, but you can find good used models from the 1960s. Embargoed and other high-quality woods are also available in older guitars. But if you're dealing with a knowledgeable seller, be prepared to pay more than bargain rates, or even more than the cost of a new instrument.

Getting a good-quality used guitar makes even more sense when you just want to save a few bucks. At this time the list price of high-quality, new guitars runs from two to three thousand dollars. Dealers cannot, as a rule, discount instruments in this range more than 20 percent and still expect to stay in business. A used instrument, on the other hand, should generally command about 50 percent of its list price. It may have some wear and scratches but so will a new one eventually. As an extra bonus, the instrument will already be played in for you. And you won't have to worry about putting the first scratch on it yourself.

Finally, a word to those who perpetually search for a better guitar because they grow unhappy with the way their guitar sounds. Look within, and consider that the problem may not lie with the instrument. Many of the people who worry excessively about finding the guitar with perfect tone would, in my opinion, be better off spending their energy on changing their strings more often and on improving their own tone by getting their pick or finger strokes more perpendicular to the string.

OWNING MORE THAN ONE GUITAR

Many pros and enthusiasts are perfectly happy owning just one guitar. Others want variety.

There are ample reasons, besides being a collector, to own more than one guitar. Specialized fingerpicking and flatpicking guitars sound and feel completely different. Flattop, classical, electric, and archtop guitars *are* completely different. A cheap guitar to throw in the trunk of your car for travel or vacations can make sense. A good-quality utility or road guitar can also make sense for professionals who wish to conserve their fine personal instrument. Or maybe you just find it stimulating to switch back and forth between more than one instrument.

So don't let them laugh at you. Buy as many guitars as you want and can afford.

VINTAGE GUITARS

Decent guitars may reach their stride at age twenty, but they still don't get any respect until they're fifty or sixty. The so-called "vintage" acoustic guitar market originally consisted of instruments from before the Second World War. (Among guitarists, the term *pre-war* refers to guitars made before World War II.) Dealers are increasingly using the term *vintage* for more recent instruments as well, especially for electric guitars.

The demand for instruments perceived as vintage—though the term itself didn't come into use until the 1970s—originated in the 1950s when folk music revivalists were learning to copy earlier musical styles and wanted period instruments to play on. They soon discovered that the old instruments usually sounded better than new ones and could be bought cheaply. After all, there were no vintage guitars in those days—just used ones.

Eventually cults developed and there emerged wizards and lore-masters who could recite all the brand names under which the old Larson Brothers workshop marketed their instruments, or date a Martin at twenty paces just from the squareness of the headstock. (The corners of Martin headstocks got more rounded over the years as the template wore down.) Guitars, to this mindset, were no longer tools for creative musicianship. They were degraded to the status of collectibles, as if they were nothing more than doggie figurines, bubble gum cards, or Rembrandt paintings.

One of the Holy Grails of vintage guitar collecting, an abalone-inlaid Martin from the late 1920s. *Photo by Larry Sandberg*

The Nature of a Collectors' Market

When you get into a collectors' market, you're playing a whole new game. Prices are based on quantified standards like the rarity of a particular feature or the number of instruments in a given year's production run rather than the individual instrument's sound quality.

It bears remembering that being old doesn't automatically make a guitar great. The instrument has to have been great from the moment it came out of the factory. It's arguable that a higher proportion of the top-line instruments that came out of the factories in the vintage days were great guitars than in later decades. But that still doesn't mean that the vintage crop doesn't have its share of mediocre-sounding instruments and outright dogs.

Some vintage dealers evade the issue of sound quality by dismissing it as "subjective." *Of course* tastes and preferences in sound are subjective. But that doesn't mean that there are no standards. It doesn't mean that a panel of good guitarists won't agree that a dog is a dog, and be able to hear its snarl fifty feet away.

Sometimes this works to a player's advantage. Instruments most valued as collectibles are those in original mint condition. Cracks, dings, refinish jobs, or non-original frets may bring price down, regardless of sound quality. Until the past decade, it was still sometimes possible for players to get their hands on superb-sounding vintage instruments at relatively low prices compared to new instruments. Now almost any old instrument is worth a considerable amount, often more than its value as a playing instrument.

The Nature of Collectors

"The first thing we do, let's kill all the lawyers," cried a revolutionary rabble-rouser in one of Shakespeare's historical plays. Some musicians feel the same way about guitar collectors. As with lawyers, the argument has its merits. At their best, collectors are informed experts, and sometimes tasteful musicians as well, who preserve important artifacts of Americana and musical history. At their worst, they are boorish ignoramuses who, as another English poet once put it, know the price of everything and the value of nothing.

The vintage waters can have some perilous undertows. They have a few sharks swimming in them, and some poisonous blowfish too. Can you detect new frets, a new fingerboard, or a contemporary refinishing job? Do you know in what year Martin went from bar frets to T-frets, or altered its X-bracing pattern? Was the original bridge plate maple or rosewood? Has someone carved a new ebony bridge to replace an ivory original? When did Martin change from the pyramid bridge to a belly bridge? Can you spot a Prairie State that's been altered from an archtop to a flattop? Do you know the date of each modification in the Gibson script headstock inlay? Even more important, can you trust the person who's pricing and selling the guitar to tell you these things, or to recognize them in the first place? One of the greatest dangers when shopping for vintage instruments is run-of-the-mill music store dealers who do not customarily deal in old instruments and who price them even higher than the specialized vintage dealers do.

In 1991 someone was advertising a 1945 Martin D-28 with "pre-war specs" for $5,200 in my local paper's classifieds. This is one of the classic "herringbone" dreadnoughts, so-called because of the herringbone-pattern ornamental edge binding that Martin used on its 28-series instruments until 1946. But though Martin kept using the pretty binding until 1946, they quit using their scalloped bracing in 1944, and they altered their original X-brace placement in 1939. These are the qualities that give the (older) herringbone dreadnoughts their sought-after sound. The instrument, therefore, didn't really have pre-war specs—especially not the ones that count most, the ones that determine its sound. Is the seller putting you on, or is he or she just ignorant? In any case, you could be in trouble if you don't know better.

On the other hand, if it's worth a lot of money to you to be seen in the parking lot at bluegrass festivals playing an old Martin with herringbone binding, then go ahead and buy it. It may sound great, anyway. But with a little looking, could you have found an equally great-sounding instrument at a lower price? Possibly.

Vintage Guitars as Investments

Vintage instruments generally maintain their value at resale if you buy at a good price to begin with. However, if you pay a top-dollar collectors' price from one of the pricier dealers, you'll find that you generally have to undercut that price to move the instrument quickly, so you might take a loss if you can't afford to wait.

If you spend much time listening to vintage instrument dealers, you'll hear talk of buying guitars as investments. (Many other dealers, to be fair, shy away from this kind of talk.) The vintage market got a big ego boost around 1970 when Sotheby Parke-Bernet and Christie's, high-class auction houses specializing in fine art, antiques, and other artifacts used by the wealthy to store their wealth, added vintage guitars and banjos to their catalogs. But guitars and banjos never really took off in that upscale environment and have now settled into making only cameo appearances in the seasonal violin and rare instrument auctions.

Dealers sometimes cite statistics that purport to demonstrate that a vintage instrument collection is a good hedge against inflation. Some of these statistics are based on dubious premises. Figures based on the original prices of the instruments or on pre-vintage-craze prices of thirty years ago are irrelevant if the price you're going to pay now is top-dollar dealer's price. Other projections are based on turnover, which means you'd be dealing rather than collecting—a completely different activity. Buying low and selling high is always a good way to make a buck.

It's important, by the way, not to take these caveats about dealers too generally. There are some fine, honorable, and knowledgeable people among them, especially among those who have been in the business the longest. Some of the old-timers have even left, or refocused their interests, because the market got to be too statistically oriented for them, or too crazy, or otherwise stopped being fun. Others keep on doing the best kind of business they can.

By all means, put your money into vintage instruments if you love them. But don't do it if you're only motivated by money, because generally you can make better money in other ways. If demand continues as it has, you'll probably stay on top of inflation anyway—especially if you know enough to buy the right models at the right prices. But when it comes to trends in musical taste, only the hardiest of prognosticators would venture to guess where the fickle finger of fate will point next. If the next craze turns out to be the return of the big bands, collectors will probably be wishing they were sitting on a garage full of Paris Selmer wind instruments instead of all those useless old Martin, Gibson, Vega, Stahl, and Prairie State guitars that no one will want any more than they did in 1956.

Why Some People Think Old and Vintage Guitars Are Better

Vintage aficionados argue that the best older and vintage guitars are made of better woods than most modern guitars and are constructed more skillfully. In a few cases, as with pre-war Martins, the older instruments have certain design characteristics that may be available today only on a limited number of models, if at all. Some sizes and shapes are hard or impossible to come by today, unless you commission an instrument from a custom luthier.

You also have to add the magic acoustical qualities of aging to all these considerations. It may have to do with the polymerization of wood resins and lacquers, their crystallization and molecular alignment along lines of vibration, and the continued evaporation of elements of the wood sap and finish long after the instrument is completed. It's never been fully explained, even in the case of Stradivarius and Guarnerius violins, the most-studied instruments in history. But to the ears of some, the sound of the best vintage instruments has a magic that cannot be duplicated.

Charles Sawtelle in the Hot Rize band bus at the Gettysburg, Pennsylvania, Bluegrass Festival in 1985, playing a mid-1930s Martin D-18 with a rare sunburst. Although he was an innovative bluegrass stylist and a pioneer in introducing modern sound reinforcement and recording techniques to the bluegrass world, Sawtelle always preferred to play older instruments. *Photo by Larry Sandberg*

Other ears are less sensitive to the magic of the vintage sound, or are just as happy if not happier with the sound of a fine modern instrument. But once you've played through your first thirty or so old instruments it's impossible not to sense that they have at least a different, and perhaps greater, character than modern instruments. Therein lies their greatest charm. It seems that in the old days specifications were not rigidly adhered to and there was greater respect for the eye and hand than for blueprints, molds, and templates. The artisans and foremen had greater authority to make personal decisions. From instrument to instrument of the same model, neck width and depth, body and top wood thickness, fingerboard contour, finish color, bracing dimensions, and other important aspects may differ considerably—much more so than on today's factory instruments. And so, of course, do the sounds of the instruments. Their personalities run much deeper and are more distinct.

Why Some People Think New Guitars Are Better Anyway

Some people feel that fine modern factory guitars are made better than older ones were because the technology is better: quality control is more even; specs are standardized; the acoustic qualities of lacquers are tested scientifically; woods are hygrometer tested; factories are climate-controlled, and everything comes out the way it's supposed to.

This is probably true of low-price and mid-price guitars. For fine factory guitars, it's like arguing that Trump Tower is better made than Rheims Cathedral because architectural and engineering techniques have improved. But fortunately there are still guitar makers who are trying to build the equivalent of Rheims Cathedral.

Custom luthiers, as well as designers in the best of the high-quality factories, have studied the great instruments of the past and learned from them. With a little bit of looking you can find superb-sounding modern instruments that have a lot of magic already in them, even fresh out of the factory. Some of them already sound better than some vintage instruments, even without yet having the chance to age or be played in. The best of today's guitars are very impressive—far more impressive than the general run of instruments from the 1960s, 1970s, and 1980s.

There's also the very important matter of the instruments' playing feel. Today's market insists on low action and fast, low-contour necks that approach the ease of playing on an electric guitar; most manufacturers are doing their best to oblige this desire as well as they can. Older instruments were generally built with thicker, clubbier necks (especially in the days before the modern truss rod), and the standard of taste in those days accepted a stiffer action as well. You can find a certain number of vintage instruments that happen to feel fast anyway, and others can be made to feel faster with a good setup job and perhaps some minor surgery. But generally speaking, if like most people you prefer the feel of a modern guitar, than it's modern guitars you should be looking at.

Finally, new guitars look new and old guitars usually look kind of beat up. In some circles (bluegrass, for example, where folks are folks and heart is still more important than appearance for many of those folks), beat up instruments are acceptable and even desirable. But in most performance situations where you go before the general public, you'll find that people are miffed or outright offended if instruments, outfits, and attitudes aren't bright and shiny.

MODERN LUTHIERY: THE NEW GOLDEN AGE?

The 1990s witnessed phenomenal growth in the skill, prestige, and success of custom luthiers. Some have larger or smaller reputations, some have inflated reputations, some are better and some are worse. Some build full-time while others also do repair work for their bread and butter. Some are superb woodworkers whose instruments are works of art but sound only OK; others make instruments that sound as great as the great guitars of the past—and even though they may not have that old sound this year, they may start sounding old next year. Vintage guitars were new once, too.

There are many good reasons to think that we are now in a second golden age of American luthiery. Certainly the new luthiery appeals to those for whom the greed, numerology, and know-nothingism that characterizes too much of the vintage market has become distasteful. There are many in the vintage market who no longer find it fun themselves.

Modern luthiery strikes me as by far a more joyful enterprise, more full of interesting, committed souls, many of whom love sharing their profession. Not that elements of mystique and snobbery and pushiness aren't there, too; no one familiar with human nature would expect otherwise. Be that as it may, musicians who fifteen years ago wouldn't have looked at anything but a vintage instrument are now able to enjoy new ones.

More interesting still is that collectors, perhaps bored with the vintage market, are commissioning instruments from custom luthiers and enjoying the adventure of putting their money on new speculation instead of old predictability. Think of art collecting. You can put your money into Impressionists and be pretty sure you'll come out OK if you buy wisely. But if you're really interested in art, you can collect contemporary artists, based on your acumen and taste, and feel much more alive about it. You can't be sure about it, though. You can only be confident about your own judgment. It seems a more interesting way to live.

LONGEVITY

Respect for vintage guitars also creates an expectation, possibly a doomed one, that today's guitars will become heirloom instruments. It may not be a reasonable expectation. Guitars, by their very nature, want to self-destruct. Flamenco guitarists long ago learned to accept a short life-span for their lightly built instruments and classical guitarists have come to understand that their somewhat more robust instruments may, within their owners' lifetimes, also play out. It happened, notoriously, to Segovia's favorite instrument.

Perhaps all guitarists should reach the *flaminquista's* mental accommodation in their own thought. Many of today's guitars are fairly lightly built in order to sound good from the get-go without the playing-in time of a heavier, more tightly constructed instrument. Others copy vintage attributes, like light bracing designs, which were once abandoned because they were thought too fragile. Some use completely new designs, especially in bracing, that have not passed the test of time. Sometimes these attributes represent marketing as much as luthiery decisions. In any case, they are largely untested and their robustness remains to be proven. It's good to accept that guitars, even expensive ones, may not last forever. That was probably true of vintage guitars from the first, pre-war golden age of luthiery as well. We only respect and admire the ones that survived. How many of the ones whose tops collapsed fifty years ago, whose sides split, and whose brace separated from the tops and backs are there left to admire today? Most of them probably became firewood.

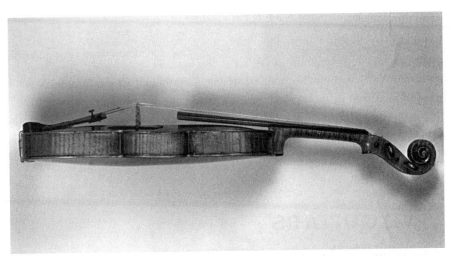

This Maggini violin has been around for a few hundred years. It's easy to see that the string forces compress it inward. Inside, a "soundpost"—a dowel inside the violin body—adds to the top's ability to resist imploding. Flattop guitars, on the other hand, by their very nature have to endure string pressure that wants to pull the instrument apart. It's a wonder they don't explode. *Violin courtesy Fred Oster; photo by Larry Sandberg*

PROS AND CONS OF BUYING A USED GUITAR

	USED	VINTAGE/COLLECTIBLE	NEW
Price	Cheaper when bought at fair value. Be careful not to pay vintage price for an instrument that is merely used.	Most expensive when good-condition instruments are involved. Sometimes better deals are possible on styles that are not currently in vogue or on instruments that are not in original condition.	More expensive, though some top-of-the-line models now cost as much or more than beat-up vintage instruments that may sound better. When comparing to used and vintage instruments, be sure to compare at discounted street price, not manufacturer's list.
Value	More likely to retain approximate current value if purchased at a fair price from a private individual. May appreciate in long term if a good instrument.	Will maintain value or appreciate in long term if purchased at reasonable price. May be quickly sellable only at a loss if you paid top dollar.	Immediate or short-term depreciation likely. However, a fine instrument is likely to appreciate in the long term.
Condition	Whatever you get.	Whatever you get.	Brand spanking shiny new, for a while.
Sound	Usually played in.	Usually played in.	Needs playing in.
Prestige	Big in hip circles, and then only if you have a hip instrument.	Big among those who know what it is or know how much you paid for it.	Good if you value newness and think used means tacky.
Structure	Depends on instrument and age. Modern plywood is probably more stable than the solid wood used on cheap instruments of the 1950s and 1960s.	Woods probably better and better aged. Glues and neck reinforcement probably inferior to modern instruments.	As a rule, most new low- and mid-range instruments have better glue and neck reinforcement than instruments from the 1950s and 1960s.
Features	Small bodies, certain woods and ornaments, etc., are less commonly found among today's production models than among used instruments.	Same as for used.	Modern truss rods, low-contour necks, and built-in electronics are only available on new or very recent used models.
Outlook	If after five, ten, or sixty years of use the neck is still good and the body is relatively uncracked, the instrument will probably stay stable unless you change climate, strings, etc.	Same as for used.	You don't know what's going to happen. Manufacturer's warranty and reputation are your only security.
Warranty	Usually no, unless you negotiate individually for dealer warranty. Most mail-order dealers sell on approval.	Same as for used.	Yes, from manufacturer.

FINE GUITARS

Becoming an Expert

This is not a book about vintage guitars. There's enough information there for a couple of books of their own, so I won't try to make you an expert.

If you want to learn more about vintage guitars, start with the books, magazines, and book and instrument dealer catalogs listed in the Resources section at the end of this book. Don't forget to see what your public library has. But that's only the barest of starts. You then have to make it your business to seek out places where there are vintage guitars and absorb everything you can about them. Get your hands on as many as possible. After a year or so, things will begin to fall into place, assuming that you can spend time around enough instruments. But remember that the real experts—and I'm not one of them—have about thirty years' head start on you. And they've got banjos, mandolins, electric guitars, and a few other instruments under their belts as well.

The same is true of contemporary guitars. Living in a city where there a number of local guitar builders helps. Check the yellow pages and magazines to look for boutique guitar stores that sell a few custom instruments or that specialize in them. Seek out custom instruments among musicians—some luthiers have waiting lists so long that you'll never see their products in stores.

Great Names of the Past

For most people, vintage flattop guitars mean vintage Martins and maybe a few Gibsons. Yet there were many more guitar manufacturers in the first heyday of the American guitar. Here are a few names from the past that you should know about. If you start hanging around with guitar buffs you'll hear these names often, sometimes spoken with reverence. You may even come across some of these instruments yourself. Some of these brands have died more than once, only to be revived over the years by new companies for different product lines, so don't be surprised if you still see them today—even on instruments imported from Asia. Remember that some of these makers are better than others and some produced several lines and models in a variety of quality ranges.

> Bacon & Day (mainly a banjo maker)
> Bruno (C. Bruno & Son; a few were subcontracted by Martin)
> Ditson (subcontracted by other makers including Martin)
> Harwood
> Haynes
> Kalamazoo (Gibson's economy line)
> Larson Brothers (marketed under the brand names Prairie State,
>   Euphonon, Stahl, and Maurer)
> Lyon & Healy (also includes various subcontracted models)
> Orpheum (mainly a banjo maker)
> Regal (Mostly cheapies, but their top-of-the line Recording King
>   was good. The brand name has gone through many changes of
>   style and ownership over the years.)
> Stella (Comment as for Regal, above.)
> Vega/Vegaphone (mainly a banjo maker)
> Washburn (not the same as the present Washburn company)
> Weymann (mainly a banjo maker)

This Harmony guitar from the mid-1960s (?) sounded terrific—while it lasted. *Photo by Larry Sandberg*

Junk Chic

You might from time to time run into people who collect low-grade and obscure guitars. Twenties Oahu Hawaiian guitars with palm tree paint jobs, 1950s Supro resophonic guitars that you can float in your bathtub, booming 1930s Stella twelve-strings, clean-sounding 1960s Harmony Sovereigns (if you can find one with a straight neck): these guitars are subject matter enough for a book of their own. Some are better than fine guitars for producing period sounds.

These instruments have a fascination all their own. Many are quite rare, if only because they weren't made well enough to survive long. (And, being cheaper, they were also more prone to being abused and discarded.) Some, like goat cheese, have strong and unmistakable characters. They provide incredible opportunities for one-upsmanship. If you want to learn about Martins and Gibsons, you can memorize a half dozen books and read some articles and hang out on the scene for a while and be three-quarters of the way toward being an expert. (That last quarter is always the hardest, though.) If you want to be an expert on old Regals, Stellas, and Kalamazoos, where are you going to even start?

11 At the Point of Purchase

DEALING WITH DEALERS

Finding a Good Dealer

A good retail business is run with the idea that it's possible to turn a decent profit by providing honest, professional service to the customer. Many, perhaps most, guitar stores are like this.

I wish there were some litmus test to separate the good dealers from the bad ones, but there isn't. A stock of both relatively inexpensive and high-quality new and used merchandise, an affiliated teaching staff, and a repair center (especially one authorized by major brands) are usually good signs, but not always. A sloppy-looking hole-in-the-wall could be the lair of a sleazoid, or merely the business place of an unkempt musician who loves guitars, manages to make a living with a high turnover of mostly used instruments at fair prices, and has never been able to raise the capital for major brand franchises.

Keep away from stores that stock mostly cheap off-brand Asian imports and whose stock of major brands and high-quality guitars is small or nonexistent. These are usually bad signs. Mall stores tend to be not so great but it's not fair to generalize. The big box, mass-market chain has a life of its own, with its own advantages and disadvantages. Sometimes you can get a good deal there, particularly on your kid's first or second electric guitar.

All other things being equal, you'll usually (though not always) get a better choice of merchandise and more knowledgeable service from a specialized guitar shop than from a band instrument dealer who also stocks a sideline of guitars.

Try to get a feel for the atmosphere of the establishment. Do they just want to sell people a piece of goods and move them out the door, or do they seem to want to cultivate repeat business from a loyal clientele? Does the dealer get uptight when you ask questions, or are you learning more about guitars each time you visit? Assuming that you treat the instrument and the people with respect and show that you're serious about learning and about making a purchasing decision, will they let you play their guitars?

The best bet, of course, is to ask around. Local music teachers and professional musicians are often good sources.

Finally, a dealer should be willing to tune the instrument and play it for you, and to let you sit in a corner and try it out yourself. Twenty years of listening to beginners try out guitars has most dealers ready to climb the walls at the drop of an E chord, but they still owe you this courtesy. In return, you should treat the instrument carefully, watch out for zipper, belt buckle, and pick scratches, and play in an inoffensive manner.

Negotiating Setup

An honest dealer will not knowingly sell you a faulty instrument. But business ethics (which are, after all, to ethics as military music is to music) don't compel them to be scrupulously certain that every instrument is set up absolutely perfectly. Most of the student-level instruments in guitar shops (and in the hands of students, for that matter) could be improved by about twenty minutes' worth of attention to nut and saddle from a competent technician.

Thirty-five years ago it was much easier than it is now to find a good guitar shop that would not put an instrument—*any* instrument— up on the wall until it had been set up and adjusted to be the best it could be. Because this required time and effort, these shops could not discount their instruments as highly as other shops that sold guitars right out of the box. The Crazy Eddie mentality has pretty much sacrificed service to discount in today's marketplace, so dealers now rarely pay that degree of attention to any but the highest-priced instruments—if even then.

However, dealers who have a repair shop or a skilled staff member may be happy to make small adjustments at no charge if it means making a sale. If a little more work is required (say, replacing a nut or saddle or some fairly extensive shaping), even a nominal charge might not be out of line on a discounted instrument. Don't be afraid to say something like "I like the sound of this guitar, but can it be made more comfortable to play?" Most dealers will either oblige or explain to you why they think that the guitar should be left the way it is. Some may explain that, given the selling price of the instrument, they will have to charge for the adjustment. On the face of it, accept this as reasonable.

Negotiating Approval or Warranty Terms

Some dealers will allow you to return an instrument *for credit* after a few days if it turns out you don't like it (and, of course, if you haven't damaged it in any way). This is a very reasonable stance. If you're not certain that you know what you're doing and if you need some time to get used to the instrument or seek advice, a for-credit return is a good deal to look or ask for. But (except in the case of faulty merchandise) asking for a total refund would be out of line with normal business practices.

When you purchase a new instrument, you're usually protected by a manufacturer's warranty. In the case of a used instrument, you are protected by whatever warranty you can negotiate with the dealer and obtain in writing. In addition, most states and localities give you certain rights in addition to warranty terms; for example, grossly faulty merchandise is held to be "unmarketable" in some states, and you may be entitled to a full refund on your purchase price. Unfortunately, it may be necessary to aggressively research and insist on your rights, perhaps with the help of a legal advisor, before you can obtain them. Purchasing with a credit card may also give you some additional protection against faulty merchandise.

Negotiating Trade-In

I'm strongly in favor of beginners starting off with a fairly inexpensive instrument and moving up later, when they have a better idea of what they want. Some dealers offer accommodating trade-in policies after six months or a year. Find out about them while you're still shopping around for your first guitar. In some cases they're just a way for the dealer to make money; other dealers have more reasonable terms.

If you move up to a pricey instrument, I'd suggest you seriously consider hanging onto your original instrument as a knock-around guitar, if your budget allows.

Sales and Marketing Techniques

As you make the rounds of music stores, you'll see that each manufacturer's line has a fairly bewildering array of features that include woods, ornamentation, grades of tuning hardware, and structural features such as scalloped braces. These feature sets exist in the guitar business for the same purpose they exist in the bicycle, camera, and electronics equipment businesses: to establish market positions and provide the dealer with sales points to use with customers.

The marketing game is based on two key concepts: "price point" and "step-up features." Price points are increments that reflect the customer's budget: do you have two, three, or four hundred dollars to spend? Step-up features are distinguishing features within price ranges: for only $100 more, you can have scalloped bracing, Schaller tuners, and rosewood instead of mahogany. A manufacturer will usually try, if possible, to come up with at least one important (or important-seeming) feature to distinguish its guitars from it's competitors' guitars in a given price bracket. For example, manufacturer X may be offering the only instruments with scalloped bracing at the $700 level.

The acoustic guitar is a fairly simple and conservative instrument, so manufacturers can't really get into the degree of technological competition that causes the rapid turnover of product lines and specifications that you find in, for instance, the camera market. Even so, you'll find that there are changes in product line from year to year as each maker strives to come up with competitive new features at each price point.

In my opinion, many of the step-up features offered on low-range and midrange guitars are fairly meaningless when considered by themselves. There *are* differences in tuning hardware but you can live with whatever you've got. The sound differences between mahogany, rosewood, and maple are less pronounced and consistent in laminates than they are in solid woods, though certainly each of these woods appears more or less pleasing to your eye. Fine points of bracing only make a real difference when the rest of the instrument is well-enough made overall to respond to them. You're better off trying to develop a sense of what makes a given instrument sound and feel best to you when you hold it in your lap and play it, rather than trying to sort out catalog descriptions and feature sets.

The marketing techniques described here are used mostly to sell mass-market, imported laminate guitars. In the case of fine instruments, there is more of an assumption that sales are going to be made to expert buyers, and the differences between instruments more truly reflect genuine differences in quality and construction.

Discounts

Most factory guitars are sold to dealers at terms that permit discounting from list price. How much, if any, of a discount you obtain depends on competition and trade practices in your area and on the dealer's standard practices. It's always worth trying to negotiate in a businesslike way on price. Wholesale discount schedules may vary among makers, meaning that dealers' retail discounts have to vary in accordance.

As a rule, you should expect to receive a discount in inverse proportion to service and other side benefits. Some big-box, high-volume retailers customarily discount 30 to 40 percent, as do some mail-order houses. However street prices in your area might be 20 percent off at best and, in a place where there's little competition, you might be lucky to get much of a discount at all. The availability of mail-order and Internet merchants, however, mean that competition is pretty much everywhere these days.

Remember that if you're buying a case, strings, and any accessories, these are also subject to price negotiation. Look at the total price when you're all done. There's no point in haggling for a discount on the guitar and losing it all back on the accessories.

Mail-Order Brides

I've always lived in or near a population center with an ample selection of competitively priced instruments to choose from. If you're out in the sticks, you're facing a much more limited set of choices. You're better off if you can sample an instrument before you buy it, but if your neighborhood offers a meaninglessly small range of instruments to sample from, then maybe you'll be better off taking your chances with a mail-order bride (or groom). A mail-order or Internet merchant should offer approval terms that allow you to return the instrument within a few days if you don't like it for any reason. Usually you eat the freight and insurance fees, hardly a bitter pill to swallow.

If you order by mail, you should have complete and unconditional approval privileges (except if you mar or damage the instrument) and it should be understood that the refund, minus freight and insurance, should go back to you at your discretion, not into credit from the retailer toward another purchase. Warranty and any other terms should be spelled out to your satisfaction. Using a credit card gives you some protection in case of dispute. To avoid misunderstanding, you should also clarify whether it's going to be your responsibility or the seller's to deal with the shipping agent in case of damage in transit.

CHECKING OUT THE GUITAR

The problems described here are discussed in greater deal in other sections of this book. This is just a quick checklist of things to look for and ask about.

Structure

1. Are the woods laminate or solid? Ask! Industry standards in labeling and describing merchandise in catalogs and on the sales floor are far too lax when it comes to woods.
2. Are there any cracks or other obvious faults?
3. As you sight down the neck from the fingerboard toward the bridge, does the neck seem to conform to the standards discussed in the earlier sections of this book on neck angle and fingerboard relief? (See Chapter 5, page 81.) It takes an expert to tell if it's perfect or not, but you should be able to see at least whether something appears to be grossly wrong.
4. Do the tuners work smoothly and sensitively?
5. Is anything obviously loose? Does it rattle when you shake it? (Be gentle!)

Playing Qualities

Is the guitar comfortable to play? Pay attention to how it feels under both the fretting and picking hands. Analyze your feelings in term of the following:

1. How far and how hard it is to depress the strings.
2. The distance between strings.
3. The contour of the neck.
4. Do the strings seem too light or too heavy? You will have to learn from experience to judge the feel of a guitar itself independent of the string gauge. Ask the dealer what the string gauge is.
5. Does the guitar sound clean? Are there mechanical buzzes or rattles that might come from something loose? Do the strings buzz against the frets when you play only fairly loud? (You can expect a certain amount of buzz if you really wham the guitar.)
6. Does the guitar sound good?

Next, think about the following distinctions. The way you are going to learn to recognize these things is by comparing different guitars. Trying to learn what these words mean by playing only one guitar will get you nowhere.

1. Is it loud enough? Don't expect an inexpensive guitar to produce the volume of a better guitar. Just ask whether it seems loud enough to satisfy you. It probably does.
2. Is it soft enough? This is a hard test. A fine guitar gives a sense of fullness and presence even at a low volume. Expect an inexpensive guitar not to be as satisfying when you play it softly. But if it sounds too weak to give you pleasure, reject it.
3. Is the tone balanced? Try to detect whether the loudness of the low notes comes at the expense of the highs. This is a lot to ask of you because it implies that you have a cultivated ear and enough playing technique to produce emphasis on either the high or low strings at will. Do the best you can. Try to hear whether the high strings have the same fullness that the low strings have. Play some chords and see whether the note on the second string can be heard as clearly as the others, or whether it gets lost. (On a nylon-strung guitar, by the way, a weak third rather than second string is a more accurate giveaway of poor balance.)
4. Is the tone pure? Listen for rawness or abrasiveness, particularly on the high strings. Comparison will teach you to hear the difference between a ringing sound and an abrasive one.
5. Does the guitar sustain? Listen for how long its sounds linger in the air, and in your ear, after you've strummed or plucked it. Try playing one high note, say the first string tenth fret, and listen to how long it lasts. (However, if you're a beginner with weak fingers, you

may not yet have enough strength to hold down the strings long enough for the notes to die naturally. Do the best you can.)

6. Does the guitar sing? Sustain is the most important component of the singing quality, but (once you've made sure the guitar is accurately in tune) also listen for the total sense of fullness and strength in individual notes and for how well the different notes within a chord seem to fit together. Listen also for a clean, ringing quality that hangs in your ear like a pleasant aftertaste. The guitar's voice should have a sense of presence; it should sound as if it's right next to you, not as if you're hearing it through a closed door.

7. Is the guitar clear? Try strumming just the three bass strings with different chords. Do you hear three clean notes or a muddy glob of sound?

What If You Can't Play Yet?

No two ways about it, you've got a problem. You should try to learn to play at least a little on a rented or borrowed guitar before you go out to buy one. Or enlist the help of an experienced friend. If you're planning to take lessons, ask your prospective teacher for help. (It would be unprofessional, though, to ask your teacher to put more than a nominal amount of time and energy into looking and checking. Offer to pay the teacher's usual hourly rate for this service. It'll probably be well worth it.)

If none of these options are available, you are simply going to have to depend entirely on your dealer. If you have a good dealer, you'll do just fine.

12 Taking Care of Your Guitar

AROUND THE HOUSE

You'll probably never find a repair shop that doesn't urge you to keep your guitar in its case whenever you're not playing. To hear them talk, you'd think that it shouldn't be taken out of its case ever. But these are the people who see busted-up, shattered, bent, stepped-on, dropped, and spilled-on guitars day after day, and they have a pretty good idea of how many of those accidents occur when instruments have been left in a corner, across a chair, or against a bookcase instead of being put back in their case.

You are, however, entitled to temper their advice with your own judgment. After all, just because many home accidents happen on the stairs doesn't mean you should quit using the stairs. If you take out your guitar once a day for a one-hour playing session, it makes sense to put it back in its case when you're done. But if your habit is to grab the guitar for a few minutes every now and then in the course of the day, then you'll want it accessible. It might be reasonable to trade off risk for convenience, just as long as you know what you're doing. Sometimes when you have five or ten minutes to kill, the handiness of your guitar determines whether you'll play it or grab some junk food out of the fridge instead. You tell me: which of these choices makes you a Better Person?

Bearing in mind that your guitar is more vulnerable when you leave it lying around, here are a couple of tips for minimizing the dangers.

1. A favorite place for musicians to keep their guitar cases is laid horizontally across the arms of an armchair. It's a convenient height, and the guitar is protected. Tabletops are good for this too, but it's much more likely you'll have a free armchair than a free tabletop. Taking up an armchair with your guitar is easier to get away with if you're single.
2. If you keep your case on that armchair, you'll find it easier to get the guitar in and out impulsively if you keep only one latch locked.

(To get away with this, though, you've got to train yourself to latch up the case completely whenever it comes off the armchair.) Don't *ever* leave a guitar in a case with the top down and all the latches undone. You're too likely to pick up the case and have the top fly open and the guitar fall out. Does this sound like a paranoid warning? Ask a repair shop how often it happens!

3. If you want to leave your guitar leaning up against a wall or bookcase, at least find the safest spot for it. A corner is good, and a corner behind an armchair is better. Make sure there's no radiator or other heat source (including even a lamp) too close, and clear the area of moveable objects that might fall.

4. Think about investing in a store-bought guitar stand. Spend a few extra bucks to get one that's got soft coated surfaces at all contact points and that has enough weight, coupled with a low-enough center of gravity, to be stable. Lightweight cheapies don't do the job as well. Stands that rest on rails or four points are more stable than tripod stands.

5. Some people like to hang their guitar on the wall—though it's definitely better to do this with a second, knock-around guitar than with your primary instrument. Find an out-of-the-way spot away from heat sources, humidity, direct sunlight, and any other possible dangers. Remember that forced-air heat rises against the walls and can dry out a guitar much faster than nature intended it to. Mount something soft, like a foot-square piece of bulletin-board cork, on the wall where the guitar's back will touch it. Make sure the backing won't harm the guitar's finish, as some synthetics, especially vinyl, might. Hang the guitar from a secure hook and a secure material (a strong leather thong, venetian blind cord, or coated 18-gauge grounding wire, for example) tied securely around the third and fourth string tuning pegs. Alternatively, use a store-bought neck mount instead of hanging the guitar from a nail or peg. Check to see that everything is secure every so often, and when you put the guitar back on the wall, make sure that it's hanging securely before you let go of it. Even so, there are risks. Nothing is 100 percent secure. I like to keep a couple of guitars on the wall and, so far, I've been lucky.

If you have cats, dogs, ferrets, kids, airhead friends and relatives, or other strange creatures wandering around your home, rethink the above suggestions accordingly.

TEMPERATURE AND HUMIDITY

Changes in Climate

Changes in humidity are the greatest danger to your guitar. High humidity, especially when combined with heat, can loosen glue joints.

Sometimes humidity can even cause wood to swell and distort. Low humidity is also bad for guitars, since the resulting shrinkage causes cracking and seam separation. The greatest danger, though, is an abrupt and extreme change in humidity—especially from damp to dry.

Heat causes wood to expand while cold causes it to contract, so avoid abrupt temperature changes as well. In addition to cracking, temperature change can cause a condition called crazing or temperature checking, in which the finish develops tiny cracks similar to the texture of the cracked lacquer finishes of old paintings. It happens because the wood and finish expand and contract at different rates. The effect is generally only skin-deep but it doesn't look good. In severe cases it can actually leave the wood vulnerable. When you bring a chilled guitar in from the cold, try to leave it in its case for a while so it can warm up gradually.

Cracking isn't the only problem caused by climate. Different woods (for example, a spruce top and ebony fingerboard) expand and contract at different rates, and are likely to pull apart as well as to impart cracking stress on each other. And since wood expands and contracts along its grain pattern, abutting sections of wood with unmatched grain patterns (like back and sides) will expand and contract in different directions with similar results. (See Chapter 4 for more information on wood behavior.)

January Is the Cruelest Month

An arid climate, especially the arid microclimate of a heated home in wintertime, is another of the guitar's greatest enemies. There are various humidifiers on the market that you can insert into your guitar without a moist surface actually coming in contact with the wood. All of them are basically neater and more elegant variations on the idea of a wet sponge. (Damp-It is probably the best-known brand, though there are others.) The problem with all of them is that if you forget or are unable to keep the device consistently moist, you may be in worse trouble than you would have been without it. Home humidifiers have similar pros and cons. Bear in mind that home humidifiers, whether of the steam or ultrasonic variety, don't have much effect outside the room they're in. Whole-house humidifiers are a different story.

Somehow I've gotten through forty years of owning guitars with only a very few minor cracking problems that might have happened even with a humidifier.

Plywood won't crack from dryness, at least not all the way through. However, there are those who feel that the sound of plywood guitars deteriorates when they get excessively dry and that humidifying improves them.

It goes without saying that you should keep your guitar away from radiators, hot air ducts (and the walls around them), freezing drafts, attics or garages with no climate control, and so on.

No Cure for the Summertime Blues

I once had a knock-around guitar made by one of the cheap American manufacturers of the 1960s. It survived the first couple of decades of its life in the arid Southwest, but during its first summer in the steampits of northeastern Pennsylvania the back absorbed so much moisture that it swelled up into ripples like sand dunes. Then when it dried out in forced-air winter heat, the back straightened out a bit, developed lots of cracks, and shrank away from the sides. The top and neck also moved around some. After one more summer-to-winter cycle, it became unplayable and not worth fixing.

Three fine sixty-year-old flattops and a fine thirty-year-old archtop also made the Southwest-to-Northeast move. They stayed perfectly stable after the move and for ten years after, except for some very minor action changes with the seasons. The flattops moved back to the Southwest again and are doing fine. I hope I stay in that good a shape when I'm their age.

The other great summer guitar-killer is the superheated car trunk or interior. Guitar glues are not permanent. They are deliberately intended to be soluble under conditions of heat and humidity so that instruments can be disassembled and repairs made. The way a repair shop gets a neck loose, for example, is to pry it off with a spatula dipped in boiling water, with additional injections of hot water from a syringe, under infrared heat lamps. The effect of leaving your guitar inside your car in the hot sun is very similar. So is leaving your guitar outdoors on a sunny lawn or patio in its case. Don't do it.

Good Guitars Finish Last

The best way to deal with climate change is to buy a well-made guitar in the first place. Aged, properly finished, air-dried, quartersawed wood has the greatest stability. In less expensive instruments, a decent grade of laminate (plywood) stays more stable than a bad piece of solid wood. Cheap plywood with a junk core is worst of all.

Instruments built under factory-controlled humidity conditions tend to stay more stable than those built under high-humidity conditions. (Around 40 percent relative humidity is the textbook figure; some shops work a little higher.) As a rule, American and Japanese guitars are built in factories with sufficient humidity control, as are the better Korean and Taiwanese instruments. Not so the cheap Korean and Taiwanese junkers.

Being careful certainly helps the guitar, but remember also that a healthy mental attitude helps *you*. Take reasonable precautions but avoid paranoia. Remember that the guitar is there to be used, and that things that get used, no matter how precious, are subject to peril.

ROUTINE CLEANING
AND MAINTENANCE

Spit 'n' Polish

Well, save the spit for your parade-dress shoes, but polish is a good thing to apply to your guitar now and then. Nothing personal, but I've never understood people who let their guitars get grungy. I don't care so much that they look bad, but they're less pleasant to play when they're covered with dust, dried sweat, dead skin tissue, banana oil, chip dip, and other pickin' party souvenirs. And even if you don't care about how grunge feels or looks, you'll find that your wood vibrates more freely, your fingerboard plays more smoothly, and you're more attractive to (most) potential mates if you keep your guitar clean.

Go over your guitar with a little polish a couple of times a year. Several of the major guitar manufacturers make polishes that work well with contemporary nitrocellulose or acrylic lacquers. Oily polishes, like the ones marketed as "lemon oil," work better on unfinished surfaces like bridges and fingerboards, and may also be satisfactory for vintage instruments. Note any special directions. Generally, you don't need a lot; just enough to help the rag get the grit off.

I once heard of a viola player who used olive oil on an ancient instrument, but I've never tried it. Over-oiling unfinished areas with a natural oil will eventually clog up the wood. Waxes are no good—they coat the guitar—nor are heavy-duty treatments like tung oil that are more properly associated with finishing than with maintaining cleanliness.

Usually just a little polish on a clean cotton rag will do the job of keeping your guitar looking and feeling clean. Wipe it on and then wipe it off with a clean, dry rag. You can keep your frets and fingerboard feeling neat and smooth by rubbing it down with a polish-moistened wad of 0000-grade (extra-fine) steel wool. Don't let it scratch any of the finished parts of your guitar and don't wipe it down with the same rag you use for polishing the finish, because the rag will pick up steel particles that will scratch up your guitar. Oil the bridge too. Keeping the fingerboard and bridge regularly oiled may also help get them through a period of dry climate without cracking. Bridges and fingerboards, particularly ones made of ebony, are prone to cracking.

When a guitar gets really dirty, you might need more than elbow grease. Many music stores carry one brand or another of heavy-duty guitar/violin polish containing a little grit to get the real grunge off. This stuff creates the same trade-off problems for your guitar that rubbing compound does for your auto: it invariably removes a bit of the finish along with the grunge, even though it's not supposed to. So use it only when absolutely necessary. (I used to know a repairman whose favorite grunge remover was toothpaste. I mention this for anecdotal value, not as a suggestion.)

It's also good to blow or vacuum the dust out of the inside of your guitar whenever there's an accumulation, which might mean every couple of weeks or every few years depending on your environment. There's more to this than just being compulsive. Dust globs can accumulate potentially harmful moisture.

You'll also find that you wind up with a friendlier-feeling guitar, and longer-lasting strings as well, if you make sure your hands are clean before you take out your guitar and keep away from finger foods during a playing session.

Tuning Machine Maintenance

Your tuners have gears—probably of the usual metal screw-and-worm variety, though some of the modern lightweight enclosed gears are nylon. Gears wear out over the years and they wear out faster if they're made of nylon or cheap metal, or are poorly machined. Unless you have enclosed ("self-lubricating") gear trains, you can help them feel smoother and live longer if you wipe off the grit once or twice a year and relubricate them. White grease (such as the Lubri-Plate brand) is better than machine oil because it doesn't run. Just before a string change, spread a small dab over the gear worm using the end of a toothpick. As you wind and unwind the gear during the string change, the worm and screw will become coated with grease. Wipe off the excess when you're done.

Some tuners have a friction-adjusting screw in the peg shaft at the end of the peg button. It should be tight enough to put a comfortable amount of friction into the peg but should not be tightened down all the way. Adjust all six of them to your satisfaction once or twice a year. Each tuner should feel smooth but not loose enough to have any play. You'll also find that you can tune more quickly and easily if all your tuners feel about the same. If your guitar has a slotted headstock then it probably has classical-style tuners. The danger with these is that the adjusting screw that holds the gear screw in place can get loose and start to rattle, or even fall out. Get into the habit of making sure it's properly adjusted as part of your maintenance routine whenever you change strings.

Most machines are held in place by small mounting screws on the back of the headstock (or on the side for classical-style machines), and perhaps by a hex nut collar on the front of the headstock as well. Check them as part of your routine maintenance to make sure they haven't worked loose.

CASES

If you own an instrument of even medium value, you should have a hard case for it—what the music trade calls a "hard shell" case, abbreviated "HSC" in dealers' catalogs. The old-fashioned wooden ones work about as well as the new molded synthetic ones that some manufacturers (like Martin) offer, and both wood and synthetics come at different levels of quality. Synthetic cases are more waterproof but can warp if left in the sun; they also tend to absorb and hold heat much more than wood cases, whether from direct sunlight or simply from a summer car interior. (You should never leave a guitar out in the sun in its case anyway, but remember to never overheat an empty case either—no matter what it's made of.)

At the low end are inexpensive cardboard cases—"soft shell" cases or "SSCs"—that don't really offer much puncture or extreme trauma protection. You should buy a hard case for a fine guitar, although lots of people store guitars in SSCs for years. They'll do for around-the-house storage and an occasional car trip.

Strength is only one issue in a hard case. There also has to be a sufficiently thick layer of soft, resilient material between the outer shell and the guitar in order to provide a cushioning effect. The role of the cushioning material is extremely important; a mere shell, no matter how strong, will not sufficiently protect the instrument unless a resilient intermediate layer is also present. The padding must also hold the instrument tightly enough to keep it from moving around within the case.

The quality of the latch hardware, hinges, and other fittings also contributes to the effectiveness and longevity of a case. Latches with a hinged catch, like the ones on steamer trunks, are preferable because they're a little harder to accidentally dislodge. Some people use case covers to protect their cases from wear and from the elements; case covers also help protect the latches.

Expect to pay upward of $100 for a new hard case. Used ones are hard to find, but try looking for one first. It doesn't matter if a case looks a little beat up as long as it's sound. There's always duct tape, especially for that professional, road-warrior look.

At the high end are the specialized travel cases for professional use. The best-known are the triangular fiberglass cases made by Mark Leaf, the molded fiberglass cases made by the Calton company, and the trunklike cases made by Anvil and other companies. They're all heavy, but the Anvil-style cases are heaviest; they're really for guitarists who have roadies to carry their equipment. Because their latches and handles lie flat, they are technically the only style of case that meets ATA (American Transportation Association) safety specs.

Another kind of case to consider is the padded, soft carrying bag known among professionals as a "gig bag." Gig bags are light and convenient, but dangerous—a broken neck or headstock being the main peril. Certainly they can make sense for knock-around instruments, and they aren't as risky to the bodies of solid-body electric guitars as to those of acoustic guitars. But the neck, if you'll permit me to run a metaphor through the Cuisinart, is their Achilles' heel. Many musicians find the convenience of gig bags worth trading off against the risks, and have gone a lifetime without damaging an instrument. Others haven't.

Just as important as the case's material is the way it holds the guitar. A guitar, like the brain in its skull, can be damaged if it is shaken around within its case. The case should fit snugly, like a shoe, and there should be some resilient, trauma-absorbing material between the shell and the instrument. If you acquire a mismatched case that's a little too loose, experiment with towels, closed-cell foam, or some other suitable padding until the guitar doesn't move around. (Don't use vinyl or other such material that could harm your guitar's finish.) It's especially important that the neck shouldn't move around—be sure to check it for up and down as well as sideways movement and, if necessary, add a little padding to the top over the spot where the neck rests in order to hold it in place. It's good if you can find a case that supports your guitar precisely under the heel, but most cases don't.

Also be careful of what you put into your case. Loose pens, capos, strap buckles, and tape cassettes can do lots of cosmetic damage and may even cause some real trauma. Don't carry liquids in your case. Vinyl articles and straps, as well as some other plastics, chemically interact with some finishes and may cause severe blemishes if left in contact with the instrument. Buckle-less leather or cloth straps are safest.

Finally, remember to loosen the strings whenever you ship your guitar or place it in foreseeable danger—in an airplane cargo hold, for example. If the guitar does suffer trauma there, whatever happens will only be made worse by the tension of the strings. The endpin, because it sticks out beyond the body, is also a vulnerable point and can cause damage if the guitar is shaken within the case or if trauma causes the end of the case to compress. Some guitarists remove the endpin before shipping or air travel.

CRACKS AND BREAKS

Accept the fact that with time and use (or abuse) things will go wrong, just as they do with your car, your body, and your elected public officials. (See Chapters 5 and 6 for more information about what can go wrong with your guitar.)

A guitar with almost any crack or break, no matter how bad, can be repaired or restored—even if it means replacing an entire neck or top. The question is whether it's worth the repair shop's time, skills, and material—which translates into *your* money—to do the job. You also have to find a person suited to the job. Most repair people know how to deal well enough with the equivalents of cuts, bruises, and the common cold, but extensive restoration work calls for luthiery skills that only select members of the profession possess.

Routine Crack Repair

Get it into your head that, in spite of all precautions, guitars sometimes crack. It's not necessarily the wood's fault nor the maker's. It's nature. It's wood's *thing* to crack. A crack may diminish your guitar's resale value; but, if properly repaired, it won't diminish the instrument's acoustic or structural integrity.

It's a good idea to have cracks and separations taken care of as soon as you notice them. Serious cracks need professional attention—especially long cracks, cracks where the wood has separated, and cracks where the wood is not on the same level on either side of the split. They need to be clamped after gluing and perhaps reinforced by tiny wooden "studs" (also called "cleats") glued into the inside of the crack through the sound hole. The worst cracks, where the wood has separated and left a gap, need to be repaired by inserting wood splints into the gap. These repairs involve special tools and complicated techniques. Leave them to a pro.

However, you may be able to deal with baby cracks on your own. Most cracks begin as tiny hairline splits. If you're handy, self-confident, and promise not to get mad at me when your finish shows some glue marks when you're done, you can fix it yourself. If you follow these steps you may be able to stop the crack from growing larger, or at least slow it down. Just try rubbing in a thin bead of white, polyvinyl resin glue (like Elmer's) and then quickly wipe off the excess with a moist rag. (White glue is better for tiny cracks than an aliphatic resin glue—like Tite-Bond brand—because it's less viscous and therefore penetrates tiny cracks better. But for most other repairs, the pros prefer aliphatic resin glue.)

You should probably only mess around like this on an inexpensive guitar that has lost its pristine glow. In most cases, you're probably better off letting a pro do the job.

Bridge and Fingerboard Cracks

You may be able to slow down a bridge crack with the above method for a while, but the bridge crack always wins in the end; so, you're probably better off having it repaired or replaced promptly. Sometimes a repair shop can save a cracked bridge by gluing, clamping, and running thin dowelling through it to reinforce the joint—it depends on the bridge shape and where the crack is. But usually cracked bridges need to be replaced. It's a routine procedure. Replacement bridges in common shapes and sizes are easily available from trade suppliers, but replacements for exotic bridges may have to be carved from scratch, requiring expert skills.

Ebony wears and feels better than rosewood but it's also more prone to shrinkage; so, ebony fingerboards commonly develop hairline cracks over the years. People usually just leave them until they become unsightly, at which point a repair shop can easily fill them with a mixture of epoxy and ebony dust, making them invisible until they appear again five or ten years later. It's a situation you can live with.

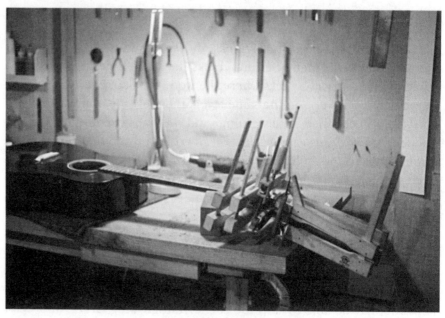
Worst-case scenario: a neck snapped at the headstock. *Photo by E. V. Dick*

The Trauma Unit

It may be wood's thing to crack, but it's definitely not wood's thing to have the pointy end of a guitar case latch shoved through its face, to fall four feet to a concrete floor, or to be swung at the speed of a fastball into a mike stand. Let any of these things happen and you'll break your heart as well as your guitar.

Somehow, I've gotten this far in life without these experiences. (Knock wood. Or, come to think of it, maybe that's not such a good idea.) But my friends who have had these experiences all speak of a sinking feeling in the pit of the stomach, a slowing down of reality, an adrenaline rush, and a rising feeling of mingled anger and despair. In the end, they all got their guitars back in perfect playing condition, and with few scars to show for it.

This isn't a repair book, so it doesn't go into repair techniques in detail. But it's important for you to know that just about anything in the way of repair is possible. Whether it's cost-effective or not for a given instrument is another story. And, of course, a job as serious as replacing an entire top is roughly the equivalent of a brain transplant. For better or worse, your guitar won't be the same guitar any more with a new top.

Trauma is one area where laminate guitars can be a problem. Plywood resists cracking and is probably also a bit stronger than solid wood when it comes to taking a hit, but once you do manage to punch your way through it, it doesn't just break; it shatters. Remember that in plywood, the plies are glued with their grain structure perpendicular to each other for maximum strength, similar to the plies in corrugated cardboard. Each individual ply fractures along its own grain pattern, so instead of getting the comparatively neat, easy-to-patch gap you would have in solid wood, you wind up with a messy, jagged-edged hole that looks like a cartoonist's representation of an explosion. The only solution is to cut out and replace an entire section.

Twenty years ago only student guitars were laminate and repair shops usually advised you to replace the instrument or settle for a quick-and-dirty repair solution. Now that laminates are also used for fairly pricey, good-sounding instruments that are worth repairing, most repair people have had to learn to accept plywood repair and do their best.

PART

2 **Market Survey**

HOW TO USE THIS SECTION

This part of the book provides information about many of the major manufacturers of fine guitars, their history, and their contributions to the history of the American guitar. Those companies that have made the greatest historical contributions or that make the most interesting and significant instruments get pride of place. Also included are some basics about many of the makers and importers of beginner and midrange guitars, including the imported, laminate-body guitars that make up a large part of today's guitar sales. In addition to the information on these wholesalers, there is also information on custom luthiers and limited-production shops. There can't be even a pretense of completeness in this chapter; essentially, it's just to give you an idea of what's out there.

The first edition of this book gave detailed information and specifications on the various models available from the various manufacturers in a second section that was, essentially, a purchaser's guide. And as happens with retail purchasing guides—especially in the case of importers and offshore manufacturers—this information became outdated too quickly.

Fortunately, the World Wide Web now makes it unnecessary to repeat this experience. In this revised edition, less is more. This book now lists the Web sites of manufacturers for whom addresses are currently available, so you can keep up with the latest models and other developments on the Net.

Because of this change model specs are dealt with here only when they're of historical or documentary significance. Historically, for example, the size, shape, and overall development of the American guitar is inextricably bound up with the development of Martin's model specifications, so there's no way to avoid—nor would anyone want to avoid—setting forth in detail Martin's system of model designations. Now that other companies are moving into the forefront of American guitar manufacturing, their models too must be considered in detail when appropriate. For history and for overall perspective, this is a worthy guide. But for the latest catalog information, get it where you can get it best: on the Web.

Please remember that the following listings don't claim to be comprehensive. They do claim to include the most widely marketed brands of high-quality and American-made guitars—the ones you're most likely to encounter as you shop in neighborhood music stores, big-box music stores, boutique and professional guitar shops, and even the worst ways to shop for a musical instrument: by catalog or on the Web. (They're the worst ways because—even though mail orders do or at any rate should give you approval rights, you still can't hold the instrument in your hands before you order.) Other criteria include accessibility: attendance at the major trade shows; listings in trade directories; availability of catalogs; a presence on the Web; and so on.

In addition, there are a few extra selected listings of custom and specialty makers—eclectic and by no means comprehensive. There is also a listing of the Web sites for importers of beginner's and mid-range, primarily laminate-body, guitars.

APPROXIMATE STANDARD GUITAR SIZES

Most manufacturers use a system of size designation based on the traditions established by the Martin company. Here is a rough guide for reference.
(See the Martin section, page 226, for greater detail as it pertains to Martin guitars.)

NAME	BODY LENGTH	UPPER BOUT WIDTH	LOWER BOUT WIDTH	MAXIMUM DEPTH
* Concert or O	18³/₈	10	13¹/₂	4¹/₄
Grand Concert or OO	18⁷/₈	10⁷/₈	14⁵/₁₆	4¹/₈
Classical	19¹/₈	11	14¹/₂	4¹/₈ +
Auditorium OOO or OM	19³/₈	11¹/₄	15	4¹/₈
Grand Auditorium or OOOO	20¹/₈	11¹¹/₁₆	16	4¹/₈
Jumbo or J	20¹/₈ +	11¹¹/₁₆ +	16 +	4⁷/₈
Dreadnought	20	11¹/₂	15⁵/₈	4⁷/₈

Instruments this size and smaller are also known as parlor guitars.

HOW TO READ GUITAR SALES LITERATURE

Since you're all sophisticated readers, you know that when you visit manufacturers' Web sites, look at their sales literature, or listen to a salesperson in the wrong kind of music store, you may have to take what you hear with a grain of salt. The following examples illustrate.

Caveat Emptor

Presented below is a selection of hype from the sales literature and Web sites of several manufacturers, who will remain nameless.

WHAT THEY SAY	WHAT THEY MEAN
"Reality will slowly disappear when the player touches the strings."	Reality quickly disappeared when the copywriter touched the keyboard, or touch strings only at your own risk!
"...puts out a really big, robust sound at the same time delicate and expressive."	We can't make up our minds what kind of guitar this is, so maybe it's for you if you can't decide what kind of guitar you want.
"We've searched the world over to supply our luthiers with the finest available materials."	Traditional guitar-making woods and sources are too expensive for us.
". . . the legend . . ."	We're coasting on our reputation.
"Classic designs with modern technologies."	We switched from solid woods to laminates in our low-end models.
"Our instruments combine the skills of both craftspeople and engineers."	Our instruments combine the skills of craftspeople, engineers, and accountants.
"This guitar will make you a star."	Everyone will be famous for fifteen minutes, anyway.
" . . . finely aged woods."	We discovered a pile of old lumber at the back of our warehouse.
"Our unbounded creativity and uncontained perfectionism compel us to produce only the most finely made products."	Our guitars are more expensive than comparable products.
"An instrument that brings out all your native talent."	Six years of lessons didn't help, so what makes you think spending two grand on a new guitar will?
(No words—just a picture of a good-lookin' young guy with a guitar and a good-lookin' young woman staring adoringly at the good-lookin' young guy.)	Sex sells. Good luck, dude.

If you take manufacturers' hype with a grain of salt, you should take this book with an equal dose as well. Not all of these opinions are shared by everyone. And there's always a chance that there could be just a plain mistake somewhere as well.

In order to make the best use of this section, it's a good idea to make yourself familiar with the information in the rest of this book. For example, learning that an instrument has "scalloped bracing" isn't much good if you don't know what scalloped bracing is and how meaningful the term (or buzzword) actually may be in the case of your particular instrument. This is the sort of stuff you find out in Part I.

13 Guitar Manufacturers

BREEDLOVE GUITARS

19885 Eighth St.
Tumalo, Oregon 97701
Web www.breedloveguitars.com
Breedlove uses a unique bracing design with a cantilevered bridge truss
in order to achieve a distinctive tone that I would describe, from my
limited experience playing Breedlove models, as an unusual and very
dark sound that is selective in the frequencies it chooses to emphasize.
Breedlove offers a top line and an S Series of less expensive models.

COLLINGS GUITARS

1125 Signal Hill Dr.
Austin, Texas 78737
www.collingsguitars.com
Bill Collings began making guitars in 1973, and now specializes in producing guitars drawing heavily and unabashedly on the inspiration of
pre-war Martins in both appearance and their clean, punchy sound quality. Although original elements do appear in Collings's work, he uses his
considerable talents as a woodworker and as a judge of high-quality raw
materials to make excellent products that conform to time-tested tastes.

In addition to models inspired by the classic Martin dreadnought,
OM, and OO guitars, Collings offers a model based on the Gibson J-185,
an archtop, and the Baby Collings travel model.

DANA BOURGEOIS GUITARS

Ceased operations as this book was going to press.

J. W. GALLAGHER & SON GUITARS

Box 128
Wartrace, Tennessee 37183
www.dnj.com/gallagher

John W. Gallagher, a cabinetmaker since 1939, turned to guitars in the mid-1960s and soon developed a reputation as a maker of distinguished instruments of high quality. The small Gallagher shop, now run by J. W.'s son Don, is still a fairly small production shop. Gallaghers have been used by many folk and country performers and recording artists, including Don Potter (the studio guitarist who did such exquisite recording work with The Judds) and Doc Watson. Older (J. W.) Gallaghers are well worth searching out. Gallagher offers bodies of both rosewood and mahogany but it has always seemed that the Gallagher sound is essentially a warm yet clear one that is best shown off with mahogany.

Gallagher is best known for its dreadnought guitars, which, in both square-shouldered and slope-shouldered models, form the greater part of its catalog. The company also offers an auditorium-size finger-style model called the Ragtime Special.

GIBSON MUSICAL INSTRUMENTS

Corporate Offices:

1818 Elm Hill Pike
Nashville, Tennessee 37210
www.gibson.com

Acoustic Guitar Production:

Gibson Montana Division
1894 Orville Way
Bozeman, Montana 59715
Gibson also imports the Epiphone line of student and journeyman-quality guitars.

Background

Orville Gibson (1856–1918) was a Michigan guitarist, woodworker, luthier, and onetime shoe clerk of whose early life we know little. We do know he possessed enough acumen to persuade a group of businessmen to found The Gibson Mandolin-Guitar Manufacturing Company in Kalamazoo, Michigan, in 1902. (By the 1920s, the company was also a major banjo maker as well.) Orville Gibson was never actually a principal in the firm. Instead, he drew fees and royalties as a design consultant and made most of his contributions within the first two years of the company's existence. His design principles, which chiefly involved the careful shaping of arched tops and backs, seem for the most part to have been worked out in his private shop by the 1890s.

Orville Gibson's work with both guitars and mandolins was influenced by the arched-top and -back design of violins. The first Gibson guitars were archtop models with round sound holes. These instruments represent an evolutionary step that, like the platypus, never went anywhere. They largely disappeared from fashion by the 1920s. Dark-sounding and slow to speak, they were unable to provide the crispness and rhythmic pliability demanded of the guitar by American music as it moved into the 1930s.

By the 1920s, the legendary acoustical engineer Lloyd Loar had guided the Gibson company to preeminence as a manufacturer of banjos, archtop guitars, and mandolins. The now-classic designs of the Mastertone banjo, the L-5 archtop guitar, and the F-5 mandolin date from this period, and a number of interesting flattop guitars were also in production around this time. Gibson also pioneered the adjustable tension rod, on which it held the exclusive patent until the late 1950s.

For the most part Gibson's better flattops were overshadowed in the marketplace by Martin (as they have been throughout Gibson's history). Gibson's low end, however, was lower than Martin's (and even lower still if you take into account the cheapie Kalamazoo line that Gibson started during the Depression). Gibsons became the Model T of American guitars during this period.

The best Gibson banjos, mandolins, electric guitars, and archtop acoustic guitars are outstanding instruments, ranking among the greatest of their kind ever produced. Gibson has also made many excellent flattops. The Nick Lucas models (1928–38) and the J-200 (originating in the 1938 model then called the Super Jumbo, and still made today) are among the all-time classics. Of earlier (pre–World War II) Gibsons, even the low-end models are instruments of character.

Historically, Gibsons have had a characteristic sound that is definably distinct from Martins. What most people now think of as the Gibson sound is typified by the guitars generally known as jumbo dreadnoughts, especially the J-45 model. The jumbos are plump, large-bodied guitars, like dreadnoughts but with more rounded shoulders— pigeons as opposed to Martin's robins—but Gibson's smaller guitars have the same sound quality, too. Compared to Martins, Gibsons have traditionally been darker sounding and with less separation, sweeter, and not as loud. The woods also have something to do with this. Martin's sound has always been rosewood-oriented. Gibson's past adventures with rosewood (like the Advanced Jumbo and rosewood J-200) were brilliant, but brilliant as departures from habit. Historically, Gibson has designed its guitars around the sounds of mahogany or maple.

Gibson's corporate history has been as varied as its catalog. By the late 1940s, control of the company passed from the original consortium to a company called CMI (Chicago Musical Instruments), which installed an innovative president, Ted McCarty, in 1958. During

McCarty's sixteen-year tenure, Gibson's sales increased well over 1,000 percent, in good part because of McCarty's vision in adopting the Les Paul solidbody guitar and developing a range of other electrics as well. It's arguable that Gibson's emphasis on electric guitars was accompanied during this period by a decline in the quality of its acoustic guitars.

Gibson also acquired the Epiphone company in the late 1950s. To avoid franchise conflicts, Gibson manufactured Epiphones as an independent line until 1967.

In the late 1960s, CMI was sold to the Norlin conglomerate, which dismantled Epiphone as an entity and used the name for a line of inexpensive oriental imports based on Gibson models. Gibson quality became extremely inconsistent during this period, as so often happens when an independent, product-oriented company becomes subject to head office bean counters.

In 1986, CMI was purchased and moved to Nashville by a new consortium of music-oriented businessmen with the intention of restoring the company's lost quality and reputation. The first Nashville Gibsons did not, in my opinion, accomplish this. By 1990, Gibson had purchased Flatiron Mandolins, a high-quality company in Bozeman, Montana, to make Gibson mandolins, and soon added a guitar-manufacturing facility to take advantage of the expertise of the former Flatiron shop. The Epiphone line has been revitalized as an importer of offshore-manufactured, primarily laminate models, including copies of historical Gibson and Epiphone instruments, ranging from beginner to journeyman quality, and good instruments for what they are.

Today the Bozeman factory makes traditional-style Gibson acoustic guitars, several new models based on traditional models, and custom models. From time to time, Gibson Montana also offers limited-run editions of special models and historic re-creations, and the famous line of Gibson mandolins. Nashville is the location of their corporate headquarters, electric guitar and banjo operations, and the OMI line of resophonic instruments.

Once upon a time, your choice was between the brighter Martin sound and the darker Gibson sound. Most people seemed to prefer Martin but the partisans of the Gibson alternative were fierce and loyal. Now the market offers a wider variety of choices, but most of them are up at the Martin end of the sound spectrum. If you enjoy the Gibson sound, the only guitar good enough is still a Gibson. New guitars don't sound like old guitars, so new Gibsons are not necessarily going to sound like old Gibsons. But the essential Gibson character has been preserved. Gibson fans exist in many styles other than blues, but the Gibson sound is especially favored by blues players because of the thick sound of the high strings. It's as close as you're going to get to the thick sound of a resophonic guitar without actually playing one—and having to deal with the somewhat soupy and slow-to-speak character of those instruments.

The author with a 1992 Gibson L-1. *Photo by Abbie Lawrence*

At century's beginning, the Gibson line is still based strongly on tradition. The round-shouldered jumbo dreadnoughts, centering around the classic J-45, as well as smaller-bodied models like the bluesy L-00, the Blues King Electro, and the Nick Lucas model, epitomize the dark side of the Gibson tone. Square-shouldered dreadnoughts like the Dove and Hummingbird models are very different from both the dark-sounding members of the Gibson family and the Martins that they resemble in shape: they offer a clean, unseparated chord sound that still sounds sweet and compressed when strummed hard. The SJ-200 is the latest incarnation of the historic J-200, an instrument that has had many fans over the years. Emmylou Harris has strummed hers in many a show while Gary Davis took fantastic fingerpicking flight on his, a disparity of styles that illustrates the instrument's versatility. There are other models too, mostly to be understood as variations on these main types, and an economy line called the Working Musician series has joined the catalog as well.

Old Gibsons for Gibson Lovers

Many older Gibsons have become collector's items: harp guitars; oval-hole archtops; certain ornamental models; rare, cultish, and (for the most part) superb f-hole models with Lloyd Loar's signature on the label; J-185s and rosewood models because they're good and only a few were made; and so on.

But older Gibsons are also good player's guitars. There are people playing every kind of music—even in bluegrass, where the Martin dreadnought reigns supreme—who just plain prefer the sound of their Gibson. There are traditional country blues stylists who find that the Gibson balance, thumpy bass strings, and thick, sweet sound of the high strings are much more suitable to their style than anything they can get out of other guitars. There are rhythm guitarists who find that the compressed, fisty chord sounds of their J-200 or Everly Brothers model punch their way into places in the ensemble that the Martin sound will never reach. And there are lots of player/collectors who own three, five, or a dozen Martins, and also one or two Gibsons from the 1930s, 1940s, or early 1950s that they use for a knock-around guitar or for a change of pace.

Some older Gibsons, particularly smaller and less glamorous models, were once good bargains; but unfortunately (for you and me, at least) the entire Gibson collectible market has taken an upswing in recent years. It is still sometimes possible to get a reasonable deal. For some reason, fewer Gibson flattops seem to have held up over the years than Martins. It's been suggested that they just weren't as well made to begin with, but that's not necessarily the case. Gibsons have probably tended to suffer more hard use, abuse, neglect, and disrespect from their owners over the years.

GODIN

See LaSiDo, page 224.

JAMES GOODALL GUITARS

Box 3542
Kailua-Kona, Hawaii 96745
www.goodallguitars.com

James Goodall, with earlier experience as a painter and woodwind maker, has been making guitars on an increasingly larger scale since 1972. He now operates a small factory in Hawaii that at the end of 1999 was turning out about five guitars a week, achieving his tonal goals through various innovations in bridge, top, and bracing designs. It's a sound that can be described as strong, vocal, and midrangy. Goodall's current lines include a grand concert, standard (large auditorium-size), and jumbo series, each available in a variety of woods and with various options.

GUILD GUITARS

Sales:
7975 N. Hayden Rd.
Scottsdale, Arizona 85258
Factory:
60 Industrial Dr.
Westerly, Rhode Island 02891
www.fender.com

The Guild company was formed by guitarist and music-store owner Al Dronge and former Epiphone executive George Mann in 1952, after the demise of the original Epiphone company. They were able to hire many of Epiphone's craftspeople and, according to rumor, to acquire some of Epiphone's molds, templates, and fixtures as well. Guild got off to a good start on the strength of its archtop models and was compelled by increased production demands to move from New York City to larger quarters in Hoboken, New Jersey, in 1956.

Once in larger quarters, the company started to make classical and flattop guitars as well. From the beginning Guild's top-of-the-line flattop was the jumbo-sized model. Smaller guitars were also available, but Guild didn't add a dreadnought to the line until the mid-1960s.

Guild was purchased by the Avnet conglomerate in 1967, at which time production moved to its present Westerly, Rhode Island, facility. Founder Al Dronge died in a plane crash in 1972 while commuting between his New Jersey offices and the Westerly factory.

In 1986, Guild was purchased by a small, guitar-oriented consortium, but passed through some hard times and by decade's end was sold to the Faas Corporation, which also owned the Randall amplifier company. Now Guild is owned by the Fender company, which, of course, is famous for its solidbody electric guitars. Guild also operates a custom shop in Nashville that turns out one-of-a-kind commissions, limited editions, and top-of-the-line instruments with customized features.

Old Guilds never really became collector's items, and newer used ones, for some reason, don't have a great cachet either. Perhaps it's the fact that some of the midrange models use laminate sides. Whatever the reason, it means that used Guilds can sometimes be a real bargain and new ones, especially in the lower and middle price ranges, are good value for the money as well.

The best-sounding individual Guilds have their own sound: powerful, balanced, clean, and without the separation and bark that distinguishes Martins. Guilds can sound terrific in their own way and have their own unique feel as well. Most of Guild's models, especially the distinctive jumbos, are good strumming guitars. I've always liked the sound and feel of Guild's twelve-strings. Guild has also made archtop models worth anyone's consideration. Guitarists as diverse as Eric Clapton, Holly Dunn, Randy Travis, John Denver, Richie Havens, Bonnie Raitt, Dave van Ronk, Mississippi John Hurt, and John Renbourne have used Guild flattops.

The nomenclature of Guild's turn-of-the-century product line makes it hard to grasp because—unlike most other makers—Guild does not use numerical order to clearly express its range of woods and features. Its products consist of the D line of dreadnoughts, the M and F series of small-bodied fingerpicking guitars, the JF series of robust jumbo-bodied instruments, and the highly reputed line of twelve-strings. Acoustic-electric instruments in dreadnought, smaller-bodied, and thinline shapes are available as well. Guild also makes acoustic and electric bass guitars and solidbody guitars and imports the DeArmond line of beginner and midrange electric guitars.

LARRIVÉE (JEAN LARRIVÉE GUITARS LTD.)

780 E. Cordova
Vancouver, British Columbia V6A 1M3
Canada
www.larrivee.com

Larrivée was founded in 1968 by classically trained luthier Jean Larrivée. Trained as a classical guitarist and then in classical luthiery, Jean Larrivée opened his first commercial workshop in Toronto in 1970 and, having become acquainted with that city's folk music community, made his first steel-string guitar in 1971. Starting with the Martin X-brace as his first model, he began to experiment on the basis of his classical training and arrived at a 90-degree cross-bracing design that, with subsequent refinements, remains at the heart of his bracing system.

After moving to British Columbia in 1977, Larrivée became interested in tooling and large-scale production systems; however, during the 1980s, a gloomy time for acoustic music, he had to concentrate mostly on electric guitars to pay the bills. In 1989 he was able to return full-time to acoustic guitars and became a major player in the market during the 1990s.

It should come as no surprise to anyone with a good ear for guitar sound that Larrivée's background was in classical guitar. The Larrivée sound, which—of course—comes through more meaningfully in his higher-end models, is very warm and mellow without a lot of ringing. In some ways it makes me think of the traditional electric jazz guitar sound, where there are certainly highs present in the tone, but not strummy highs. (Remember, though, that different body woods also bring out this quality to a greater or lesser degree.) In any case, the Larrivée sound is a distinctive one, not like a Martin and not like a Gibson, and one that you'll either like or you won't.

Once a maker of high-end guitars, Larrivée's tooling now allows it to compete across a wide price spectrum with many models available at the low end as well. As with Taylor and other companies largely dependent on tooling and automated processes, the quality of woods and of sound tends to rise consistently in proportion to price, though there is bound to be the occasional exception.

Larrivée offers a range of models in dreadnought, jumbo, and auditorium sizes as well as parlor (OO-size) and small dreadnought sizes. All are available in different series representing differences in woods, feature sets, possible cutaways, and other options. There is also an acoustic bass guitar, the Pete Anderson model inspired by 1940s western guitars with cowboy motifs, and a classical model.

LASIDO (GODIN, SEAGULL, AND SIMON & PATRICK)

19420 Ave. Clark-Graham
Baie D'Urfé, Québec H9X 3R8
Canada
www.lasido.com and www.simonandpatrick.ca
You've probably never heard of LaSiDo, but they're one of North America's largest guitar manufacturers. (I guess they must sell their guitars to all those people in the Yukon and Northwest Territories.)

LaSiDo keeps a fairly wholesale profile and a relatively small dealer list. A great deal of the company's effort is concentrated on supplying precut or ready-to-assemble parts to companies that then market the assembled guitars under other brand names. Their Seagull and Simon & Patrick model lines represent good value, especially in beginner- and student-quality instruments, when you find them. If their top-of-the-line models are consistent with the quality of their lower-price models, they would well be worth looking at.

LaSiDo also makes several other lines: Norman steel-string acoustics; Art & Lutherie steel-string acoustics; and La Patrie classical guitars. Again, if their quality within price ranges is consistent with that of other LaSiDo products, these too would be well worth looking at.

The Godin line of primarily electric guitars also includes several electro-acoustic instruments of considerable interest. Several models in the Multiac series of steel- and nylon-string models are designed especially to drive the industry-standard Roland guitar synthesizer, while functioning as plugged-in acoustic guitars as well. Constructed out of routed-out, solid-mahogany bodies with two sound chambers and well-conceived built-in electronics, they also have a small but warm acoustic voice. The acoustic design is such as to promote an effective, pleasant, sustained sound when plugged in; the plugged-in sound can be used simultaneously with the synthesized sound or either can be used separately. The design is also less prone to feedback than that of traditional guitars. Other Multiac models are available as purely electro-acoustic guitars without the built-in synth driver. For driving a synthesizer or even for purely electro-acoustic applications, these are guitars well worth considering; as acoustic synth drivers, they seem to be the best game in town.

In addition, Godin also produces the similarly-designed ACS series of nylon-strung, synth-driving guitars with extra-heavy tops to further reduce feedback. Classical guitars are generally the worst offenders when it comes to feedback, so the ACS is currently the only chambered guitar worth considering for high-volume, nylon-strung synth applications. (The only remotely comparable instrument, the Gibson Chet Atkins model, has no synth driver and its completely solid body—which does of course minimize feedback— has no acoustic presence.)

A Seagull parlor-size guitar.
Photo courtiesy LaSiDo

LOWDEN

8 Glenford Way
Newtownards, Co. Down BT23 4BX
Northern Ireland
http://web.ukonline.co.uk/akker.net/lowden.htm
George Lowden is a Northern Irish guitar builder of high-quality instruments characterized by a sound that manages to maintain warmth, brilliance, sweetness, and a cutting quality, all at once. It's not easy to manage this, so Lowden guitars are definitely worth searching out, especially by fingerstyle players.

The availability of Lowden guitars in the United States has been inconsistent over the years. Lowden began building in 1973; then, during the early 1980s, a line of Lowden-designed, Japanese-made guitars came and went. A fair selection of Lowden instruments—can again be found at selected dealers. Several models in various woods and with various options, including electronics, are available. Lowden likes to build fairly large (grand auditorium and jumbo) size guitars; it seems customers also like to buy them, so the smaller models are harder to find in stock but are also worth looking for.

Please note that their Web address gives all appearances of being a tentative site at this time. Look for a more substantial site, perhaps even as lowden.com, in the near future.

C. F. MARTIN & COMPANY

Nazareth, Pennsylvania 18064

www.mguitar.com

Martin also imports the Sigma line of beginners' guitars.

The history of the Martin company is to a large extent the history of the American guitar through the 1970s. Martin, more than any other manufacturer, has defined the flattop guitar as we know it today. Probably well over 90 percent of the steel-strung guitars sold today are influenced by (or are outright copies of) Martin's looks, proportions, and bracing patterns. In addition, the vintage acoustic guitar market is concerned primarily with Martin guitars. For these reasons, Martin gets the largest share of space in this section.

Martin Scholars

Because of continuous family—one might even say dynastic—management and the stability of Martin's work site, the history of the Martin business and its product designs are documented to a much greater degree than this short sketch suggests. Martin product lore takes up a book of its own—for deeper reading consult Mike Longworth's *Martin Guitars: A History*. Once you've memorized that, you'll need an apprenticeship of several years of hands-on experience to really become an expert on old Martins—especially if you want to know enough of Martin's product history to swim safely in the shark-ridden seas of the vintage Martin guitar market. This chapter includes the major points but there are many more details to learn, including details of the past models no longer in production.

C. F. Martin and the Martin Bracing System

Many Europeans came to young America because of religious strife, but it was a craft guild jurisdictional dispute that led Christian Frederick Martin (1796–1873) to emigrate from Saxony to New York City in 1833. Like his father before him, he was a guitar maker and a member of the cabinetmakers' guild in Mark Neukirchen, a town full of small woodworking industries because of its proximity to the German forests. The town's violin makers' guild wanted the guitar business all for itself, and Martin decided it was better to run than fight. He was right.

Martin got off to a good-enough start running a general-service music store and guitar workshop in New York but didn't much care to live there, even then. In 1839 he moved his workshop to Nazareth, a congenial Moravian German community in Pennsylvania's Lehigh Valley. The Martin company has remained amidst the flat fields and rolling hills so reminiscent of the terrain of Martin's native land to the present day. (Incidentally, Martin kept stamping its instruments "C. F. Martin & Co., New York" until 1898, because its instruments were distributed by an independent New York City office until then.)

Christian Frederick Martin (1796–1873). *Photo courtesy C. F. Martin & Co.*

C. F. Martin brought with him to New York a guitar shape and a simple diagonal bracing system that he had learned from his own master, the Viennese luthier Johann Stauffer. But by the time he moved to Nazareth his instruments no longer looked like Stauffer's on the outside and he was experimenting on the inside as well. By the end of the 1850s, what we now know as the characteristic Martin X-bracing pattern had taken shape. It was used more and more over the years and by the end of the century it had become a standard feature on all Martin guitars.

Remember that early Martin guitars were originally made to be gut-strung. The X-brace was not conceived for use with steel strings. In that sense, it was an accident waiting to happen, and it was a fortunate accident indeed. Some early Martins can tolerate being strung with low-tension steel strings (like compound or extra-light sets). They function effectively, sometimes magnificently, this way, but usually with a voice and tonal balance not particularly suited to today's fashions in either sound or playing touch. Guitars were generally built smaller in those days, as well.

As nineteenth-century tastes began to approach modern ones, Martin guitars tended to become somewhat stronger and heavier—even more so in the years after 1918, as the public's taste turned more and more toward steel strings. But the instruments weren't consistently and officially beefed up until the late 1920s, when Martin formally accommodated its product line to steel strings by embedding an ebony reinforcing strip in the neck. The reinforcement became a metal T-bar in 1934, a square channel bar in 1967, and finally an adjustable tension rod inside a channel bar in 1985. (See Chapter 5, page 82, for more information on neck reinforcement.)

Martin tops of the pre-war era tended to belly—that is, to bulge a little below the bridge under the pressure of the medium-to-heavy-gauge steel strings fashionable at that time. (Most guitars belly a bit, and it's OK.) Bellying wasn't really bad for the guitars, but too many owners found it disturbing. In 1939 Martin accommodated by moving the crossing point of the two main braces that make up the X about an inch farther away from the sound hole. This created space for a larger bridge plate and also made the amount of bridge area between the braces smaller. (The original configuration is known as the "high X-brace" or "forward-shifted" position.)

Lightness of the bracing also contributed to the tendency to belly. Part of the standard Martin bracing design involved scooping out scal-

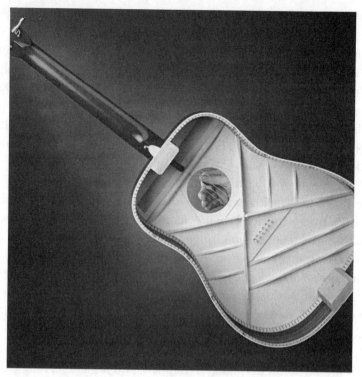

Standard X-bracing on a contemporary Martin dreadnought. *Photo courtesy C. F. Martin & Co.*

lops of wood from the tops of the bracing struts, giving the strut an overall parabolic shape like that of a suspension bridge. This is known as "scalloping" the bracing. In 1944 Martin stopped scalloping the braces and increased their thickness from ¼ of an inch to 5/16 of an inch in order to keep the tops from bellying as much.

Many feel that, as a result of these two bracing changes, the tops lost some punch and volume and the high notes became less transparent and well-balanced. (Some also feel that this was abetted by a changeover to Sitka from Adirondack spruce tops at about this time, though this issue is more questionable.)

Since the mid-1970s, Martin has again offered scalloped bracing on selected models. Some models even re-create the pre-1939 bracing position. Many other manufacturers now offer scalloped, parabolic bracing as well.

It's good to remember that guitar sound is the result of the interaction of many complex variables. Scalloped bracing is only one of them. It may produce a meaningful tonal difference or it may be merely a buzzword, depending on the manufacturer and on the individual instrument. And even though the scalloped bracing does make a difference on Martins and other fine instruments, whether you prefer the sound or not is still a matter of taste. There are a number of excellent, good-sounding players out there who could and would have a scalloped instrument if they wanted to, but don't. Others don't care; they buy the guitar that makes them happy and, having done so, remain happy.

When you're listening to guitars, don't listen for whether the bracing seems to be scalloped. Listen for whether you like the sound of the instrument. Among the memorable older Martins I've played in the past few years was one made in 1956, long after the bracing ceased being parabolic and the X position shifted. To my ears, the only ears that matter, it still had the old sound of pre-war guitars with the original configuration.

The Mystique of Pre-War Martins

"Pre-war," in the guitar world, always refers to World War II. Martin guitars of the era between the two world wars set the standard by which all other flattop guitars were judged until recently. The last decades of the twentieth century witnessed many changes in the tastes of both players and the listening public for guitar tone. Recorded rather than intimate live guitar sound became the ideal. Schools of steel-string guitar playing whose styles are light-stringed sweetness, or a more even attack-sustain shape to the sound, or syrupy sweet long notes, also came to prominence. True, the old Martins have some of these qualities to some degree, even to a high degree in certain individual instruments. But what the great ones mostly have is punch, brilliance, clarity, and cutting power. Even the deep lows of an old dreadnought cut more than they rumble when heard in an acoustic music context. Today, amidst changing tastes, the Martin tonal paradigm remains valid, if not as widespread as it once was.

It runs against every spiritual presupposition of the luthiery art that the greatest instruments of their type ever made should have come out of a factory rather than from the single-minded, single-handed shop of a private luthier; but somehow, that's what happened.

The Martin factory is an assembly line in the sense that no one person is responsible for a given guitar. Martin line employees are not luthiers; they are skilled craftspeople who have been trained in a particular operation. Each operation—neck shaping, top gluing, inlaying, and so on—is done by a different person. But, because it moves more slowly than, say, Henry Ford's line, the resemblance to an assembly line ends there. As in other guitar factories, fine models are set aside to stabilize in between major operations.

The more handwork and personal concern there is in a manufacturing process, the more variation there is in the character and even the quality of the individual products. This give us the fascinating differences that exist among individual fine guitars, even of the same model, and that existed to a far greater degree in the pre-war era. It also means that some old Martins sound better than others and this, in turn, means that some old Martins sound worse than others.

Most players feel that there's a definite sound characteristic of pre-war Martins. But there are also a lot of great-sounding Martins that were made after that time, and some sound better and more pre-war than some of the pre-war ones do. You can also find unexceptional instruments and some real dogs among pre-war Martins. Because the market for them is a collectors' market based in part on cosmetic condition, production statistics, and other non-musical considerations, you can expect to see these dogs offered at top dollar, too. To debate just what *better* or *worse* means in terms of taste is irrelevant. The point is that differences do exist and you'd better learn to hear them and be able to decide what you like and what you don't—especially if you're planning to pay the top dollar that an old Martin fetches.

Is it possible to get a new Martin that's as good a guitar as a vintage Martin? Yes and no. No, because age does certain things to a guitar that only age can do; no new guitar can ever be like an old one until it *is* an old one. Yes, because some individual modern Martins are better than some individual old ones. (It's also important to remember that Martin is no longer the overwhelmingly biggest game in town.) But all that being said, there's a certain unique character to the older instruments that cannot be recaptured.

Besides the sound, Martin's traditional cosmetic features of herringbone-pattern marquetry and inlay of abalone and mother-of-pearl have also achieved a mystical status (even though they are not causally related to sound quality), and are widely copied throughout the guitar industry. (See Chapter 7, page 135, for more information about inlay and ornamentation.)

The Martin Dreadnought Guitar

As American music moved into the early decades of the twentieth century, public taste demanded larger and larger guitars. The age when young ladies entertained guests in the front parlor with light classical pieces was over. The age of country and western singers whose strumming had to be heard over the din of a honky-tonk crowd was about to begin.

The new generation of solo singers wanted a booming, powerful bass to fill in under their voice. Mountain string band guitarists wanted the same sound to help them fill the space that, in later styles, would be filled by a string bass player, and they also needed lots of raw power just to be heard. The names Martin gave to its guitars over the past several decades tell the story. For a long time, Martin's largest size was the concert guitar. By today's standards, it's a very small guitar. Then came the grand concert size, and finally the auditorium size. (I guess they didn't have stadium rock concerts back then.) But people hungered for an ever bigger sound. Note the progression over the years.

MARTIN'S LARGEST-SIZED GUITARS SINCE 1854

Concert (0)	introduced 1854
Grand Concert (00)	introduced 1877
Auditorium (000)	introduced 1902
Largest size custom Ditson	1916–30
Dreadnought (D)	introduced 1931
Grand Auditorium (J)	introduced 1980
Jumbo M (now OOOO)	introduced 1985

Eric Clapton playing a Martin dreadnought. *Photo courtesy C. F. Martin & Co.*

Flash back to 1916. In that year, Martin began to custom build a small number of oddly shaped guitars for the Oliver Ditson company, a sheet music retailer. These instruments had a very broad waist (similar to some early nineteenth-century French guitars), and were made in small, medium, and large sizes. They bore the Ditson name and were at first not even stamped with Martin-series serial numbers. Conflicting testimony survives about whether the design was the brainchild of Ditson guitar department manager Harry Hunt or Martin foreman John Deichman, but one or the other of these gentlemen seems to deserve a prominent place in guitar history. The shape ranks second only to Christian Martin's X-brace as the most influential design innovation in the history of the flattop guitar.

Forward to 1931. The country was caught up in the Depression. Ditson was no longer ordering guitars, and not too many other people were, either. Martin factory shifts were cut down to part-time and a desperate management had gone so far as to develop a prototype line of rosewood trinkets (they were never actually marketed) in order to try to boost total revenues. Stimulated by the perception that the world wanted larger guitars and by the desire to try anything new that might increase sales, Martin introduced its own version of the largest-size Ditson model. They named it after HMS *Dreadnought*, a famous battleship of World War I. (According to factory legend, the name had to begin with D because the custom Ditson models were already referred to in-house as the D-series.)

The pace of dreadnought sales began to pick up through the early 1930s as the public began to get used to the mahogany-bodied model D-1 and the rosewood-bodied D-2. At that time the dreadnoughts, like many of Martin's other instruments, were still being made with twelve-fret necks. But these were the waning years of twelve-fret guitars, and by 1934 most models, including the dreadnoughts, were fitted with fourteen-fret necks and a concomitantly smaller upper bout size (smaller to make room to expose the two extra frets). In that year Martin changed the mahogany dreadnought model designation to D-18 and the rosewood to D-28. Sales were taking off by then; the public had adjusted to the new behemoths. The D-18 and the D-28 have remained as Martin's best-known workhorse guitars to the present day.

The dreadnought shape has now become the usual shape people think of when they think of steel-strung guitars. Many other makers have copied it, though in the case of cheap imitations it's merely the shape, and not the sound, that's being copied. It's often thought of as the most desirable guitar shape, but in fact there are many advantages to other shapes as well, whether it be the equally large jumbo guitar or other, smaller sizes. The dreadnought style is almost every bluegrass guitarist's first choice, but other styles may make more sense for other styles or as all-purpose guitars.

Martin Since 1950

Martin moved into the 1950s with a line of guitars ranging from the small concert size to the massive dreadnoughts. Sales were about six thousand instruments a year during that period thanks to the musical tastes of the times, but they began to pick up when the 1960s generation came along. They picked up so well, in fact, that by the middle of the decade there was a three years' back order for new guitars and a new factory was built in Nazareth to accommodate the demand.

At about this time Martin also introduced the D-35 model, essentially a D-28 with a three-piece (rather than the traditional two-piece) back. Brazilian rosewood was beginning to get scarce and it was hard to find sections large enough to make the back of an instrument as large as a dreadnought. Three-piece backs are attractive—when properly selected the wood grain makes a pleasing contrast and the extra seam creates the opportunity for an extra strip of ornamental marquetry at the joint. In a clever bit of marketing, Martin added a few more cosmetic features (like fingerboard binding) and charged *more* for an instrument whose origins lay in a desire to economize on rosewood. (In the end, the difference between the D-28 and D-35 is generally one of looks more than of sound or sturdiness, so you should simply get whichever pleases you. Martin sales literature used to claim a consistently more bass-heavy sound for the D-35s, but this is debatable.)

The late 1960s were a time of change. Martin had always used Brazilian rosewood for its top-of-the-line models, but export restrictions made it impossible to obtain Brazilian wood on as large a scale as Martin required. The company began to use the somewhat lighter-colored, more highly textured Indian rosewood instead. Some players and luthiers believe that there is no perceptible sound difference between Brazilian and Indian rosewood, and both woods seem equally durable. Others think there is consistently greater sustain and brilliance in Brazilian. Others might agree with my friend Denny Stevens's view that Brazilian sounds "different but not necessarily better."

Nonetheless, as soon as Indian was introduced, Brazilian Martins acquired a cachet and a premium collector's value apart from any real value as a playing instrument.

Aside from looks, there is one more valid reason for preferring the last of Martin's Brazilian rosewood guitars to the first of the Indians. When the change occurred, Martin was in its peak production years: over 22,000 instruments in the record year 1970, as opposed to around 6,500 per year during the 1950s, and 7,500 in the late 1980s. Many feel that during these high-production years from the late 1960s into the mid-1970s, a higher-than-usual percentage of mediocre—mediocre in sound and also production quality—Martins came out of the factory. There was even a period when the bridge-setting jig got out of whack and bridges went on in a slightly wrong place, making it impossible for the instruments to be played in tune! However, there were also many excellent instruments produced during those years. Anyone who has been around the music retail business has shared the experience of seeing customers reject reasonably priced, fine-sounding, Indian rosewood guitars in favor of more expensive Brazilian models that sounded no better, or sometimes even worse.

During the 1970s public taste began to shift definitively away from smaller guitars, and Martin began to produce fewer and fewer of them, to the point where they are now offered only as special-order or limited-edition instruments and are hard to find in the catalogs of other manufacturers as well. For decades, Martin relied on the dreadnought to serve the large-guitar market, and its next-largest guitar was the auditorium size, which by today's standards is a small instrument. It was probably a point of pride that Martin was reluctant to develop jumbo-size instruments, leaving them to Gibson and Guild. The problem was that Gibson and Guild, and now the Japanese as well, were offering both dreadnoughts and jumbos. It made little sense, especially in the shrinking market of the 1970s, to leave the entire market share of jumbo guitars to the competition.

In 1977, Martin introduced its grand auditorium M-series guitars, with large, jumbo-size bodies comparable in breadth to the Gibson J-200 jumbo prototype and its Guild and Japanese derivatives, but more shallow in depth. Martin already had the molds and templates for such a body size. They had been used for a long-defunct series of archtop guitars that Martin had offered, with limited success, in the 1930s and 1940s. The idea came in part from Berkeley craftsmen Jon Lundberg and Marc Silber, who had been putting flat tops onto archtop Martins and similarly sized archtop Prairie State guitars. Their conversions demonstrated that this body size could produce a large sound with most of the dreadnought's bite and volume but with fewer of the dreadnought's problems with bass-heaviness. But for those who want a bassier instrument closer to the dreadnought's sound, Martin waited only two years after it introduced the M series before launching the J ("Jumbo M") series, having the same breadth as the M but every bit as much depth as a dreadnought. Today the Jumbo M guitars are known as the J series, and the M series is known as the OOOO ("quadruple-oh") series.

Martin's aggressive marketing of the M and J series was only part of a new set of marketing strategies the company had to come up with during the 1980s. Competition had been fierce. The offshore companies, then mainly Japanese, completely dominated the low-end plywood market. (Martin developed an imported Sigma line that was a very small player in this market). In the midrange, the all-solid-wood guitar became a creature of the past, and Martin had to counter Guild and the better Japanese models by introducing its Shenandoah line of guitars with solid tops and plywood bodies. Shenandoah parts were brought in from abroad and assembled at the Martin plant. However, the Shenandoah line died during the 1990s. At the high end, Martin had to compete against an army of private luthiers and limited-production makers who did not exist in earlier generations, as well as against the excellent products of the Santa Cruz and Taylor companies, who were aiming for a share of the high-end market.

Martin also has to compete with its own past not just in terms of image but in basic terms of moving sales units. Vintage Martin fanatics will only be happy with a genuinely old model, but ordinary players with a little patience looking for a good used instrument can usually find a more recent Martin at a far lower price than comparable new instruments.

Martin's response to the conditions of the 1980s and early 1990s was to position itself solidly as a "conservatively innovative" high-end company, and it's done a good job of keeping its balance on the high-wire rope of this apparent self-contradiction.

The early 1990s saw an increasing number of limited-edition revivals of structural designs and cosmetic features from the pre-war period. Abalone and pearl inlay, which were discontinued in the early 1940s, were reintroduced on a limited scale as early as the mid-1960s, and are now even used on some standard models. Scalloped bracing, herringbone inlay, pre-1939 high-X bracing, bridge plate modifications, and other features also became available as standard features on several models and as options on others. By the end of the century, Martin had consolidated these features in an entire range of guitars known as the Vintage Series.

Martin has also sought to capitalize on the legendary collectibility of its older instruments by offering a bewildering array of special-issue and limited-edition models. The entire special-issue program is highly promotional and somewhat gimmicky in nature, reflecting the company's current strong emphasis on special promotions largely resting on its past reputation. Included are instruments with special structural or cosmetic features, labels and interiors bearing the signatures of Martin staff, re-creations of older instruments, instruments made of unique or unusual materials, and so on. In addition to Martin's own programs, every so often one of the major acoustic guitar dealers will order a special custom run of some model with special features for sale by that dealer only.

The gimmick lies in the fact that special-issue instruments may be touted as collectors' items of the future. Whether this will be the case, and to what degree their value will increase compared to the value of other guitars, will depend on factors that are unrelated to the qualities of the instruments themselves. You should buy an instrument because you like it, not primarily as an investment.

Martin has also kept up with changing tastes. The shallow-contoured, "low-profile" neck was introduced in 1985 to accommodate the tastes of a generation of guitarists used to the light strings and fast necks of electric guitars. (Santa Cruz and especially Taylor make guitars with fast necks as a rule; Taylor in particular positions itself as an "easy-to-play" guitar.) Martin just can't allow market share to slip over this issue without putting up a fight. But because many guitarists prefer the feel of a standard neck and the tonal advantages of stiffer action, Martin did not give it up completely. In addition, Martin departed from its earlier traditions by introducing cutaway models for guitarists who like to play on the highest frets. But the most striking departure from tradition, which also took place in 1985, was the adoption of the adjustable truss rod. Even though the Gibson patent on the adjustable truss rod had long been expired, Martin steadfastly refused to adopt it, asserting that a properly made, properly aged guitar would not need one. In Martin's own case, at least, the assertion was true—a great deal of the time. The old Martins have been extremely stable, particularly when they haven't been too-heavily strung. Nonetheless, seasonal changes do occur with all wooden instruments, and neck adjustments are also routine when changing string gauge or replacing frets. And the new thin necks, with less wood mass to help them stabilize themselves, would be intrinsically less stable than the old-style, thicker necks. This is probably why the adjustable rod and new neck style were introduced at the same time.

Martin also revived koa wood on a number of models during the 1980s and, for a while, issued an entirely new series of maple-bodied guitars in many of its most popular sizes and shapes. The traditional Martin sounds are the brilliant sound of rosewood and the sweet, full sound of mahogany—if you wanted the bright, unseparated sound of maple you used to have to go to Guild, Gibson, or the Japanese. No longer. It was another matter of market share. In the guitar market of the 1990s, no one could afford to relegate any segment of business to the competition.

At century's beginning, the Martin company continues to make many good, some excellent, and a few great guitars as it accommodates itself to changing tastes in the sound and visual design of the acoustic guitar, new manufacturing techniques, and very worthy competition. At this time it has organized its products into ten distinct product lines. (See page 237 for Martin's size and style designations.) Among Martin's diverse lines are many guitars of good quality within their price ranges, and the traditional Martin sound continues to be popular. Martin's quality curve remains bell-shaped—just as it was in the days of its classic, pre-war models—and among the products in its top lines can be found guitars of excellent quality.

Other Martin Products

Over the years Martin has made or distributed instruments other than guitars. There was even a nineteenth-century flirtation with zithers! Mandolins (of various sizes and styles) were a big item for a while, particularly in the 1920s, and Martin mandolins have always had their partisans, especially among players of sweeter European styles who don't care for Gibson's bluegrass bark.

Martin also did well with ukuleles, taro-patches, and tiples (in various sizes and styles) during the Hawaiian music craze of the 1920s, having jumped on the bandwagon in 1916 just as the fad was beginning. The Hawaiian craze was also responsible for the H-series Hawaiian guitars Martin produced during the 1920s and 1930s. Most of the surviving H-series instruments have by now been converted to standard configuration by their owners.

There were also several adventures with archtop and electric guitars over the years, none of which really went anywhere; Martin's sideline of four-string tenor guitars, however, are among the best ever made.

Martin has made several styles of nylon-strung guitar over the years, but in sound and feel they were well removed from the mainstream tastes of classical guitarists. Many non-classical guitarists who like nylon strings are attracted to them; Willie Nelson's quietly brilliant solo guitar style is strongly rooted in the sound of his Martin classical. Classical models are currently available in several ranges. Martin also offers four-string acoustic bass guitars; several models in different price ranges are currently in the catalog.

Today Martin imports the inexpensive Sigma beginner's guitar line; markets strings, pickups, and preamps; and offers guitars with special features through its custom shop. Martin also makes the Backpacker guitar, a travel guitar that differs from those offered by most other makers in that it features a tiny body cavity (a minus, since it takes away from the robustness of its sound) but a full-size fingerboard (a plus, since this makes it much more congenial to play than the child-size fingerboards of most other travel models).

Name That Number: Martin's Size and Style Designations

Since the days of C. F. Martin himself, the Martin company has used a system consisting of an alphanumeric prefix and suffix system (for example, D-28) to designate its models. Martin enthusiasts bandy these letters and numbers about the way cyclists talk about gear ratios, computer nuts about processor speed, and fitness freaks about aerobic threshold. If you don't know how the Martin numbering system works, you're just not cool, so pay close attention to this section.

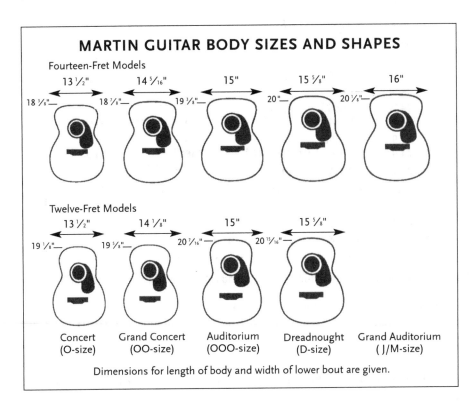

MARTIN GUITAR BODY SIZES AND SHAPES

Fourteen-Fret Models

Twelve-Fret Models

Concert (O-size) Grand Concert (OO-size) Auditorium (OOO-size) Dreadnought (D-size) Grand Auditorium (J/M-size)

Dimensions for length of body and width of lower bout are given.

The prefix, which generally consists of letters except when it includes the addition of the number 12 to indicate a twelve-string model, refers to the instrument's size and shape, which Martin calls "size." The suffix, which was traditionally numeric, refers to the wood, ornamentation, and other details of material, which Martin calls "style." For example, in model OOO-28 (pronounced "triple-oh twenty-eight"), the OOO tells you that the guitar is auditorium size and the 28 tells you that the guitar has a rosewood back and sides, an ebony bridge and fingerboard, and certain other details of ornamentation. In recent years Martin has taken to adding letters to the style suffix as well, usually in order to identify special characteristics (for example, *V* for Vintage Series instruments with certain pre-war characteristics) or celebrity models (*EC* for the Eric Clapton model).

SE	For "Signature Edition." Special collector's edition with underside of top signed by Martin officers and staff.
T	Tenor (four-string) guitar.
V or Vintage	Instrument with certain pre-war characteristics.

By the end of the 1990s, Martin had established nine distinct lines, which they described with an update of their traditional alphanumeric system. The lines, and their most salient distinguishing features, are as follows, in order of price range. Various sizes and styles are available within each line.

*X Series	Beginners' guitars with synthetic laminate tops and sides.
Road Series	A better grade of student and amateur guitar with solid tops and laminate backs and sides.
15 Series	All solid mahogany tops, backs, and sides; Martin's way to bring in all-solid-wood guitars in a price range roughly comparable to the 1 Series.
1 Series	Journeyman-quality guitars with solid tops and laminate backs and sides; available in a larger variety of sizes and styles.
16 Series	Solid wood tops, backs, and sides; a more economical version.
Standard Series	This series essentially continues the traditional variety of styles and sizes that has defined the Martin guitar.
Vintage Series	Similar to the Standard Series, but incorporating such pre-war structural and cosmetic features as herringbone binding, high X-bracing, and scalloped braces.
Special Series	Limited editions, historical copies, unusual woods, and so forth.
Ac/Electric	Built-in electronics on journeyman-quality instruments.

* The X Series of synthetic-bodied guitars is not at all competitive in their price range. These aberrations, recently introduced at the time of this writing, stand some chance of being laughed out of the marketplace by the time this book sees print. Unfortunately, the current Martin leadership seems prone to make gimmicky marketing decisions rather than concentrate on the fine guitars Martin is still capable of building when it sets its mind to it—although, with the introduction of the X Series, one begins to fear this may become a lost art in Nazareth if the company does not refocus its priorities.

Martin Serial Numbers

A chronological index of Martin serial numbers, beginning with the number 8,000 arbitrarily assigned in 1898, is available on Martin's Web site. There are actually people who can keep these numbers in their head, much as others keep sports statistics in theirs.

OVATION AND ADAMAS

Box 507
Bloomfield, Connecticut 06002
www.KamanMusic.com

Ovation and Adamas guitars are manufactured by the Kaman Corp. Kaman also imports the similarly designed Applause line of beginner-level guitars as well as the Takamine line of laminate-body guitars.

The fortunes of Kaman Corporation founder Charles H. Kaman were based on a new design for a helicopter rotor blade, but he was also an avid guitarist who had turned down a chance at a performing career in order to go to college. When Kaman's board decided in the late 1960s that diversification into consumer products would help balance the ups and downs of aerospace contracting, it was natural that Charles Kaman's background would lead the company toward guitars.

In the spirit of its aerospace heritage, Ovation is a pioneer in the use of factory automation and of synthetics for guitar construction. The standard Ovation models have spruce tops, graded in quality to match the price category of each model. A variety of new bracing patterns were developed through acoustical research. The radical Ovation bodies are made of a single, bowl-shaped molding of the synthetic fiberglass material that Kaman uses for covering its rotor blades. After a great deal of design testing by engineers this highly sound reflective material was shaped to focus the sound waves out through the sound hole. Letting the sound "out" is not necessarily the most important function of a sound hole—it's there to form what acousticians call a reflex chamber or Helmholtz resonator. In any case, the guitar works well. Ovation called it the "Lyrachord" body.

Ovation was also a pioneer in the use of built-in pickups, having developed the technique, now in common use by other manufacturers as well, of seating an individual piezo-electric pickup for each string in the bridge. Ovations are good guitars to consider, especially if you're in the market for an instrument that you'll primarily be playing amplified. Kaman continues to be a leader in the development of built-in amplification and connectivity.

In 1975, Ovation introduced its Adamas model, a revolutionary (and pricey) design with a top of synthetic graphic-fiber laminates sandwiching a birch veneer inner core and an unusual array of small sound holes in the upper bouts. They call it the "Fibronic" soundboard. It looks strange, but sounds good: crisp, clear, extremely well-balanced, and with effective built-in pickups. It's not a deeply soulful sound, but it's a very even and efficient one.

Some purists hate the very idea of Ovation guitars, and the Adamas models most of all. I've always thought of them as a species apart and like them for what they are. The Ovation body shape can be a bit tricky to hold steadily in the lap but it may not bother you much, and it probably won't bother you at all if you use a strap. People either like Ovations or they don't, and some of the people who do are well-known and accomplished players.

Graphite Fiber

Graphite fiber is a modern synthetic perhaps best known for its use in fishing rods and tennis rackets—in other words, as a wood substitute in precisely those applications that, like a guitar, require a combination of stiffness and elasticity. The material is created by high-temperature treatment of polyacrylonitrate fiber, which produces graphite fibers about a tenth of the thickness of a human hair. These fibers are then embedded in an epoxy resin.

Graphite resins have been used by several makers for guitar necks (mostly on electric guitars), in addition to Ovation's use of it on Adamas tops.

The better Ovations have achieved wide acceptance as trustworthy, roadworthy, journeyman-quality instruments—especially by guitarists who use Ovation's built-in pickups and preamps. Ovation and Adamas models are currently offered in several price lines and include twelve-string and bass models, the Trekker travel model, parlor-size and classical models, mandolins, and built-in preamplifier options with an interesting array of features.

SANTA CRUZ GUITAR COMPANY

328 Ingalls Ave.
Santa Cruz, California 95060
www.santacruzguitar.com

Luthier Richard Hoover and repairmen William Davis and Bruce Ross started the Santa Cruz Guitar Company in 1976. Davis left the company in 1978 followed by Ross in 1989. The company's philosophy, however, is still based on its original principle of turning out fine work by luthier-level craftspeople in a limited-production setting. Like its peers in the trade, Santa Cruz has expanded its operations greatly during the 1990s. It makes beautifully crafted, excellent-sounding guitars, inspired for the most part by Martin designs and the Martin sound. At their best, Santa Cruz guitars can have a slightly more luscious, less cutting sound.

Much of the company's success is based on its association with Tony Rice, the leading exponent of new acoustic guitar music, who endorses the model named after him. This lightly built dreadnought is designed in collaboration with Rice and modeled after his own legendary Martin, an eccentrically modified instrument once owned by the legendary Clarence White. But prospective buyers should consider other Santa Cruz models as well.

Santa Cruz currently offers models in the traditional Martin-inspired shapes OO, OOO, OM, and dreadnought. In addition there is

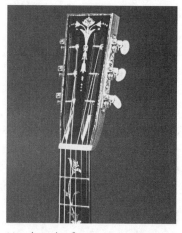

Headstock of a Santa Cruz guitar. *Photo courtesy Santa Cruz Guitar Co.*

the Janis Ian model (fourteen-fret parlor or O size with cutaway), the twelve-fret PJ parlor model, a 12-fret dreadnought, the deep F model, the cutaway FS model that acoustic jazz players in particular should consider, the H model fingerstyle guitar, and the Bob Brozman baritone model with a twenty-seven-inch scale designed for tuned-down playing. Each model is available with various wood and appointment options.

Santa Cruz offers several archtop models and in the year 2000 they introduced a line of ukuleles as well. A scheduled vintage jumbo guitar model had not yet entered production as this book went to press.

TACOMA GUITARS

4615 E. 192 St.
Tacoma, Washington 98446
www.tacomaguitars.com

Tacoma, an upstart company, seized a large part of the market share in the 1990s through new, well-conceived designs and an ability to offer good sound for the money, especially at the middle and lower segments of its price range. Production economies resulting from the advantages of all-new startup tooling probably had a lot to do with it as well. If you want to spend a lot of money on a high-end instrument, look elsewhere; that's not what Tacoma is about, at least, not at this time. But if you're looking for good value in an all-solid-wood instrument with a street price of under $1,000, Tacoma is one of the brands you should certainly consider.

The Tacoma line consists of both dreadnought and smaller-bodied instruments available in various woods and with different degrees of decoration. Despite the plastic decoration that graces some models, the overall feeling of Tacoma instruments is of an underlying economy and austerity. Some models sound brighter and clearer, heading toward the Martin end of the sound spectrum; many of the others have a tone with the pronounced midrange emphasis that most blues guitarists and fingerpickers favor. Many Tacoma models are traditional in appearance, although their midrange quality is especially prevalent in the modernistic-looking Chief models, with their asymmetrical bracing and off-center sound hole. These are the first such all-wood guitars to be mass produced for the general market. (Ovation pioneered such designs earlier in mass production for its Adamas series of synthetic-bodied and graphite guitars.)

Tacoma also offers archtop models, mandolins, electro-acoustic instruments, and thinline models. There is also the distinctive Papoose model, a tiny instrument sometimes called a piccolo guitar, that, far from being merely a toy or travel model, has now taken on a sound and life of its own, especially in the recording studio.

TAYLOR GUITARS

1940 Gillespie Way
El Cajon, California 92020
www.taylorguitars.com

Bob Taylor and Kurt Listug founded Taylor Guitars in the mid-1970s. At the middle and top of their line, their well-made, good-sounding instruments are first-rate and give their competition a good run for the money—especially Martin, which had been undisputed king of the market share hill before Taylor took off.

The Taylor company got off to a slow start in the late 1970s, and sat fairly dead in the water during the acoustic music doldrums of the early 1980s, but really began to pick up as its principles acquired enough production and marketing savvy in the late 1980s to keep pace and then stay ahead of the acoustic music explosion of the 1990s.

Taylors sound good and are made of good woods, but they probably owe most of their success to the fast necks and congenial action that they have made a strong sales point. Dealers originally liked them because the bolt-on necks—the first to appear on good-quality acoustic guitars—were easy to fix. The Taylor sound, characteristically somewhat silkier and less punchy than the traditional Martin-Collings-Santa Cruz spectrum, may also be a factor. Played live, Taylors tend to sound very much the way many acoustic guitars sound on record after an audio engineer has processed their sound in the mix, and therefore they are well suited to certain modern sensibilities. One thing for sure is that lots of people like that sound.

To their design and sound, Taylor adds careful attention to tooling, a high reliance on automated processes, a strong sense of production economies, and well-orchestrated promotion and artist relations strategies—all reasons why Taylor has achieved the degree of success it has. In 1999 Taylor announced a revolutionary new neck design that promises even more consistent playability and easier maintenance. (See Chapter 5, page 89, for more details.)

As Taylor celebrated its twenty-fifth anniversary at the turn of the century, it offered various lines of guitars with a wide variety of sizes, shapes, woods, and features. These included the 300 to 900 series, special koa and walnut series, and, at the top of the line, the Signature and Presentation series.

Because Taylor's control of material and quality is so tight, you'll find that Taylor price ranges, even more than those of most other companies in these days of tight quality control, accurately reflect the overall quality of the instruments—even their sound quality. All things never being equal even in the most automated-part guitar world, however, this can never be the case all the time.

Taylor also offers bass guitars, twelve-strings, and the Baby Taylor, a small travel guitar designed to be tuned slightly higher than usual that could also work as a high-quality child-sized guitar.

RESOPHONIC GUITAR MANUFACTURERS

National Reso-Phonic Guitars

www.nationalguitars.com

Original Acoustic Instruments (Dobro Brand)

Distributed by Gibson.
www.gibson.com

Regal

Distributed by Saga Musical Instruments.
Box 2841
South San Francisco, California 94083

14 Custom Luthiers

Thirty years ago very few steel-string guitars were being built by individuals in North America. Now there are scores of luthiers populating the landscape. Some even make a full-time living at it, though many also do repair work as well.

While some luthiers create instruments and then offer them for sale, others—especially those with long waiting lists—create instruments only on demand. Commissioning a personal instrument is no light undertaking. You need to trust the luthier, be confident of getting a good product, and know what to ask for. Some guitar makers work within a narrow range of options. Choosing such a luthier makes it more likely that you'll get a predictable product. Others will work with you to create a wider range of options and variations, or perhaps even to try for a unique instrument or a specific sound.

Some makers charge more and some less, but generally speaking you can expect to begin at between two and three thousand dollars for a good handmade instrument. Prices can also be considerably higher, depending on the maker's reputation, the complexity of the instrument, and so on. Classical makers seem to be able to get more, as a rule. Archtops also cost more, and legitimately so; carving and tuning an arched top and back are an intense and laborious process.

Luthiers come in many varieties with lots of different philosophies as well. Some are conservative, and want nothing more than to make another Martin or Gibson, though with care. Others have their own take on tradition, or are daring and original. Some follow the latest developments in lutherie; others scoff at them. Some build with a unique and consistent sound. Obviously, some are better and some worse than others.

Most important, some are local and some are not. Finding someone to make a guitar you want means trusting them. An established public reputation is generally a good sign, as with practitioners in any other field, although you do sometimes need to be able to see beyond reputation.

Familiarity is a keystone of trust, and that's why it can make a lot of sense to commission an instrument from someone with a reputation within your own community, and of whose work you have seen many examples.

Almost all luthiers are prepared to work with you to a greater or lesser degree in developing an instrument to suit your needs and style. You don't always have to know exactly what you want in the way of size, shape, and materials, since often a good luthier can make valuable suggestions based on an analysis of your playing style and musical tastes.

If you're leery about laying out a hefty down payment for an instrument that doesn't even exist yet, look for a maker who is putting an existing instrument up for sale or who is brokering an instrument for a past client who wants to sell.

WHY COMMISSION A CUSTOM GUITAR?

You probably shouldn't if you have to ask! But here are some reasons why you might:

- You're an experienced player and for years you've wished to have a certain neck shape or cutaway or cosmetic feature that's not available ready-made.
- You may think, and justly so, that you've found a luthier whose guitars are just plain better-sounding than factory guitars, or happen to have exactly the sound you want.
- You're an amateur guitarist and guitar fan, you care about guitars, you play well enough to justify having a good instrument (or maybe not), you make good money, the kids are out of school, the car only has 10,000 miles on it, and this time you're going to damn well treat yourself for a change. (Or, you're self-indulgent and can afford one more toy.)
- You're convinced that your luthier's instrument will increase in value over the years at a rate significantly exceeding the rate of inflation. (A bad reason and probably a bad bet.)
- You love guitars, you collect them, and you're burned out on the vintage guitar market.

Whatever the reason, it's clear that plenty of guitarists do it—there are probably more luthiers at work, and doing good work, than there have been at any other point in history.

FINDING LUTHIERS

Asking around at guitar shops in your area is a good way to find local people. Checking the ads in the guitar magazines, especially *Acoustic*

Guitar, also helps. (See the Resources section, page 265, for more information on acoustic guitar–focused periodicals.) And there's always the Web. In addition, there are two luthiers' organizations. They are:

Association of String Instrument Artisans (ASIA)
www.guitarmaker.org
Guild of American Luthiers (GAL)
www.luth.org.

ASIA tends to have an East Coast and GAL a West Coast membership, though not exclusively so. Both publish journals that also include luthiers' advertising, of interest mainly to professional luthiers though perhaps to technically minded aficionados and collectors as well. Both Web sites include luthiers' advertising and links.

Many luthiers have achieved national reputations. But one of the best things about the current guitar-making scene is that a good many luthiers seem able to get by simply by serving the musicians of their own community. For the most part, I've stayed within my neighborhood in asking luthiers for photos of their work to illustrate this book, and most of those participating are friends or acquaintances. Luthiers whose work is illustrated in this book include:

Edward V. Dick
  (EVD String Instruments)
1869 S. Pearl St.
Denver, Colorado 80210
(303) 777-7411
www.evd303.com

Harry Fleishman
4500 Whitney Pl.
Boulder, Colorado 80303
(303) 499-1614

Linda Manzer
65 Metcalfe St.
Toronto, Ontario M4X IR9
Canada
(416) 927-1539
www.manzer.com

Larry Pogreba
Box 861
Lyons, Colorado 80504
(303) 823-6691

John Rumley
c/o Denver Folklore Center
1893 S. Pearl St.
Denver, Colorado 80210
(303) 777-4786

D. W. Stevens
Salem, Oregon
(503) 540-7504

Selected Importers, Distributors, and Manufacturers of Student, Mid-Line, and Laminate-Body Instruments

Following is a list of manufacturers and importers of beginner-, midrange-, and journeyman-quality laminate-body guitars. These have received short shrift here because they are essentially import companies, which tend to lack the kind of personal history and character, and the design personality, that the higher-end companies have.

It's very important for you to recognize that just because they're given short shrift here does not mean you should give their guitars short shrift in your consideration of possible instruments for you. In the journeyman ranges (and in their own price ranges), they are competitive with instruments from those manufacturers who also make higher-end instruments. They are certainly competitive with any of the lower-price or mid-price guitars offered by those high-end manufacturers who also offer models at this level. It's also important to remember that, while laminate guitars never sound as good as really good all-solid-wood guitars, they can sound better than a poor all-solid-wood guitar.

Many professional musicians work in the studio with instruments from the makers listed in this section. I own a good laminate guitar myself.

Alvarez/Alvarez Yairi
www.alvarezgtr.com

Applause Guitars
Distributed by Kaman
www.KamanMusic.com

Aria
www.ariausa.com

Blue Ridge Guitars
Distributed by Saga Musical
   Instruments
Box 2841
South San Francisco,
   California 94083

Epiphone
Distributed by Gibson
www.gibson.com

Fender Musical Instruments
www.fender.com

Fred Gretsch Enterprises,
Ltd.
www.gretsch.com

Ibanez
Web www.ibanez.com

Norman
Manufactured by LaSiDo
   (See Chapter 13, page
   224)

Seagull
Manufactured by LaSiDo
   (See Chapter 13, page
   224)

Sigma
Distributed by Martin
www.mguitar.com

Simon & Patrick
Manufactured by LaSiDo
   (See Chapter 13, page
   224)

Takamine
Distributed by Kaman
www.KamanMusic.com

Washburn
www.washburn.com

Yamaha
www.Yamaha.com

GLOSSARY

When a word used in a definition also appears as a glossary item on its own, it is printed in capital letters and boldface type.

ACOUSTIC: Term used to describe nonelectric guitars or music that is basically nonelectric. An **ACOUSTIC-ELECTRIC**, **SEMI-ACOUSTIC**, or **ELECTRO-ACOUSTIC** guitar has built-in electronics intended to make it sound more like a miked acoustic guitar than an electric guitar. See also **ELECTRO-ACOUSTIC**.

ACOUSTIC-ELECTRIC: See **ELECTRO-ACOUSTIC**.

ACTION: Ease of playing as a function of the height of the strings above the **FINGERBOARD**. While this may be measured objectively, the player's perception of action is also affected by strings, **SCALE**, and the condition of the **FRETS**. See also **SETUP**.

ARCHTOP: A guitar with a wood top arched by carving or pressing, usually thicker than the top of a **FLATTOP**, and with cellolike **F-HOLES** rather than a round **SOUND HOLE**. In f-hole models and some roundholes, the back is usually likewise arched. F-hole guitars are the typical choice of mainstream jazz guitarists. Roundhole or oval-hole archtops, which often had a dark, wooly sound, went out of fashion after Gibson introduced the f-hole model in the 1920s. However, lighter-sounding models are now being made by some contemporary **LUTHIERS** and factories.

ARPEGGIO: A chord played one note at a time, usually with a rippling sound (Italian for *harplike*, more or less).

BACKBOW: See **WARP**.

BALANCE: The relative volume, tonal strength, and **SUSTAIN** of the high and low strings of the guitar. Also, the distribution of the guitar's weight.

BARREL: See **PEG**.

BARS: Properly speaking, the smaller or secondary **STRUTS** that make up the guitar top's **BRACING** system and the braces used on the guitar's back. Most people don't usually make this fine distinction and loosely call them braces anyway, as in *back-braces*. See also **TONE BARS**.

BASS: The lowest range of notes. Also used to refer to the lowest three strings of the guitar, and also short for the string bass or **BASS GUITAR**.

BASS GUITAR: 1. An instrument with an oversized **ACOUSTIC** guitar–like body and long four-string neck, tuned like a bass fiddle. 2. Another name for the electric bass. 3. An obsolete name for a seven- to ten-string guitar, where the extra strings are **BASS** strings.

BELLY: The area of the top in back of the **BRIDGE** (toward the **ENDPIN**). Or, a bulge in this area caused by string tension on the bridge.

BELLY BRIDGE: The standard guitar pin bridge shape, so called because it's basically rectangular with a curved-out portion (belly) along one side.

BEND: To push or pull a string along the **FINGERBOARD** parallel to the **FRETS** using a finger of the fretting hand, in order to alter the pitch for a sliding or bluesy effect.

BINDING: Strips of plastic, wood, or nitrocellulose added at the edges of a guitar's back and top where they join the sides, and sometimes also at the edges of the **FINGERBOARD**. See also **MARQUETRY** and **PURFLING**.

BLANK: A roughly shaped piece of wood to be used, for example, for a guitar's neck, prior to the final fine shaping, carving, and finishing. In fine guitars, the neck blanks are machine-cut but the final shaping is done by hand.

BOOKMATCHED: This term applies to sections of a single piece of wood that has been cut in half down the narrow dimension and then opened out like a book. The resulting symmetrical structure looks good and, more importantly, minimizes the possibility of cracking. The sides and back of a fine guitar are bookmatched. In less expensive, laminated guitars, bookmatching the top layer of **LAMINATE** is only cosmetic and adds nothing to the instrument's durability.

BOTTLENECK: See **SLIDE**.

BOTTOM BLOCK: Another term for **END BLOCK**.

BOUTS: The upper or lower parts of the guitar's body, separated by the **WAIST**. (Sometimes affectionately called the bust and hips.)

BOW: See **WARP**.

BRACING: The pattern of **STRUTS** underneath the top of a guitar, which has both acoustical and reinforcing functions. Bracing patterns include the **X-BRACING** typical of **FLATTOP** guitars and the **FAN-BRACING** typical of classical guitars. (See also **BARS**.)

BRAZILIAN: Casually, short for Brazilian rosewood or for a guitar with a Brazilian rosewood back and sides.

BRIDGE: The wooden structure mounted on the **SOUNDBOARD** that holds the strings.

BRIDGE PLATE: A flat piece of wood (preferably maple or rosewood) glued to the underside of the top beneath the **BRIDGE** for structural support.

BUZZ: The sound a string makes when it vibrates against a **FRET** farther up the **FINGERBOARD** than the fret against which it is being depressed. Usually the result of neck warp, or poorly adjusted action or relief. Often also used loosely to refer to any rattle or foreign sound, for example from loose **BRACING** or a loose **TUNER**.

CARVED-TOP: See **ARCHTOP**.

CENTER SEAM: The point at which the two halves of the top or back are joined.

CHANNEL ROD: One type of **REINFORCING ROD**, consisting of a U-shaped or hollow rectangular metal bar. An adjustable **TRUSS ROD** may be run through the inside of the channel rod.

CHECKING: Small cracks in the finish of the guitar caused by the different coefficients of expansion of the finish and of the wood itself when the instrument is subjected to sudden or extreme temperature change. (In the wood industry, Checking refers to hairline cracks in milled lumber caused by improper kilning.)

CLEAT: See **STUD**.

CLUBBY: Used to describe the feel of a thick, roundly contoured, club-like guitar neck.

COMPENSATED SADDLE: See **SADDLE**.

COURSE: A close-together **SET** of one to three strings that are fretted and plucked as a unit; for example, a pair of strings on a twelve-string guitar.

CRAZING: The pattern caused by **CHECKING**.

CROSS-BRACING: A term to avoid, since some people use it to mean X-BRACING and others to mean **TRANSVERSE BRACING**.

CROWN: The top (visible) portion of the **FRET**. Crowning refers to dressing the tops of the frets with a file and emery paper to ensure good tone and smoothness of playing.

CUTAWAY: The area of the upper **BOUT** cut away in a crescent-shaped indentation in order to make the upper **FRETS** accessible. A pointy-shaped cutaway is called Florentine; one with a smoothly curved horn is called Venetian.

DI: Pronounced "dee-eye"; see **DIRECT INPUT**.

DIAMOND: Another term for **HANDSTOP**, used because the classic Martin-design handstops are carved into a diamond shape. Also sometimes used for **STUD**, because most **LUTHIERS** cut studs in a diamond shape, as well as for the diamond-shaped **POSITION MARKERS** used on older Martins and widely imitated by other makers.

DIRECT INPUT: The technique of running a guitar's **PICKUPS** directly into the mixing console of a sound system or recording studio without the intermediary step of using an individual guitar amplifier and speaker. However, preamps, various equalization devices, and other sound processing devices are frequently used in the **SIGNAL PATH**.

DOBRO: Although this is a trademark for resophonic guitars made by the Original Musical Instrument Company (OMI), *dobro* has become a generic word for any resophonic guitar played in the Hawaiian style.

DOTS: See **POSITION DOTS**.

DREADNOUGHT: Name for a large-bodied, narrow-waisted guitar shape developed by Martin in the 1930s, which is now the most common shape in the industry.

DRESSING: Smoothing and shaping the **FRETS** with a file or emery paper.

EDGE BINDING: See **BINDING**.

ELECTRO-ACOUSTIC: Used by many manufacturers to describe a shallow-bodied, cutaway guitar with built-in electronics. However, usage is not entirely consistent within the industry. See **ACOUSTIC**.

END BLOCK: A block of hardwood placed inside the guitar body at the tail end in order to both reinforce the sides where they join and to provide an anchor point for the pin that holds the guitar strap.

END JOINT: An ornamental strip of wood or other binding material that joins the two side pieces where they meet over the **END BLOCK**. Not used on all guitars; some just have a simple seam.

ENDPIN: A pin seated in a hole at the lower end of the guitar for the purpose of attaching a strap.

EQUALIZER: An electronic sound processing device that boosts or suppresses selected frequencies.

F-HOLE: The shape of the **SOUND HOLE** in violin-family instruments and most **ARCHTOP** guitars, formed like an old-fashioned script letter *f*. On some guitars the holes are shaped with an art deco flow to them, more like an elongated teardrop. Also short for a guitar with f-holes; in practice, a synonym for an archtop guitar. See also **ARCHTOP**.

FAN-BRACING: See **BRACING**.

FAST NECK: A neck with any or all of these qualities: thin contour, low **ACTION**, or extra-wide **FRETS**. More typical of jazz and electric rather than **ACOUSTIC** guitar necks. Fast isn't necessarily better; it's a matter of personal preference.

FIGURE: The visual design formed by the grain pattern in a piece of wood.

FINGERBOARD: The strip of wood along the top of the guitar neck in which the **FRETS** are seated. Also called the **FRETBOARD**.

FINGERPICKING, FINGER-STYLE: Any style of guitar playing in which the strings are plucked by the fingers (with or without **FINGERPICKS**). Sometimes refers more specifically to the spectrum of melodically expressive ragtime/blues/country musical styles encompassed by such musicians as Elizabeth Cotton and Chet Atkins.

FINGERPICKS: Metal or plastic picks that are worn on the thumb and fingers of the picking hand.

FLATTOP: An **ACOUSTIC** guitar with a flat top (and almost always a round or roundish **SOUND HOLE**), as opposed to an **ARCHTOP** guitar.

FLOATING PICKUP: A magnetic **PICKUP** mounted on the end of the **FINGERBOARD** or on the **PICKGUARD** of an **ARCHTOP** guitar so that it won't interfere with the vibrations of the top.

FOLK GUITAR: In this book, and often elsewhere, a steel-string **FLATTOP** guitar. Occasionally elsewhere, especially in materials from the 1960s, the term refers to wide-necked, small-bodied, **TWELVE-FRET**, steel-string guitars like the Martin 0-16NY.

FORWARD BOW: See **WARP**.

FOURTEEN-FRET: See **TWELVE-FRET**.

FRET: T-shaped metal strip with a studded tang seated in the **FINGER-BOARD** against which the strings are depressed. Most guitars have twenty or twenty-one frets, of which fourteen are clear of the body. See also **TWELVE-FRET**.

FRETBOARD: Another word for **FINGERBOARD**.

FRICTION PEGS: Violin-style wooden tuning pegs held in place only by friction. Today used only on flamenco guitars.

GERMAN SILVER: A strong, silvery-looking, stainless nickel-steel alloy desirable for **FRETS** and other fittings. There is no actual silver content in this alloy. Also called **NICKEL SILVER**.

GOLPEADOR: Spanish for tap-plate (literally, "striker").

GRADUATION: The technique of altering the thickness of a guitar's **SOUNDBOARD** in different areas in order to promote a maximum balance of strength and acoustical response.

HANDSTOP: A protruding piece of wood carved into the guitar neck in order to add extra thickness and reinforcement at its most vulnerable spot, the point where the **HEADSTOCK** angles back.

HARMONIC: The sound produced by the total length of the vibrating string (the "fundamental"), or any of the sounds of its independently vibrating fractional sections (**OVERTONES**). Also used specifically to refer to the bell-like overtone produced by a plucked string that is touched lightly (not fretted) at one of its exact fractional points; for example, the harmonic produced at the twelfth fret (half the string length).

HARP GUITAR: A guitar with extra, unfretted strings, usually **BASS** strings, attached to an extra neck or necklike extension of the body.

HAWAIIAN GUITAR: See **SPANISH GUITAR**.

HEAD: Another word for the **HEADSTOCK** or **TUNING MACHINE**. See **MACHINE HEAD**.

HEAD BLOCK: A block of hardwood placed inside the guitar body opposite the **HEEL**, in order to reinforce the sides where they join and to provide a joining point for the heel. The heel is traditionally mortised into the **HEEL BLOCK** with a dovetail joint. On cheap guitars and on some good guitars of unusual design, the neck may be otherwise glued or even bolted on.

HEAD PLATE: The veneer used to cover the front of the **HEADSTOCK**, sometimes (though not necessarily) made of the same wood as the sides and back. The head plate is strictly ornamental and may be omitted, or a paint or finish may be used instead (though usually only on cheaper guitars). This term is rarely used; people usually just speak of headstock veneer.

HEADSTOCK: The section at the end of the guitar neck that holds the **TUNING MACHINES**.

HEEL: The widened-out portion at the base of a guitar's neck where it joins the body. On some instruments the bottom of the heel may be covered with an ornamental piece of wood veneer or ivoroid binding called the **HEEL PLATE**.

HEEL BLOCK: See **HEAD BLOCK**. Sometimes **HEEL BLOCK** is used specifically to refer to a configuration often used in classical guitars, where the block is carved out of the same piece of wood as the neck.

HEEL PLATE: See **HEEL**.

HERRINGBONE: A herringbone-pattern **PURFLING** strip used on **PRE-WAR** Martin 28-series guitars, and more recently revived by Martin and other makers. Also short for a Martin guitar with such purfling, especially a pre-war D-28.

IN-LINE: A parts-supplier term applied to **TUNING MACHINES** that are mounted three to a **PLATE**.

INTONATION: The ability to play in tune. Bad intonation on a guitar may be caused by improper **FRET** or **SADDLE** placement, a warped neck, or worn-out strings.

JUMBO: The name for a common, large-bodied, deep-waisted guitar shape.

KERF: See **LINING**.

LAMINATE (noun): Veneered wood or plywood. Also refers to necks made out of several wood sections glued together. Good multi-piece laminate necks are sturdy and, unlike plywood bodies, perfectly respectable. Laminated **HEADSTOCKS** are somewhat less desirable but are still quite acceptable.

LAP STEEL: See **STEEL GUITAR**.

LINING: The strip of wood glued around the edges of the inside of the body of the guitar, in order to provide support and extra gluing surface where the back and top join the sides. Linings are usually **KERFED**, which means that they have indentations cut into them so they can be easily bent to the shape of the guitar.

LOOP BRIDGE: The **BRIDGE** shape typical of classical guitars, in which the string is run through a hole parallel to the **FINGERBOARD** and then looped around itself to hold it in place.

LUTHIER: A maker of stringed instruments.

MACHINE or **MACHINE HEAD:** The string tuning mechanism, including the knob, gears, and winding post.

MARQUETRY: Decorative strips of patterned wood inlaid into the guitar's body, usually in **ROSETTES** or at joining points such as edge **BINDINGS** and center seams.

MOP: An abbreviation, used especially in dealers' catalogs, for mother-of-pearl.

MOT: An abbreviation, used especially in dealers' catalogs, for mother-of-toilet seat.

MOTHER-OF-TOILET SEAT: Fanciful but commonly used term for fake, plastic mother-of-pearl, especially the highly iridescent and artificial-looking variety.

MULTIPIECE: Word used to describe laminated necks. See **LAMINATE**.

NECK BLOCK: See **HEEL BLOCK**.

NECK REINFORCEMENT: See **HANDSTOP**.

NEW YORK MARTIN: A C. F. Martin and Co. guitar made before 1898. In that year, Martin terminated its agreement with the New York–based company that had distributed its guitars since its beginning and finally changed its guitar imprint from "C. F. Martin & Co., New York," even though the company had been in Nazareth, Pennsylvania, since 1839. The model code suffix NY is used by Martin to designate recent models patterned after pre-1898 originals.

NICKEL SILVER: See **GERMAN SILVER**.

NUT: The grooved rectangle of ivory, bone, ceramic, plastic, metal, or hardwood that spaces the strings at the **HEADSTOCK** end of the **FINGERBOARD** and defines one end of the string **SCALE**.

NUT EXTENDER: A grooved metal collar that sits over the **NUT**, raising the **ACTION** to a height suitable for slide playing.

OFFSET SADDLE: See **SADDLE**.

OPEN TUNING: A manner of tuning the guitar strings to the notes of a chord rather than to their usual pattern, which does not constitute a chord. Characteristic of certain blues, Hawaiian, steel, and bottleneck styles, and also used extensively in contemporary British Isles and new-age styles. The term is usually also used loosely to refer to other unusual tunings, even when they don't produce a real chord.

ORCHESTRAL GUITAR: An outmoded term referring to **ACOUSTIC ARCHTOP** guitars, especially loud, heavy models for big band use.

OVERTONE: The sound of each vibrating fraction of the string length. (A guitar string vibrates not only along its entire length but also along its fractional sections.) These overtones combine with the "fundamental" (the sound of the entire string length vibrating) to give each guitar its unique sound.

PARAMETRIC EQUALIZER: An equalizer that selects the bandwidth of the frequency it governs as well as the frequency itself. See **EQUALIZER**.

PEARL: Among guitarists and **LUTHIERS**, short for mother-of-pearl. See **MOP**.

PEDAL STEEL: See **STEEL GUITAR**.

PEG: The cylinder part of the **TUNING MACHINE**, around which the strings are wound. Also called **BARREL** or **TUNING PEG**.

PEGHEAD: See **HEADSTOCK**.

PICK: Usually short for **FLATPICK**, although this might also refer to a **FINGERPICK**.

PICKGUARD: A plate of plastic (rarely hardwood, formerly tortoiseshell) glued to the top near the **SOUND HOLE** to protect it from **PICK** and finger abrasion.

PICKUP: An electronic transducer device that converts the sounds of the guitar strings (or, in some cases, the oscillation of their magnetic fields) to electrical signals that are fed into an amplifier.

PIN BRIDGE: The standard **BRIDGE** style for steel-string guitars. Ball-end strings are run through holes in the bridge into the guitar body. The ball ends are held in place against the **BRIDGE PLATE** on the underside of the top, while removable pins are inserted to hold the strings in position against the bridge plate.

PLATE: The strip of metal on which several **TUNING MACHINES** may be mounted (though **TUNERS** may also be separate). Also, an obsolescent word for **SOUNDBOARD**.

POSITION DOTS, POSITION MARKERS: The **DOTS** or inlays located on the **FINGERBOARD** (usually below frets 5, 7, 9, 12, and perhaps also 3, 15, 17, and 19) to provide visual guidance for the player's fingers.

PRE-WAR: Made prior to World War II. Most manufacturers were involved in the production of war materials; when they retooled after the war, perhaps with new personnel, quality and/or specifications were usually somewhat different, and often not as good.

PURFLING: Ornamental strips of inlay, usually around the edges of the top and/or back where they join the sides, inside of the **BINDING**. In casual usage, people may not carefully distinguish between the terms **BINDING, PURFLING,** and **MARQUETRY**.

PYRAMID BRIDGE: A **PIN BRIDGE** design in which the **BRIDGE** feet are ornamentally carved into pyramid shapes; this was characteristic of Martin guitars up to the late 1920s.

QUARTERSAWED: Wood sawed so that the edge grain is perpendicular to the cut. The most desirable way of milling wood for guitars.

REINFORCING ROD: A steel bar, ebony strip, or similar strengthening device set in a routed-out channel in the neck under the **FINGER-BOARD** to help keep the neck straight under pressure from the strings. Sometimes used synonymously with **TENSION ROD**. A few nineteenth-century guitars were also made with a completely different form of metal or wood reinforcing rod set banjo-style inside the body, running from the **HEEL BLOCK** to the **END BLOCK**.

RELIEF: A small amount of apparent **WARP** deliberately built into the **FINGERBOARD** to avoid string rattle in certain circumstances, and to make the higher **FRETS** more playable. A fingerboard should not be perfectly straight.

REVERSE BOW, REVERSE WARP: Another term for **BACKBOW**. See **WARP**.

RIBS: A term sometimes used for the sides of the guitar.

ROSETTE: Ornamental **MARQUETRY** pattern surrounding the **SOUND HOLE**.

SADDLE: The strip of ivory, bone, plastic, or other synthetic material seated in the **BRIDGE**, across which the strings rests. The saddle is usually mounted on an angle. This slightly lengthens the lower strings to allow for their different coefficient of length-to-mass, which helps them play in tune.

SCALE: Short for "scale length," the length of the vibrating portion of the string, from **NUT** to **SADDLE**. Scale technically refers to the guitar maker's model or template for placing the **FRETS**, which is mathematically derived from the length of the vibrating portion of the string. Most guitars are built more or less in conformance with three standards: Martin short scale (24.9 inches for most smaller guitars); Martin long scale (today's most common scale length, 25.4 inches), and classical concert scale (26 inches). Also, a musical scale, as in common usage.

SEMI-ACOUSTIC: See **ACOUSTIC**.

SEPARATION: A quality in an instrument in which the notes played simultaneously in a chord are perceived distinctly and individually, rather than as a homogeneous whole. How much separation you want is a matter of taste.

SET: The precut, roughly shaped sections of wood that will be used for the back and sides of the guitar. In the highest-quality instruments, sets will be **QUARTERSAWED** (to minimize shrinkage and the possibility of cracking) and cut from the same log (to maximize visual and structural uniformity and the symmetry of whatever shrinkage does occur).

SETUP: The sum of adjustments that govern the **ACTION** and playability of the guitar, including: **NUT** and **SADDLE** height, **TENSION ROD** adjustment, and choice of string gauge. Other relevant factors, such as neck set, **FINGERBOARD** planing, and **FRET** dressing, are in the realm of more serious repair work and aren't usually considered part of setup.

SHOULDERS: The parts of the guitar's sides along the top of the upper **BOUT** where they abut the neck **HEEL**.

SIGNAL PATH: The path followed by an electrical current carrying sound information; for example, the pathway through the various cables and devices from a guitar **PICKUP** through a phase shifter, a digital delay unit, and into an amplifier.

SKEWING: A sideways (rather than convex or concave) **BOW** or distortion of the neck. See **WARP**.

SLIDE GUITAR: A style of playing in which the strings are not depressed against the **FRETS**, but instead are fretted with a movable, hard object held by the fretting hand. This may be a cut-down glass bottleneck or pill bottle worn on the pinky or third finger, a steel cylinder, a jackknife held between the fingers, a store-bought guitar slide, or **STEEL**, and so on.

SOLID: In the context of this book (and of the guitar industry), "solid" refers to genuine lumber as opposed to veneered **LAMINATE** or plywood.

SOLIDBODY: An electric guitar with a body constructed of a solid piece of wood, offering no sound-chamber resonance so that its amplified sound is totally produced by its electromagnetic **PICKUP**.

SOUNDBOARD: The top of the guitar, on which the **BRIDGE** is mounted.

SOUND CHAMBER: An enclosed or semi-enclosed chamber that amplifies and colors sound vibrations; for example, the body of a guitar.

SOUND HOLE: The hole in the top of an **ACOUSTIC** guitar, which affects tone production of the sound chamber and the elasticity of the top. Usually round (or, at least, roundish) on a **FLATTOP** guitar. **ARCHTOP** guitars generally have two f-shaped sound holes like a violin.

SPANISH GUITAR: A troublesome, obsolescent term that has caused confusion out of all proportion to its innocence. It doesn't necessarily refer to a guitar made in Spain or used to play Spanish music. The term originated in the 1920s to distinguish *any* kind of guitar held in the normal upright playing position. A **HAWAIIAN GUITAR** is also any kind of guitar as long as it's held flat (face-upward) across the lap and fretted with a steel bar held against the strings.

SPATULA: The part of the **FINGERBOARD** that extends over the body of the guitar (usually beginning at the fourteenth or twelfth **FRET**).

SPLINT: A shaved sliver of wood glued into a crack to in order repair it. Used when the crack is too wide for simple gluing and clamping.

STEEL: The heavy, metal bar or cylinder used to note the strings on a **STEEL GUITAR**. Also short for **STEEL GUITAR**.

STEEL GUITAR: An electrified instrument consisting essentially of a neck and strings without a body, played horizontally. You play a steel guitar by holding a heavy, metal cylinder (the **STEEL**) against the strings. The **LAP STEEL** is a simple version held on the player's lap. The more complicated **PEDAL STEEL** has more strings, the basic pitches of which are altered by pressing different combinations of pedals and levers with feet and knees.

STRAP BUTTON: A pin attached to the guitar's neck near the **HEEL**, or sometimes to the side close to the **NECK HEEL**, for the purpose of attaching a strap. See also **ENDPIN**.

STRUTS: See **BRACING**.

STUD: A small rectangular- or diamond-shaped chip of spruce, ideally with beveled edges, glued in the inside of the guitar body to reinforce a repaired crack.

SUSTAIN: The guitar's ability to keep a string sounding once it's been plucked.

SYMPATHETIC STRINGS: Extra strings that are not plucked or fretted, but that are set in motion by the vibration of the strings that are played. The sitar is a good example of a sympathetic-string instrument.

T-BAR: One type of **REINFORCING ROD**, consisting of a T-shaped metal bar.

TABLE: An obsolescent word for **SOUNDBOARD**, used mainly by classical guitar **LUTHIERS**.

TAIL BLOCK: See **END BLOCK**.

TAILPIECE: A device that hold the ends of the strings on **ARCHTOP** and, occasionally, older **FLATTOP** guitars. Conventional on archtops, but usually the sign of a cheaply made flattop (Maccaferri-style guitars being one exception).

TAP-PLATE: Protective plate of wood, plastic, and so on similar to a **PICKGUARD**, used on flamenco guitars to protect against the effects of percussive sounds made by the fingernails.

TENOR GUITAR: A small-bodied, four-string guitar tuned like a tenor (four-string) banjo.

TENSION ROD or **BAR**: Also commonly called **TRUSS ROD**. A steel (sometimes ebony, graphite, and so on) rod inserted under tension in a channel cut the length of the neck in order to inhibit warping of the neck under string pressure. Most manufacturers now use a steel rod in which tension is adjustable to compensate for aging and changes in climate or string gauge. In this book, as often elsewhere, rod or **TRUSS ROD** is used loosely to describe any kind of neck reinforcing rod, including nonadjustable metal or ebony bars.

TERZ GUITAR: (Pronounced "tertz," from the German.) A small guitar, fashionable in the nineteenth century, tuned three tones higher than usual. The smallest-sized antique Martins were terz guitars.

TONE BARS: In a **FLATTOP** guitar, the ancillary **STRUTS** under the lower **BOUT** of the guitar, other than the two main struts that form the **X-BRACING**—although most people usually use the term **BRACING** loosely to encompass both the X-braces and the tone bars. In an **ARCHTOP** guitar, the two longitudinal struts that in most such guitars solely comprise the bracing system.

TRANSDUCER: The technically correct term for **PICKUP**. A transducer is any device that converts one form of energy to another; in this case, sound into an electrical signal.

TRANSVERSE BRACING: An early form of **BRACING** in which a few **STRUTS** run laterally, or at a very slight angle off the lateral, underneath the **BELLY**. Transverse bracing reinforces the top structurally but doesn't help much acoustically.

TREBLE: The highest range of notes. Also used to refer to the highest three strings of the guitar.

TRUSS ROD: See **TENSION ROD**.

TUNER or **TUNING MACHINE**: See **MACHINE HEAD**.

TUNING PEG: See **PEG**. Also sometimes used loosely to mean the entire **MACHINE HEAD**.

TWELVE-FRET, FOURTEEN-FRET: These terms refer to the two major neck styles. The number indicates the number of **FRETS** clear on the neck before the neck joins the body (ignoring any **CUTAWAY**), and not to the total number of frets on the **FINGERBOARD**. Classical guitars, a few contemporary steel-strung guitars (especially those with wider fingerboards), and early steel-strung guitars have twelve frets. Most contemporary steel-strung guitars have fourteen frets to allow greater access to high notes.

VINTAGE: A term used to describe high-quality used guitars made far enough in the past to have antique or collector's value (usually pre–World War II for acoustic guitars and pre-Beatles-era for electrics).

VOICING: The process in which a **LUTHIER** listens to the sounds of the top and **BRACING** on a fine handmade guitar as they are being carved into final shape. (In music theory and composition, voicing refers to the way notes are located within chords.)

VOLUTE: See **HANDSTOP**.

WAIST: The narrowest section of the guitar's body, between the upper and lower **BOUTS**, where it rests on your knee.

WARP: Any distortion in the shape of wood, usually in reference to the straightness of the long axis of the neck. Concave distortion is called a **BOW** or **FORWARD BOW**. Convex distortion is called a **BACKBOW**, or **REVERSE BOW**, or **REVERSE WARP** or, confusingly, also just **BOW** (as opposed to **WARP**) by some repair people. Sideways distortion or movement is called **SKEWING**.

WINDING: The outer part of a string (usually strings 3 through 6), consisting of a thin metal wire wound around a metal or fiber core.

X-BRACING: See **BRACING**.

ZERO FRET: An extra **FRET**, placed directly in front of the **NUT**, which serves as a de facto nut to determine where the scale begins.

RESOURCES

For Further Reading

BOOKS

Bacon, Tony. *The Ultimate Guitar Book.* New York: Alfred A. Knopf, 1992. Includes lavish illustrations of beautiful as well as interesting and offbeat acoustic and electric guitars.

Brozman, Bob. *History and Artistry of National Resonator Instruments.* Milwaukee, WI: CenterStream/Hal Leonard, 1994. A leading player and expert's history, with photos of pre-war National and Dobro instruments.

Carter, Walter. *Gibson Guitars: 100 Years of an American Icon.* Grand Rapids, MI: Gollehon Press, 1996. Acoustics, electrics, history, lots of wonderful color photos.

———. *The Complete History of Epiphone.* Milwaukee, WI: Hal Leonard, 1995. Acoustics and electrics, into the Gibson era, from this important manufacturer—though more important for its archtops than its flattops.

———. *The Martin Book.* San Francisco, CA: Miller Freeman, 1995. Supplements the older book by Mike Longworth and supplies the color photos Longworth lacks.

Cumpiano, William, and Jonathan D. Natelson. *Guitarmaking: Tradition and Technology.* New York: NY Music Sales, 1994. A well-received book covering both classical and steel-string guitars.

Duchossoir, A. R. *Guitar Identification.* Minneapolis, MN: Hal Leonard, 1983. A short, basic guide to the dating of serial numbers and salient historical characteristics of Fender, Gibson, Gretsch, and Martin acoustic and electric guitars.

Evans, Tom, and Mary Anne Evans. *Guitars: Music, History, Construction, and Players from the Renaissance to Rock.* New York: Facts on File, 1977. This book is out of print, but if you do get a copy you'll find much commentary and lots of pictures, though black and white, of wonderful guitars.

Freeth, Nick, and Charles Alexander. *The Acoustic Guitar.* Philadelphia, PA: Courage Books/Running Press, 1999. Selected—but wonderfully selected—instruments, beautifully photographed, that illuminate the past to very recent history of the guitar. Commentary to the photos provides historical background.

George, David. *The Flamenco Guitar.* Madrid, Spain: Society of Spanish Studies, 1969. The history, spirit, and sociology of the flamenco guitar as well as flamenco music, flamenco life, and the Gypsy mystique; also some details on guitar making.

Gruhn, George, and Walter Carter. *Acoustic Guitars and Other Fretted Instruments*. San Francisco, CA: GPI/Miller Freeman, 1993. Beautiful pictures of beautiful instruments, older and newer.

———. *Gruhn's Guide to Vintage Guitars*. San Francisco, CA: GPI/Miller Freeman, 1993. Typology and descriptions from the leading expert on vintage guitars.

Grunfeld, Frederic V. *The Art and Times of the Guitar*. New York: MacMillan, 1969. A witty, readable social history primarily covering the classical guitar and its music, with some attention to other forms and styles as well.

Kamimoto, Hideo. *Complete Guitar Repair*. New York: Oak Publications, 1978. A readable, reasonable, and comprehensive book. Its price and accessibility make it a likely candidate for your bookshelf. Even though you shouldn't attempt any difficult repairs yourself, and should think twice about making even simple adjustments, a book like this can give you insights into how your instrument works.

Longworth, Mike. *Martin Guitars: A History*. Minisink Hills, PA: Four Maples Press, 1987. Detailed information on Martin's history, specifications, and production figures from the beginning through the mid-1980s, based on direct access to the company's official records, foremen's logs, and so on. Essential information if you're planning to purchase or cultivate an interest in used or antique Martins.

Moust, Hans. *The Guild Guitar Book: The Company and Instruments*. Milwaukee, WI: Hal Leonard, 2000. At last, a book for Guild fans, and one that begins to give Guild some of its historical due.

Sandberg, Larry, and Dick Weissman. *The Folk Music Sourcebook*, rev. ed. New York: Da Capo Press, 1989. Discography, bibliography, and other information about people, places, retailers, and organizations as well as the music itself. Includes recommendations for instructional materials (books, tapes, videos), records, and so forth. A good place to get started in learning about the traditional side of acoustic music.

Santoro, Gene, ed. *The Guitar*. New York: Quill/Quarto, 1984. Separate sections by various authors on classical, jazz, blues, country, and rock guitarists and styles. Personality-oriented.

Schneider, John. *The Contemporary Guitar*. Berkeley, CA: University of California Press, 1985. In the course of expounding his personal theory of tone production, the author deals with guitar construction, repertoire, and the compositional conventions of the nylon-strung and electric guitar in contemporary classical usage. Much information on guitar acoustics in general.

Sloan, Irving. *Steel-String Guitar Construction*. New York: E. P. Dutton, 1975. A useful guide especially for the beginning luthier; includes sources for tools and materials.

Teeter, Don. *The Acoustic Guitar: Adjustment, Care, Maintenance, and Repair, Volumes I and II*. Norman, OK: University of Oklahoma Press,

1980. Sensible advice, methods, anecdotes, custom tool diagrams, and controversial, brilliantly idiosyncratic techniques generously shared. Professional-level, though interesting to all.

Tyler, James. *The Early Guitar: A History and Handbook*. New York: Oxford University Press, 1980. A scholarly study of the guitar and its musical styles from the sixteenth through mid-eighteenth centuries.

Wheeler, Tom. *American Guitars: An Illustrated History*. New York: Harper Collins, 1992. Covers acoustics, electrics, resophonic guitars, f-hole archtops, and more. Good overall view of the subject, organized by company/brand, comprehensively illustrated, with much detail. A good place to start learning more about vintage guitars and industry history.

————. *The Guitar Book: A Handbook for Electric and Acoustic Guitarists*. New York: Harper & Row, 1978. This title is OP, but if you can find a copy you'll be able to read more on acoustics, electrics, and amplifiers, too.

Whitford, Eldon, David Vinopal, and Dan Erlewine. *Gibson's Fabulous Flat-Top Guitars*. San Francisco, CA: Miller Freeman, 1994. From 1926 to current Gibson Montana products; a rather partisan history but worth it for the color pictures.

Young, David Russell. *The Steel String Guitar: Construction and Repair*. Westport, CT: The Bold Strummer, 1987. Methods and techniques of a well-respected luthier strongly influenced by the traditions of classical guitar making.

MAGAZINES

Acoustic Guitar, Box 767, San Anselmo, California, 94960. Covers playing as well as instruments, accessories, personalities, events, reviews, and so on.

Dirty Linen, Box 66600, Baltimore, Maryland, 21239. A lively publication dealing with traditional music and associated acoustic styles.

Fingerstyle Guitar, 22760 Hawthorne Blvd., No. 208, Torrance, California, 90505. Oriented a little more toward music than instruments.

Flatpicking Guitar, P.O. Box 2160, Pulaski, Virginia, 24301. Oriented a little more toward music than instruments.

Frets. Discontinued in 1989 after a decade of publication. If you can find back issues, you'll learn a lot from them about contemporary and traditional acoustic music, instruments, and personalities.

Guitar Player, 20085 Stevens Creek Blvd., Cupertino, California, 95014. Deals mainly with electric and especially rock guitars, but has some coverage of acoustic guitar topics.

Sing Out!, Box 5253, Bethlehem, Pennsylvania, 18015. The voice of the urban folk song community.

Remember, in addition, the various magazines devoted primarily to styles of music or music industry topics, like *Old Time Herald, Bluegrass Unlimited, Gig,* and *Acoustic Musician,* also contain much of interest of acoustic guitarists.

Guitar Shows

The big music industry trade shows run by NAMM (National Associa-tion of Music Merchants) are open to tradespeople only. However, regional guitar shows of one to three days' duration, open to the gen-eral public, have become a usual feature on the musical landscape. Dal-las, Austin, Columbus, Decatur, Kansas City, and Houston are just a few of the cities that have recently hosted such shows; smaller ones some-times are held in smaller towns. Find out about them by reading the guitar magazines and asking your local dealers. You can also find out about guitar shows and luthiery festivals by keeping track of listings in magazines like *Acoustic Guitar.* The major show of American luthiery is the Healdsburg Guitar Makers Festival, held at the end of August in the California wine country, and sponsored in part by that magazine. It's attended not only by luthiers and music industry people but also by musicians and collectors.